BHIM RAO AMBEDKAR

Series Editor
Dr. M.H. Syed

Editor
Anil Kathuria **Bharat Singh**

Himalaya Books Pvt. Ltd.
'Ramdoot', Dr. Bhalerao Marg, Girgaon, Mumbai - 400 004
Tel : (022) 23863863. Fax : (022) 23877178
Email : himpub@vsnl.com

Edition : 2020

Published by : **H.B.P.L.**
"Pooja Apartments", 4-B, Murari Lal Street, Ansari Road,
Darya Ganj, New Delhi-110 002
Phones: 23270392, 23278631 Reliance : 30180392 to 396
Fax: 011-23256286 Email : hphdel@vsnl.com

Sole Distributers : **HIMALAYA PUBLISHING HOUSE PVT. LTD.**

Branch Offices :

Mumbai : "Ramdoot", Dr. Bhalerao Marg, Girgaon, Mumbai - 400 004.
Phone: 022-23860170/23863863, Fax: 022-23877178
E-mail: himpub@vsnl.com;
Website: www.himpub.com

Nagpur : Kundanlal Chandak Industrial Estate, Ghat Road, Nagpur - 440 018. Phone: 0712-2738731, 3296733; Telefax: 0712-2721216

Bengaluru : Plot No. 91-33, 2nd Main Road, Seshadripuram, Behind Nataraja Theatre, Bengaluru - 560 020.
Phone: 080-41138821; Mobile: 09379847017, 09379847005

Hyderabad : No. 3-4-184, Lingampally, Besides Raghavendra Swamy Matham, Kachiguda, Hyderabad - 500 027.
Phone: 040-27560041, 27550139

Chennai : New No. 48/2, Old No. 28/2, Ground Floor, Sarangapani Street, T. Nagar, Chennai - 600 017. Mobile: 09380460419

Pune : First Floor, "Laksha" Apartment, No. 527, Mehunpura, Shaniwarpeth (Near Prabhat Theatre), Pune - 411 030.
Phone: 020-24496323/24496333; Mobile: 09370579333

Lucknow : House No 731, Shekhupura Colony, Near B.D. Convent School, Aliganj, Lucknow - 226 022.
Phone: 0522-4012353; Mobile: 09307501549

Ahmedabad : 114, "SHAIL", 1st Floor, Opp. Madhu Sudan House, C.G. Road, Navrang Pura, Ahmedabad - 380 009.
Phone: 079-26560126; Mobile: 09377088847

Ernakulam : 39/104 A, Lakshmi Apartment, Karikkamuri Cross Rd., Ernakulam, Cochin - 622011, Kerala.
Phone: 0484-2378012, 2378016; Mobile: 09387122121

Cuttack : New LIC Colony, Behind Kamala Mandap, Badambadi, Cuttack - 753 012, Odisha. Mobile: 09338746007

Kolkata : 108/4, Beliaghata Main Road, Near ID Hospital, Opp. SBI Bank, Kolkata - 700 010, Phone: 033-32449649, Mobile: 7439040301

Printed at : Sri Prints & Sales, New Delhi-110 002

B. R. Ambedkar

Preface

Biography, is now a form of literature, very much in vogue. In fact, biography is a description or account of someone's life and the times, which is usually published in the form of a book. A biography is more than a mention of personal facts (life, education, work, relationships and death), it also portrays the subject's experience of events. Technically speaking, a work is biographical, if it covers, all of a person's life. Biography writing has a long history. A biography is real. Ancient Greeks developed the biographical tradition, which we have inherited, although until the 5th century AD, when the word 'biographia' first appeared, in Damascius' "Life of Isodorus," biographical pieces were called simply "lives". It is quite likely that the Greeks were drawing on a pre-existing eastern tradition. Certainly Herodotus' "Histories" contains more detailed biographical information on Persian kings and subjects. The earliest surviving pieces, which we would identify as biographical are Isocrates' "Life of Evagoras" and Xenophon's "Life of Agesilaos," both from the fifth century BC. "Parallel Lives" by Plutarch, a Greek writing under the Roman empire, is a series of short biographies of eminent men.

The Golden Age of English biography emerged in late eighteenth century, the century in which the terms "biography" and "autobiography" entered English lexicon. The classic works of the period were Samuel Johnson's "Critical Lives of the Poets" and James Boswell's "Massive Life of Johnson". Generally American biography followed English model. By World War I, cheap hardcover reprints had become popular. The decade of the 1920s witnessed a biographical 'boom'. Later, biographical writings developed a lot and today biographies are written and compiled in the finest form of the genre. In India too, biography, as a form of literature has been evolved, cultivated and polished over the years. Here is an effort to promote this tradition further.

This series of biographies of great men, great women and celebrities in all walks of life is an adventurous academic endeavour, in its own right. A team of researchers and compilers has worked for a good period of time to accomplish the project. For this purpose, hundreds of books by eminent authors and editors have been consulted and referred to. We have benefited from various works, liberally, in order to illustrate and enrich this effort of ours. Present book is devoted to the great personality of Bhimrao Ramji Ambedkar.

Bhimrao Ramji Ambedkar, also known as Babasaheb, was an eminent jurist, political leader, social activist, philosopher, thinker, anthropologist, historian, orator, prolific writer, economist, scholar, editor, revolutionary and a revivalist for Buddhism in India. He was also the chief architect of the Indian Constitution. Born into a poor Mahar — then considered untouchable — family, Ambedkar spent his whole life, fighting against social discrimination, the system of Chaturvarna — the categorisation of Hindu society into four varnas — and the Hindu caste system. Ambedkar was honoured with the Bharat Ratna, India's highest civilian award, posthumously.

This is a compact and comprehensive account of the above mentioned great life, which is bound to attract the attention of scholars, researchers, students and the general readers alike. Let's hope this humble effort would receive a warm welcome and due applause.

— ***Editors***

Contents

1

An Illustrious Life

India's foremost leader, Bhimrao Ramji Ambedkar (14 April 1891 - 6 December 1956), also known as *Babasaheb*, was a jurist, political leader, Buddhist activist, philosopher, thinker, anthropologist, historian, orator, prolific writer, economist, scholar, editor, revolutionary and a revivalist for Buddhism in India. He was also the chief architect of the Indian Constitution. Born into a poor Mahar, then Untouchable, family, Ambedkar spent his whole life fighting against social discrimination, the system of *Chaturvarna* — the categorisation of Hindu society into four *varnas* — and the Hindu caste system. He is also credited with providing a spark for the conversion of hundreds of thousands of Dalits with his Ambedkar(ite) Buddhism. Ambedkar has been honoured with the Bharat Ratna, India's highest civilian award.

Overcoming numerous social and financial obstacles, Ambedkar became one of the first "Dalit" to obtain a college education in India. Eventually earning law degrees and multiple doctorates for his study and research in law, economics and political science from Columbia University and the London School of Economics, Ambedkar returned home as a famous scholar and practiced law for a few years before publishing journals advocating political rights and social freedom for India's untouchables. He is regarded as a Bodhisattva by Indian Buddhist Bhikkus and by millions of other Buddhists.

His Birth and Greatness Foretold

On April 14th, 1891 a son was born to Bhimabai and Ramji Ambadvekar. His father Ramji was an army officer stationed at Mhow in Madhya Pradesh — he had risen to the highest rank an Indian was allowed to hold at that time under British rule. His mother decided to call her son Bhim. Before the birth, Ramji's uncle, who was a man living the religious life of a sanyasi, foretold that this son would achieve worldwide fame. His parents already had many children. Despite that, they resolved to make every effort to give him a good education.

Early Life

Bhimrao Ramji Ambedkar was born in the British-founded town and military cantonment of Mhow in the Central Provinces (now in Madhya Pradesh). He was the 14th and last child of Ramji Maloji Sakpal and Bhimabai Murbadkar. His family was of Marathi background from the town of Ambavade in the Ratnagiri district of modern-day Maharashtra. They belonged to the Hindu, Mahar caste, who were treated as so-called untouchables and subjected to intense socio-economic discrimination. Ambedkar's ancestors had for long been in the employment of the army of the British East India Company, and his father Ramji Sakpal served in the Indian Army at the Mhow cantonment. He had received a degree of formal education in Marathi and English, and encouraged his children to learn and work hard at school.

Belonging to the Kabir Panth, Ramji Sakpal encouraged his children to read the Hindu classics. He used his position in the army to lobby for his children to study at the government school, as they faced resistance owing to their caste. Although able to attend school, Ambedkar and other untouchable children were segregated and given no attention or assistance by the teachers. They were not allowed to sit inside the class. Even if they needed to drink water somebody from a higher caste would have to pour that water from a height as they were not allowed to touch either the water or the vessel that contained it. This task was usually performed for the young Ambedkar by the school peon, and if he could not be found Ambedkar went without water. Ramji Sakpal retired in 1894 and the family moved to Satara two years later. Shortly after their move, Ambedkar's mother died. The children were cared for by their paternal aunt, and lived in difficult circumstances. Only three sons — Balaram, Anandrao and Bhimrao — and two daughters — Manjula and Tulasa — of the Ambedkars would go on to survive them. Of his brothers and sisters, only Ambedkar succeeded in passing his examinations and graduating to a higher school. His native village name was "Ambavade" in Ratnagiri District so he changed his name from "Sakpal" to "Ambedkar" with the recommendation and faith of Mahadev Ambedkar, his Deshastha Brahmin teacher who believed in him.

Ramji Sakpal remarried in 1898, and the family moved to Mumbai (then Bombay), where Ambedkar became the first untouchable student at the Government High School near Elphinstone Road. Although, excelling in his studies, Ambedkar was increasingly disturbed by the segregation and discrimination that he faced. In 1907, he passed his matriculation examination and entered the University of Bombay, becoming one of the first persons of untouchable origin to enter a college in India. This success provoked celebrations in his community, and after a public ceremony he was presented with a biography of the Buddha by his teacher Krishnaji Arjun Keluskar also known as Dada Keluskar, a Maratha caste scholar. Ambedkar's marriage had been arranged the previous year as per Hindu custom, to Ramabai, a nine-year old girl from Dapoli. In 1908, he entered Elphinstone College and obtained a scholarship of twenty five rupees a month from the Gayakwad ruler of Baroda, Sahyaji Rao III for higher studies in the USA. By 1912, he obtained his degree in economics and political science, and prepared to take up employment with the Baroda state government. His wife gave birth to his first son, Yashwant, in the same year. Ambedkar had just moved his young family and started work, when he dashed back to Mumbai to see his ailing father, who died on February 2, 1913.

First School

Two years later, Ramji retired from the army, and the family moved to Dapoli in the Ratnagiri district of Maharashtra, from where they came originally. Bhim was enrolled at school when he was five years old. The whole family had to struggle to live on the small army pension Ramji received.

When some friends found Ramji a job at Satara, things seemed to be looking up for the family, and they moved again. Soon after, however, tragedy struck. Bhimabhai, who had been ill, died. Bhim's aunt Mira, though she herself was not in good health, took over the care of the children. Ramji read stories from the epics Mahabharata and Ramayana to his children, and sang devotional songs to them. In this way, home life was still happy for Bhim, his brothers and sisters. He never forgot the influence of his father. It taught him about the rich cultural tradition shared by all Indians.

Matriculation and Marriage

In due course, Bhim passed his Matriculation Exam. He had already come to the attention of some people interested in improving society. So when he passed the exam, a meeting was arranged to congratulate him — he was the first 'untouchable' from his community to pass it.

Bhim was then 17 years old. Early marriage was common in those days, so he was married to Ramabai the same year. He continued to study hard and passed the next Intermediate examination with distinction. However, Ramji found himself unable to keep paying the school fees. Through someone interested in his progress, Bhim was recommended to the Maharaja Gaekwad of Baroda. The Maharaja granted him a monthly scholarship. With the help of this, Bhimrao ('rao' is added to names in Maharashtra as a sign of respect) passed his B.A. in 1912. Then he was given a job in the civil service — but only two weeks after starting, he had to rush home to Bombay. Ramji was very ill, and died soon afterwards. He had done all he could for his son, laying the foundations for Bhimrao's later achievements.

Studies in USA and UK

The Maharaja of Baroda had a scheme to send a few outstanding scholars abroad for further studies. Of course, Bhimrao was selected — but he had to sign an agreement to serve Baroda state for ten years on finishing his studies.

In 1913, he went to the USA where he studied at the world-famous Columbia University, New York. The freedom and equality he experienced in America made a very strong impression on Bhimrao. It was so refreshing for him to be able to live a normal life, free from the caste prejudice of India. He could do anything he pleased — but devoted his time to studying. He studied eighteen hours a day. Visits to bookshops were his favourite entertainment!

His main subjects were Economics and Sociology. In just two years he had been awarded an M.A. — the following year he completed his Ph.D. thesis. Then he left Columbia and went to England, where he joined the London School of Economics. However, he had to leave London before completing his course because the scholarship granted by the State of Baroda expired. Bhimrao had to wait three years before he could return to London to complete his studies.

An Outstanding Scholar

At this time in his young life, with his mother dead, and father working away from the village where Bhim went to school, he had some good fortune. His teacher, though from a 'high' caste, liked him a lot. He praised Bhim's good work and encouraged him, seeing what a bright pupil he was. He even invited Bhim to eat lunch with him — something that would have horrified most high caste Hindus. The teacher also changed Bhim's last name to Ambedkar — his own name.

When his father decided to remarry, Bhim was very upset — he still missed his mother so much. Wanting to run away to Bombay, he tried to steal his aunt's purse. When at last he managed to get hold of it, he found only one very small coin. Bhim felt so ashamed. He put the coin back and made a vow to himself to study very hard and to become independent.

Soon he was winning the highest praise and admiration from all his teachers. They urged Ramji to get the best education fro his son Bhim. So Ramji moved with his family to Bombay. They all had to live in just one room, in an area where the poorest of the poor lived, but Bhim was able to go to Elphinstone High School — one of the best schools in all of India.

In their one room everyone and everything was crowed together and the streets outside were very noisy. Bhim went to sleep when he got home from school. Then his father would wake him up at two o'clock in the morning! Everything was quiet then — so he could do his homework and study in peace.

In the big city, where life was more modern than in the villages, Bhim found that he was still called an 'untouchable' and treated as if something made him different and bad — even at his famous school.

One day, the teacher called him up to the blackboard to do a sum. All the other boys jumped up and made a big fuss. Their lunch boxes were stacked behind the blackboard — they believed that Bhim would pollute the food! When he wanted to learn Sanskrit, the language of the Hindu holy scriptures, he was told that it was forbidden for 'untouchables' to do so. He had to study Persian instead — but he taught himself Sanskrit later in life.

Shock of Prejudice — Casteism

Bhim began to notice that he and his family were treated differently. At high school he had to sit in the corner of the room on a rough mat, away from the desks of the other pupils. At break-time, he was not allowed to drink water using the cups his fellow school children used. He had to hold his cupped hands out to have water poured into them by the school caretaker. Bhim did not know why he should be treated differently — what was wrong with him?

Once, he and his elder brother had to travel to Goregaon, where their father worked as a cashier, to spend their summer holidays. They got off the train and waited for a long time at the station, but Ramji did not arrive to meet them. The station master seemed kind, and asked them who they were and where they were going. The boys were very well-dressed, clean, and polite. Bhim, without thinking, told him they were Mahars (a group classed as 'untouchables'). The station master was stunned — his face changed its kindly expression and he went away.

Bhim decided to hire a bullock-cart to take them to their father — this was before motor cars were used as taxis — but the cart-men had heard that the boys were 'untouchables', and wanted nothing to do with them. Finally, they had to agree to pay double the usual cost of the journey, plus they had to drive the cart themselves, while the driver walked beside it. He was afraid of being polluted by the boys, because they were 'untouchables'. However, the extra money persuaded him that he could have his cart 'purified' later! Throughout the journey, Bhim thought constantly about what had happened — yet he could not understand the reason for it. He and his brother were clean and neatly dressed. Yet they were supposed to pollute and make unclean everything they touched and all that touched them. How could that be possible?

Bhim never forgot this incident. As he grew up, such senseless insults made him realise that what Hindu society called 'untouchability' was stupid, cruel, and unreasonable. His sister had to cut his hair at home because the village barbers were afraid of being polluted by an 'untouchable'. If he asked her why they were 'untouchables', she could only answer — that is the way it has always been." Bhim could not be satisfied with this answer. He knew that — it has always been that way" does not mean that there is a just reason for it — or that it had to stay that way forever. It could be changed.

Return to India — Nightmare in Baroda

So he was called back to India to take up a post in Baroda as agreed. He was given an excellent job in the Baroda Civil Service. Bhimrao now held a doctorate, and was being trained for a top job. Yet, he again ran into the worst features of the Hindu caste system. This was all the more painful, because for the past four years he had been abroad, living free from the label of 'untouchable.'

No one at the office where he worked would hand over files and papers to him - the servant threw them onto his desk. Nor would they give him water to drink. No respect was given to him, merely because of his caste.

He had to go from hotel to hotel looking for a room, but none of them would take him in. At last he had found a place to live in a Parsi guest house, but only because he had finally decided to keep his caste secret.

He lived there in very uncomfortable conditions, in a small bedroom with a tiny cold-water bathroom attached. He was totally alone there with no one to talk to. There were no electric lights or even oil lamps — so the place was completely dark at night.

Bhimrao was hoping to find somewhere else to live through his civil service job, but before he could, one morning as he was leaving for work a gang of angry men carrying sticks arrived outside his room. They accused him of polluting the hotel and told him to get out by evening — or else! What could he do? He could not stay with either of the two acquaintances he had in Baroda for the same reason — his low caste. Bhimrao felt totally miserable and rejected.

Beginning of Social Activity

He had no choice. After only eleven days in his new job, he had to return to Bombay. He tried to start a small business there, advising people about investments — but it too failed once customers learned of his caste.

In 1918, he became a lecturer at Sydenham College in Bombay. There, his students recognised him as a brilliant teacher and scholar. At this time he also helped to found a Marathi newspaper 'Mook Nayak' (Leader of the Dumb) to champion the cause of the 'untouchables'. He also began to organise and attend conferences, knowing that he had to begin to proclaim and publicise the humiliations suffered by the Dalits — 'the oppressed' — and fight for equal rights. His own life had taught him the necessity of the struggle for emancipation.

Leader of India's Untouchables

In 1920, with the help of friends, he was able to return to London to complete his studies in Economics at LSE. He also enrolled to study as a Barrister at Gray's Inn. In 1923, Bhimrao returned to India with a Doctorate in Economics from the LSE — he was perhaps the first Indian to have a Doctorate from this world-famous institution. He had also qualified as a Barrister-at-Law.

Back in India, he knew that nothing had changed. His qualifications meant nothing as far as the practice of Untouchability was concerned — it was still an obstacle to his career. However, he had received the best education anyone in the world could get, and was well equipped to be a leader of the Dalit community. He could argue with and persuade the best minds of his time on equal terms. He was an expert on the law, and could give convincing evidence before British commissions as an eloquent and gifted speaker. Bhimrao dedicated the rest of his life to his task.

He became known by his increasing number of followers — those 'untouchables' he urged to awake — as Babasaheb. Knowing the great value and importance of education, in 1924 he founded an association called Bahiskrit Hitakarini Sabha. This set up hostels, schools, and free libraries. To improve the lives of Dalits, education had to reach everyone. Opportunities had to be provided at grass roots level — because knowledge is power.

Leading Peaceful Agitation

In 1927 Babasaheb presided over a conference at Mahad in Kolaba District. There he said: It is time we rooted out of our minds the ideas of high and low. We can attain self-elevation only if we learn self-help and regain our self-respect." Because of his experience of the humiliation and injustice of untouchability, he knew that justice would not be granted by others. Those who suffer injustice must secure justice for themselves. The Bombay Legislature had already passed a Bill allowing everyone to use public water tanks and wells. (We have seen how Bhim was denied water at school, in his office, and at other places. Public water facilities were always denied to 'untouchables' because of the superstitious fear of 'pollution').

Mahad Municipality had thrown open the local water tank four years earlier, but so far not one 'untouchable' had dared to drink or draw water from it. Babasaheb led a procession from the Conference on a peaceful demonstration to the Chowdar Tank. He knelt and drank water from it. After he set this example, thousands of others felt courageous enough to follow him. They drank water from the tank and made history. For many hundreds of years, 'untouchables' had been forbidden to drink public water. When some caste Hindus saw them drinking water, they believed the tank had been polluted and violently attacked the Conference, but Babasaheb insisted violence would not help — he had given his word that they would agitate peacefully.

Babasaheb started a Marathi journal Bahishkrit Bharat (The Excluded of India). In it, he urged his people to hold a satyagraha (non-violent agitation) to secure the right of entry to the Kala Ram Temple at Nasik. 'Untouchables' had always been forbidden to enter Hindu temples. The demonstration lasted for a month. Then they were told they would be able to take part in the annual temple festival. However, at the festival they had stones thrown at them — and were not allowed to take part. Courageously, they resumed their peaceful agitation. The temple had to remain closed for about a year, as they blocked its entrance.

Round Table Conferences

Meanwhile, the Indian Freedom Movement had gained momentum under the leadership of Mahatma Gandhi. In 1930 a Round Table Conference was held by the British Government in London to decide the future of India. Babasaheb represented the 'untouchables'. He said there: "The Depressed Classes of India also join in the demand for replacing the British Government by a Government of the people and by the people... Our wrongs have remained as open sores and have not been righted although 150 years of British rule have rolled away. Of what good is such a Government to anybody?"

Soon a second conference was held, which Mahatma Gandhi attended representing the Congress Party. Babasaheb met Gandhi in Bombay before they went to London. Gandhi told him that he had read what Babasaheb said at the first conference. Gandhi told Babasaheb he knew him to be a real Indian patriot. At the Second Conference, Babasaheb asked for a separate electorate for the Depressed Classes. "Hinduism", he said, — has given us only insults, misery, and humiliation." A separate electorate would mean that the 'untouchables' would vote for their own candidates and be allotted their votes separate from the Hindu majority.

Babasaheb was made a hero by thousands of his followers on his return from Bombay — even though he always said that people should not idolise him. News came that separate electorates had been granted. Gandhi felt that separate electorates would separate the Harijans from the Hindus. The thought that the Hindus would be divided pained him grievously. He started a fast, saying that he would fast unto death.

Only Babasaheb could save Gandhi's life — by withdrawing the demand for separate electorates. At first he refused, saying it was his duty to do the best he could for his people - no matter what. Later he visited Gandhi, who was at that time in Yeravda jail. Gandhi persuaded Babasaheb that Hinduism would change and leave its bad practices behind. Finally Babasaheb agreed to sign the Poona Pact with Gandhi in 1932. Instead of separate electorates, more representation was to be given to the Depressed Classes. However, it later became obvious that this did not amount to anything concrete.

Poona Pact

By now Ambedkar had become one of the most prominent untouchable political figures of the time. He had grown increasingly critical of mainstream Indian political parties for their perceived lack of emphasis for the elimination of the caste system. Ambedkar criticised the Indian National Congress and its leader Mohandas Gandhi, whom he accused of reducing the untouchable community to a figure of pathos. Ambedkar was also dissatisfied with the failures of British rule, and advocated a political identity for untouchables separate from both the Congress and the British. At a Depressed Classes Conference on August 8, 1930 Ambedkar outlined his political vision, insisting that the safety of the Depressed Classes hinged on their being independent of the Government and the Congress both:

We must shape our course ourselves and by ourselves... Political power cannot be a panacea for the ills of the Depressed Classes. Their salvation lies in their social elevation. They must cleanse their evil habits. They must improve their bad ways of living.... They must be educated.... There is a great necessity to disturb their pathetic contentment and to instill into them that divine discontent which is the spring of all elevation.

In this speech, Ambedkar criticised the Salt Satyagraha launched by Gandhi and the Congress. Ambedkar's criticisms and political work had made him very unpopular with orthodox Hindus, as well as with many Congress politicians who had earlier condemned untouchability and worked against discrimination across India. This was largely because these "liberal" politicians usually stopped short of advocating full equality for untouchables.

In 1932, M. C. Rajah concluded a pact with two right-wingers in the Indian National Congress, Dr. B. S. Moonje and Jadhav. According to this pact, Moonje offered reserved seats to scheduled castes in return for Rajah's support. This demand prompted Ambedkar to make an official demand for Separate Electorate System on an all-India basis. Ambedkar's prominence and popular support amongst the untouchable community had increased, and he was invited to attend the Second Round Table Conference in London in 1931. Here he sparred verbally with Gandhi on the question of awarding separate electorates to untouchables. Gandhi fiercely opposed separate electorate for untouchables but accepted separate electorate for all other minority groups like Muslims, Sikhs..., etc. Gandhi feared that separate electorates for untouchables would divide Hindu society for future generations.

When the British agreed with Ambedkar and announced the awarding of separate electorates, Gandhi began a *fast-unto-death* while imprisoned in the Yerwada Central Jail of Pune in 1932 against the separate electorate for untouchables only; Gandhi is not against separate electorates for Muslims, Sikhs, and others. Exhorting orthodox Hindu society to eliminate discrimination and untouchability, Gandhi asked for the political and social unity of Hindus. Gandhi's fast provoked great public support across India, and orthodox Hindu leaders, Congress politicians and activists such as Madan Mohan Malaviya and Palwankar Baloo organised joint meetings with Ambedkar and his supporters at Yeravada. Fearing a communal reprisal and killings of untouchables in the event of Gandhi's death, Ambedkar agreed under massive coercion from the supporters of Gandhi to drop the demand for separate electorates, and settled for a reservation of seats. This agreement, which saw Gandhi end his fast, in the end achieved more representation for the untouchables, while dropping the demand for separate electorates that was promised through the British Communal Award prior to Ambedkar's meeting with Gandhi. Ambedkar was to later criticise this fast of Gandhi as a gimmick to deny political rights to the untouchables and increase the coercion he had faced to give up the demand for separate electorates.

In the Prime of His Life

Babasaheb had by this time collected a library of over 50,000 books, and had a house named Rajgriha built at Dadar in north Bombay to hold it. In 1935 his beloved wife Ramabai died. The same year he was made Principal of the Government Law College, Bombay. Also in 1935 a conference of Dalits was held at Yeola. Babasaheb told the conference: "We have not been able to secure the barest of human rights... I am born a Hindu. I couldn't help it, but I solemnly assure you that I will not die a Hindu." This was the first time that Babasaheb stressed the importance of conversion from Hinduism for his people — for they were only known as 'untouchables' within the fold of Hinduism.

During the Second World War, Babasaheb was appointed Labour Minister by the Viceroy. Yet he never lost contact with his roots — he never became corrupt or crooked. He said that he had been born of the poor and had lived the life of the poor, he would remain absolutely unchanged in his attitudes to his friends and to the rest of the world. The All-India Scheduled Castes Federation was formed in 1942 to gather all 'untouchables' into a united political party.

Architect of the Constitution

After the war Babasaheb was elected to the Constituent Assembly to decide the way that India — a country of millions of people — should be ruled. How should elections take place? What are the rights of the people? How are laws to be made? Such important matters had to be decided and laws had to be made. The Constitution answers all such questions and lays down rules. When India became independent in August 1947, Babasaheb Ambedkar became First Law Minister of Independent India. The Constituent Assembly made him chairman of the committee appointed to draft the Constitution for the world's largest democracy. All his study of law, economics, and politics made him the best qualified person for this task. A study of the Constitutions of many countries, a deep knowledge of law, a knowledge of the history of India and of Indian Society — all these were essential. In fact, he carried the whole burden alone. He alone could complete this huge task.

After completing the Draft Constitution, Babasaheb fell ill. At a nursing home in Bombay he met Dr. Sharda Kabir and married her in April 1948. On November 4, 1948 he presented the Draft Constitution to the Constituent Assembly, and on November 26, 1949 it was adopted in the name of the people of India. On that date he said: "I appeal to all Indians to be a nation by discarding castes, which have brought separation in social life and created jealousy and hatred."

Conversion to Buddhism

In 1950, he went to a Buddhist conference in Sri Lanka. On his return he spoke in Bombay at the Buddhist Temple. -In order to end their hardships, people should embrace Buddhism. I am going to devote the rest of my life to the revival and spread of Buddhism in India."

Babasaheb resigned from the Government in 1951. He felt that as an honest man he had no choice but to do so, because the reforms so badly needed had not been allowed to come into being.

For the next five years Babasaheb carried on a relentless fight against social evils and superstitions. On October 14, 1956 at Nagpur he embraced Buddhism. He led a huge gathering in a ceremony converting over half a million people to Buddhism. He knew that Buddhism was a true part of Indian history and that to revive it was to continue India's best tradition. 'Untouchability' is a product only of Hinduism.

Fight against Untouchability

As a leading Indian scholar, Ambedkar had been invited to testify before the Southborough Committee, which was preparing the Government of India Act 1919. At this hearing, Ambedkar argued for creating separate electorates and reservations for Dalits and other religious communities. In 1920, he began the publication of the weekly *Mooknayak* (*Leader of the Silent*) in Mumbai. Attaining popularity, Ambedkar used this journal to criticise orthodox Hindu politicians and a perceived reluctance of the Indian political community to fight caste discrimination. His speech at a Depressed Classes Conference in Kolhapur impressed the local state ruler Shahu IV, who shocked orthodox society by dining with Ambedkar. Ambedkar established a successful legal practice, and also organised the Bahishkrit Hitakarini Sabha to promote education and socio-economic uplifting of the depressed classes.

By 1927 Dr. Ambedkar decided to launch active movements against untouchability. He began with public movements and marches to open up and share public drinking water resources, also he began a struggle for the right to enter Hindu temples. He led a *satyagraha* in Mahad to fight for the right of the untouchable community to draw water from the main water tank of the town.

He was appointed to the Bombay Presidency Committee to work with the all-European Simon Commission in 1925. This commission had sparked great protests across India, and while its report was ignored by most Indians, Ambedkar himself wrote a separate set of recommendations for future constitutional reformers.

Sudden Demise

Only seven weeks later on December 6, 1956 Babasaheb died at his Delhi residence. His body was taken to Bombay. A two-mile long crowd formed the funeral procession. At Dadar cemetery that evening, eminent leaders paid their last respects to him. The pyre was lit according to Buddhist rites. Half a million people witnessed it.

Thus, ended the life of one of India's greatest sons. His was the task of awakening India's millions of excluded and oppressed to their human rights. He experienced their suffering and the cruelty shown to them. He overcame the obstacles to stand on an equal footing with the greatest men of his time. He played a vital role in forming modern India through its Constitution. His work and mission continue today — we must not rest until we see a truly democratic India of equal citizens living in peace together.

The Aftermath

Frequent violent clashes between Buddhist groups and orthodox Hindus have occurred over the years. When in 1994 a garland of shoes was hung around a statue of Ambedkar in Mumbai, sectarian violence and strikes paralysed the city for over a week. When the following year similar disturbances occurred, a statue of Ambedkar was destroyed. In addition, some Dalits who had converted to Buddhism have rioted against Hindus (such as the 2006 Dalit protests in Maharashtra) and desecrated Hindu temples and replacing deities with pictures of Ambedkar.

Foundation of Independent Labour Party

Dr. Ambedkar, organised the Independent Labour Party, participated in the provincial elections and was elected to the Bombay Legislative Assembly. During these days he stressed the need for abolition of the 'Jagirdari' system, pleaded for workers' Fight to strike and addressed a large number of meetings and conferences in Bombay Presidency.

Dr. Babasaheb Ambedkar's first political party, the Independent Labour Party founded in 1936, took its name from British politics. But two things lessened the importance of Britain for Ambedkar: the colonial presence of the British in India, and the preference of British liberals for Gandhi and his non-violent direct action campaigns for independence over Ambedkar and the slow parliamentary path. And it also seems likely that American optimism, and the lack of an obvious class system in America, met a natural response in Ambedkar.

Political Career

In 1935, Ambedkar was appointed principal of the Government Law College, a position he held for two years. Settling in Mumbai, Ambedkar oversaw the construction of a large house, and stocked his personal library with more than 50,000 books. His wife Ramabai died after a long illness in the same year. It had been her long-standing wish to go on a pilgrimage to Pandharpur, but Ambedkar had refused to let her go, telling her that he would create a new Pandharpur for her instead of Hinduism's Pandharpur which treated them as untouchables. His own views and attitudes had hardened against orthodox Hindus, despite a significant increase in momentum across India for the fight against untouchability and he began criticising them even as he was criticised himself by large numbers of Hindu activists. Speaking at the Yeola Conversion Conference on October 13 near Nasik, Ambedkar announced his intention to convert to a different religion and exhorted his followers to leave Hinduism. He would repeat his message at numerous public meetings across India.

In 1936, Ambedkar founded the Independent Labour Party, which won 15 seats in the 1937 elections to the Central Legislative Assembly. He published his book *The Annihilation of Caste* in the same year, based on the thesis he had written in New York. Attaining immense popular success, Ambedkar's work strongly criticised Hindu religious leaders and the caste system in general. He protested the Congress decision to call the untouchable community *Harijans* (*Children of God*), a name coined by Gandhi. Ambedkar served on the Defence Advisory Committee and the Viceroy's Executive Council as minister for labour. With *What Congress and Gandhi Have Done to the Untouchables,* Ambedkar intensified his attacks on Gandhi and the Congress, charging them with hypocrisy. In his work *Who Were the Shudras?*, Ambedkar attempted to explain the formation of the Shudras, i.e. the lowest caste in hierarchy of Hindu caste system. He also emphasised how Shudras are separate from Untouchables. Ambedkar oversaw the transformation of his political party into the All India Scheduled Castes Federation, although it performed poorly in the elections held in 1946 for the Constituent Assembly of India. In writing a sequel to *Who Were the Shudras?* in 1948, Ambedkar lambasted Hinduism in *The Untouchables: A Thesis on the Origins of Untouchability*:

> The Hindu Civilisation.... is a diabolical contrivance to suppress and enslave humanity. Its proper name would be infamy. What else can be said of a civilisation which has produced a mass of people... who are treated as an entity beyond human intercourse and whose mere touch is enough to cause pollution?

Ambedkar was also critical of Islam and its practices in South Asia. While justifying the Partition of India, he condemned the practice of child marriage in Muslim society, as well as the mistreatment of women. He said:

> No words can adequately express the great and many evils of polygamy and concubinage, and especially as a source of misery to a Muslim woman. Take the caste system. Everybody infers that Islam must be free from slavery and caste. While slavery existed, much of its support was derived from Islam and Islamic countries. While the prescriptions by the Prophet regarding the just and humane treatment of slaves contained in the Koran are praiseworthy, there is nothing whatever in Islam that lends support to the abolition of this curse. But if slavery has gone, caste among Muslims has remained.

He wrote that Muslim society is "even more full of social evils than Hindu Society is" and criticised Muslims for sugarcoating their sectarian caste system with euphemisms like "brotherhood". He also criticised the discrimination against the Arzal classes among Muslims who were regarded as "degraded", as well as the oppression of women in Muslim society through the oppressive *purdah* system. He alleged that while Purdah was also practiced by Hindus, only among Muslims was it sanctioned by religion. He criticised their fanaticism regarding Islam on the grounds that their literalist interpretations of Islamic doctrine made their society very rigid and impermeable to change. He further wrote that Indian Muslims have failed to reform their society unlike Muslims in other countries like Turkey.

In a "communal malaise", both groups [Hindus and Muslims] ignore the urgent claims of social justice.

Pakistan and Partition of India

Between 1941 and 1945, he published a number of books and pamphlets, including *Thoughts on Pakistan*, in which he criticised the Muslim League's demand for a separate Muslim state of Pakistan but considered its concession if Muslims demanded so as expedient.

In the above book Ambedkar wrote a subchapter titled *If Muslims truly and deeply desire Pakistan, their choice ought to be accepted*. He wrote that if the Muslims are bent on Pakistan, then it must be conceded to them. He asked whether Muslims in the army could be trusted to defend India. In the event of Muslims invading India or in the case of a Muslim rebellion, with whom would the Indian Muslims in the army side? He concluded that, in the interests of the safety of India, Pakistan should be acceded to, should the Muslims demand it. According to Ambedkar, the Hindu assumption that though Hindus and Muslims were two nations, they could live together under one state, was but a empty sermon, a mad project, to which no sane man would agree.

Architect of India's Constitution

Upon India's independence on August 15, 1947, the new Congress-led government invited Ambedkar to serve as the nation's first law minister, which he accepted. On August 29, Ambedkar was appointed Chairman of the Constitution Drafting Committee, charged by the Assembly to write free India's new Constitution. Ambedkar won great praise from his colleagues and contemporary observers for his drafting work. In this task Ambedkar's study of sangha practice among early Buddhists and his extensive reading in Buddhist scriptures were to come to his aid. Sangha practice incorporated voting by ballot, rules of debate and precedence and the use of agendas, committees and proposals to conduct business. Sangha practice itself was modelled on the oligarchic system of governance followed by tribal republics of ancient India such as the Shakyas and the Lichchavis. Thus, although Ambedkar used Western models to give his Constitution shape, its spirit was Indian and, indeed, tribal.

Granville Austin has described the Indian Constitution drafted by Dr. Ambedkar as 'first and foremost a social document.' ... 'The majority of India's constitutional provisions are either directly arrived at furthering the aim of social revolution or attempt to foster this revolution by establishing conditions necessary for its achievement.'

The text prepared by Ambedkar provided constitutional guarantees and protections for a wide range of civil liberties for individual citizens, including freedom of religion, the abolition of untouchability and the outlawing of all forms of discrimination Ambedkar argued for extensive economic and social rights for women, and also won the Assembly's support for introducing a system of reservations of jobs in the civil services, schools and colleges for members of scheduled castes and scheduled tribes, a system akin to affirmative action.

India's lawmakers hoped to eradicate the socio-economic inequalities and lack of opportunities for India's depressed classes through this measure, which had been originally envisioned as temporary on a need basis. The Constitution was adopted on November 26, 1949 by the Constituent Assembly.

Ambedkar resigned from the Cabinet in 1951 following the stalling in Parliament of his draft of the Hindu Code Bill, which sought to expound gender equality in the laws of inheritance, marriage and the economy. Although supported by Prime Minister Nehru, the Cabinet and many other Congress leaders, it received criticism from a large number of members of Parliament. Ambedkar independently contested an election in 1952 to the lower house of Parliament, the Lok Sabha, but was defeated. He was appointed to the upper house, of Parliament, the Rajya Sabha in March 1952 and would remain a member until his death.

Ambedkar's Survival

Ambedkar was survived by his second wife Savita Ambedkar and converted to Buddhism with him. His wife's name before marriage was Sharda Kabir. Savita Ambedkar died as a Buddhist in 2002. Ambedkar's grandson, Prakash Yashwant Ambedkar leads the Bharipa Bahujan Mahasangha and has served in both houses of the Indian Parliament.

A number of unfinished typescripts and handwritten drafts were found among Ambedkar's notes and papers and gradually made available. Among these were *Waiting for a Visa,* which probably dates from 1935-36 and is an autobiographical work, and the *Untouchables, or the Children of India's Ghetto,* which refers to the census of 1951.

A memorial for Ambedkar was established in his Delhi house at 26 Alipur Road. His birthdate is celebrated as a public holiday known as Ambedkar Jayanti or Bhim Jayanti. He was posthumously awarded India's highest civilian honour, the Bharat Ratna in 1990. Many public institutions are named in his honour, such as the Dr. Babasaheb Ambedkar Open University in Hyderabad, Andhra Pradesh, B. R. Ambedkar Bihar University, Muzaffarpur Dr. B. R. Ambedkar National Institute of Technology, Jalandhar the other being Dr. Babasaheb Ambedkar International Airport in Nagpur, which was otherwise known as Sonegaon Airport. A large official portrait of Ambedkar is on display in the Indian Parliament building. On the anniversary of his birth (14 April) and death (6 December) and on Dhamma Chakra Pravartan Din, 14th Oct. at Nagpur, at least half a million people gather to pay homage to him at his memorial in Mumbai. Thousands of bookshops are set up, and books are sold. His message to his followers was "Educate, Agitate, Organise".

2

Great Ambedkar

Ambedkar *vs* Gandhi

Ambedkar was a fierce critic of Mahatma Gandhi (and the Indian National Congress). He was criticised by his contemporaries and modern scholars for this opposition to Gandhi, who had been one of the first Indian leaders to call for the abolition of untouchability and discrimination.

Gandhi had a more positive, arguably romanticised view of traditional village life in India and a sentimental approach to the untouchables, calling them Harijan (children of God) and saying he was "of" them. Ambedkar rejected the epithet "Harijan" as condescending. Ambedkar strongly opposed Gandhi's statement about dalit 'The harijan'. Ambedkar criticised Gandhi that calling dalit as children of Hindu God (Hari) indirectly implies as dalit must be under the circle of Hindu religion, not to go away from this. Then only the dalits said to be untouchables according to the Hindu varnasrama. He tended to encourage his followers to leave their home villages, move to the cities, and get an education.

Dr. Ambedkar and Gandhi had big differences and conflicts of thoughts. The details of some of those are written by Dr. Ambedkar in his book *What Congress and Gandhi have done to the untouchables.*

Criticism and Legacy

Ambedkar's legacy as a socio-political reformer, had a deep effect on modern India. In post-Independence India his socio-political thought has acquired respect across the political spectrum. His initiatives have influenced various spheres of life and transformed the way India today looks at socio-economic policies, education and affirmative action through socio-economic and legal incentives. His reputation as a scholar led to his appointment as free India's first law minister, and chairman of the committee responsible to draft a Constitution. He passionately believed in the freedom of the individual and criticised equally both orthodox casteist Hindu society. His condemnation of Hinduism and its foundation of caste system, made him controversial, although his conversion to Buddhism sparked a revival in interest in Buddhist philosophy in India and abroad.

Ambedkar condemned Gandhi's support for the caste system and perpetuating untouchability. Dr. Ambedkar warned people, "Don't call Gandhi a saint. He is a seasoned politician. When everything else fails, Gandhi will resort to intrigue." "Don't fall under Gandhi's spell, he's not God... Mahatmas have come and Mahatmas have gone but untouchables have remained untouchables."

Ambedkar's political philosophy has given rise to a large number of Dalit political parties, publications and workers' unions that remain active across India, especially in Maharashtra. His promotion of the Dalit Buddhist movement has rejuvenated interest in Buddhist philosophy in many parts of India. Mass conversion ceremonies have been organised by Dalit activists in modern times, emulating Ambedkar's Nagpur ceremony of 1956.

Some scholars, including some from the affected castes, took the view that the British were more even-handed between castes, and that continuance of British rule would have helped to eradicate many evil practices. This political opinion was shared by quite a number of social activists including Jyotirao Phule.

Some, in modern India, question the continued institution of reservations initiated by Ambedkar as outdated and anti-meritocratic fact.

Outside India, at the end of 1990s, some Hungarian Romani people drew parallels between their own situation and the situation of the Dalits in India. Inspired by Ambedkar's approach, they started to convert to Buddhism.

In Popular Culture

Dr. Ambedkar's very name became a sign of victory of the down-trodden and long-exploited. *Jai Bhim,* i.e. Victory to Bhim has become a greeting phrase of the Buddhists all over India.

Several movies, plays, and literary forms are made based on his life and teachings. Jabbar Patel directed the English-language movie (also dubbed in Hindi and other Indian languages) Dr. Babasaheb Ambedkar about the life of Ambedkar, released in 2000, starring the Indian actor Mammootty as Ambedkar. Sponsored by India's National Film Development Corporation and the Ministry of Social Justice, the film was released after a long and controversial gestation period. Mammootty won the National Film Award for Best Actor for the role of Ambedkar, which he portrayed in this film.

Dr. David Blundell, professor of anthropology at UCLA and Historical Ethnographer, has established a long-term project; a series of films and events that are intended to stimulate interest and knowledge about the social and welfare conditions in India. *Arising Light* is a film on the life on Dr. B. R. Ambedkar and social welfare in India.

A Great Humanist

Humans as the Homo sapience evolved on this planet about 150,000 years before present. Some of the oldest civilizations known in the history of humanity have been dated 10,000 years old. Human Being is a social animal. Social animal has a tendency to govern and to be governed by a set of rules framed by the society itself. There are two fundamental types of human nature. Creative and possessive. Creative humans use human intellect for creative endeavours which enriches human thought; knowledge and wealth thereby contribute to the development of human heritage for the posterity. Possessive people, on the other hand do not believe in the use of human intellect for creative purpose. Rather, they believe in appropriation, amassing and even usurpation of the products of the labour of the creative people. This type of people posses a strong urge to become the governing class by all means in order to achieve their aims. Lesser the degree of civilization in the society, greater is the probability of succeeding this type of people in becoming the governing class. However, in a more civilized society the creative people can offer resistance to possessive people and try to safeguard their interests. This is a continuous process in the human society. Karl Marx has scientifically analysed this conflict by applying the principles of dialectical materialism to the sphere of social phenomenon and described it as the historical materialism. Slavery, apartheid, gender bias and caste system are the abominable creations of possessive peoples for the exploitation of creative people. These are man made evils created by man for the exploitation of man. Those, who have raised their voices against these evils and given a relentless fight against the prevailing social order of their times in order to free the creative peoples from the shackles imposed on them have become immortal personalities in the human history. Some of these great persons are better known as founders of religions. Gautam Buddha, Jesus Christ and Guru Nanak for example. Some have become famous as saints as Kabeerjee, Ravidasjee and Tukarama. Some have become source of inspiration and guidance to the underprivileged classes as Krantiba Jotiba Phoolay and Periyar Ramaswamy Naicker and some are revered even more than gods as Bharat Ratna Dr. Bhimrao Ramjee Ambedkar.

Gautam Buddha, Jesus Christ, Guru Nanak Kabeer, Ravidas, Tukarama, Krantiba Jotirao Phoolay, Periyar and Dr. Babasaheb Ambedkar they all belong to the great class of exalted Homo sapience called as Humanists.

Dr. Babasaheb Ambedkar was truly a multi-faceted personality. A veritable emancipator of Dalits, a great national leader and patriot, a great author, a great educationist, a great political philosopher, a great religious guide and above all a great humanist without any parallel among his contemporaries. All these facets of Dr. Babasaheb Ambedkar's personality had strong humanistic underpinnings. It is only regrettable that the press in the past as well as the contemporary has projected Ambedkar mainly as a great social rebel and a bitter critic of the Hindu religion. Critics of Dr. Ambedkar have ignored his basic humanistic instincts and strong humanitarian convictions behind his every act or speech through out his life. It is important to trace the origin and consolidation of his humanistic convictions.

Origins of Dr. Ambedkar's Humanistic Convictions: Dr. Ambedkar's father, Subhedar Ramji was a known follower of the Kabeerpanth. Many of the Kabir's Dohas are the veritable gems of rationalism and the most daring expressions of the humanitarian beliefs. Dr. Ambedkar's mind was thus deeply imbued with Kabeer's philosophy in the childhood days. On passing his matriculation examination, he was felicitated by his teacher and was presented with a copy of a book on the life of Buddha. This gift must have made a profound impact on the mind of young Ambedkar. Dr. Ambedkar stayed in America, the land of liberty, for his higher studies. There he studied the western liberal thought and the humanitarian philosophy expounded by great thinkers such as Prof. John Dewey, who was also his teacher, John Stuart Mill, Edmund Burke, and Prof. Harold Laski to name a few. The impact of this original thinker on Dr. Ambedkar's mind is evident from the frequent quotations one comes across in his writings and speeches. The contrast between the social milieu which he lived in, and the liberal academic thought he studied could not have resulted in anything but making him an ardent humanist.

Proof of Dr. Ambedkar's Unflinching Humanistic Convictions: Following events in the life of Dr. Ambedkar bears testimony to his humanitarian concerns and convictions.

Mahad Tank Satyagraha: Untouchables were barred however; the animals were allowed to use the water of the Chawdar tank in the Mahad town of Maharashtra. This glaring manifestation of inhuman attitude of the society was challenged by Dr. Ambedkar to usher a new era of social revolution. On 20th March 1927, 10,000 satygrahis assembled at Mahad under the leadership of Dr. Ambedkar and marched to the Chawdar tank to assert their human right to drink the water from the public place. The procession was attacked by caste Hindus and many satyagrahis were injured by them. There were many ex-military persons among the satyagrahis who had shown their bravery during the World War I. They could have retaliated in a befitting manner. However, Dr. Ambedkar appealed to his comrades not to indulge in violence. Only a person who is the humanist to his innermost core can show such steadfast faith in the non-violence in such situation.

The name of Mahad town is also permanently linked with human rights because one more reason. Dr. Ambedkar organised a conference of satyagrahis on the 25th December 1927 in which the Manusmriti was burned. Burning of the Manusmriti was a revolutionary step which sought to denounce the inhuman laws of scriptures and proclamation of right to equality and justice.

Poona Pact: In the field of politics also, Dr. Ambedkar remain firm with his convictions. Signing the Pune pact is perhaps the ultimate testimony of Dr. Ambedkar's humanitarian credentials. He was fully aware of the reason for Gandhi's fast and also the consequence of signing the pact, yet only on the humanitarian ground to save the life of Gandhi he did it. The essence of his political philosophy, the trilogy of Liberty, Equality and Fraternity he had borrowed from Buddha's philosophy. His political aims and objectives as expressed in the manifesto of the independent labour party founded by him. Many of the current provisions for the welfare and protection of labour have their origin in the manifesto of the independent labour party.

Fundamental rights assured to all citizens of our country is a great leap towards establishing the basic human values in the society that was based on graded inequality. As the chairperson of the Constitution drafting committee Dr. Ambedkar was instrumental in the incorporation of the principle of fundamental rights in the Constitution.

Dr. Ambedkar was a firm believer in the parliamentary democracy. That is why when the fear of fascism represented by Hitler was looming large over the world, he decided to cooperate with the British government in its fight against the fascism. Because as a humanist he could foresee the dangerous consequences of the victory of the fascism. Today some myopic people criticise Dr. Ambedkar for this. However, by criticising Dr. Ambedkar on this score, they inadvertently expose their fascist leanings.

A few months before his Mahaparinirvana he embraced Buddhism. It was a great tribute of a great humanist to the greatest humanistic philosophy of Buddha. By initiating millions of his follower in to the Buddhist fold, he asserted his faith in the humanistic values preached by Buddha in alleviating the sufferings of his lot. He thus reached the pinnacle of the humanism by becoming a Bodhisattva.

A Great Lawyer and Dalit Leader

In 1920 he went to London where he got his Bar-at-Law at Gray's Inn for Law.

While coming back to India in 1923, Ambedkar again experienced humiliation. The upper caste lawyers would not even have tea at his desk. But his greatest consolation were his clients, whom he treated with a liberal mind. His reputation and fame among the Depressed Classes began to grow. He was one of the greatest thinkers that India has produced. He visualised and struggled for a casteless and equal India.

At this time he was fully convinced that nothing could emancipate the Dalits except through a complete destruction of the caste system. He asserted: 'I was born a Hindu, but never will die a Hindu. Hinduism should become a religion of social equality. What is required is to get rid of the doctrine of 'Chatuvarna'. That is the root cause of all inequality and is also the parent of the caste system and untouchability, which are merely other forms of inequality'.

Ambedkar's Struggle for Equality

In 1924 he started the organisation 'Bahiskrit Hitakarini Sabha', for the upliftment of the untouchables. Ambedkar adopted a two-pronged strategy:

- Eradication of illiteracy and economic uplift of the downtrodden.
- Non-violent struggle against visible symbols of casteism, like denial of entry into temples and drawing water from public wells and tanks.

Ambedkar won two major victories when the High Court of Bombay gave a verdict in favour of the untouchables and made a successful non-violent march and entry into a temple. The two struggles shook the religious foundation on which the caste system is built. He formed a political party 'Scheduled Castes Federation' in April 1942. Ambedkar was also advocate of women's rights. He struggled for women's liberalisation from the caste-entrenched patriarchal system. At the conference of the Depressed Classes Women in Nagpur in 1942, he stated: 'let every girl who marries stand by her husband, claim to be her husband's friend and equal, and refuse to be his slave'.

Constitution Maker

He was the prime architect of the Constitution of independent India. In August 1947 a drafting committee was appointed to prepare a Draft Constitution. Dr. Ambedkar was the chairman of this committee. The Draft was submitted to the Governor General of India on February 21, 1948. The Constitution was finalised in November 1949 and came into force on January 26th, 1950; the day that India became a Republic. In that same year he became Law Minister in the first Cabinet after Independence, but he resigned from the ministry as Nehru's Cabinet refused to pass the Women's Rights Bill.

In the Fold of Buddhism

Ambedkar was justifiably bitter and disenchanted with Hinduism and thus he changed his religion. In October 1956 he, along with about two lakh Dalit men and women, converted to Buddhism in Nagpur. For Ambedkar Buddha was one of the main inspiring personalities in history who raised a strong voice of protest against inequality between people and between men and women.

On 6 December 1956 Dr. B. R. Ambedkar died. Dalits will always remember him as their Liberator and Champion of their rights. 'Rights are protected not by laws, but by the social and moral conscience of society', Ambedkar said.

Why Go for Conversion?: Speech by Dr. B. R. Ambedkar

In 1935 at Nasik district, Maharashtra, Dr. Babasaheb Ambedkar had declared his firm resolve to change his religion. He had declared that he was born as a Hindu but will not die as Hindu. About a year later, a massive Mahar conference was held on May 30 and 31, 1936, in Mumbai, to access the impact of that declaration on Mahar masses. In his address to the conference, Dr. Ambedkar expressed his views on conversion in an elaborate, well-prepared and written speech in Marathi. Here is an English translation of that speech by Mr. Vasant Moon, OSD to the committee of Govt. of Maharashtra for publication of Writings and speeches of Dr. B. R. Ambedkar.

> Conversion is not a game of children. It is not a subject of entertainment. It deals with how to make man's life successful. Just as a boatman has to make all necessary preparations before he starts for voyage, so also we have to make preparations. Unless I get an idea as to how many persons are willing to leave the Hindu fold, I cannot start preparations for conversion.

For a common man this subject of conversion is very important but also very difficult to understand.

Class Struggle:

There are two aspects of conversion; social as well as religious; material as well as spiritual. Whatever may be the aspect, or line of thinking, it is necessary to understand the beginning, the nature of Untouchability and how it is practiced. Without this understanding, you will not be able to realise the real meaning underlying my declaration of conversion. In order to have a clear understanding of untouchability and its practice in real life, I want you to recall the stories of the atrocities perpetrated against you. But very few of you might have realised as to why all this happens! What is at the root cause of their tyranny? To me it is very necessary, that we understand it.

This is not a feud between rival men. The problem of untouchability is a matter of class struggle. It is the struggle between caste Hindus and the Untouchables. That is not a matter of doing injustice against one man. This is a matter of injustice being done by one class against another. This "class struggle" has a relation with the social status. This struggle indicates, how one class should keep its relation with another class. This struggle starts as soon as you start claiming equal treatment with others.

Conversion not for Slaves:

The reason for their anger is very simple. Your behaving on par with them insults them. The untouchability is not a short or temporary feature; it is a permanent one. To put it straight, it can be said that the struggle between the Hindus and the Untouchables is a permanent phenomena. It is eternal, because the religion which has placed you at the lowest level of the society is itself eternal, according to the belief of the Hindu caste people. No change, according to time and circumstances is possible. You are at the lowest rung of the ladder today. You shall remain lowest forever. This means the struggle between Hindus and Untouchables shall continue forever. How will you survive through this struggle is the main question. And unless you think over it, there is no way out. Those who desire to live in obedience to the dictates of the Hindus, those who wish to remain their slaves, they do not need to think over this problem. But those who wish to live a life of self-respect, and equality, will have to think over this. How should we survive through this struggle? For me, it is not difficult to answer this question. Those who have assembled here will have to agree that in any struggle one who holds strength becomes the victor. One, who has no strength, need not expect success. This has been proved by experience, and I do not need to cite illustration to prove it.

Three Types of Strength:

The question that follows, which you must now consider, is whether you have enough strength to survive through this struggle? Three types of strength are known to man: (i) Manpower, (ii) Finance, and (iii) Mental Strength. Which of these, you think that you possess? So far as manpower is concerned, it is clear, that you are in a minority. In Mumbai Presidency, the untouchables are only one-eighth of the total population. That too unorganised. The castes within themselves do not allow them to organise. They are not even compact. They are scattered through the villages. Under these circumstances, this small population is of no use as a fighting force to the untouchables at their critical moments. Financial strength is also just the same. It is an undisputed fact that you at least have a little bit of manpower, but finances you have none. You have no trade, no business, no service, no land. The piece of bread thrown out by the higher castes, are your means of livelihood. You have no food, no clothes. What financial strength can you have? You have no capacity to get redress from the law courts. Thousands of untouchables tolerate insult, tyranny and oppression at the hands of Hindus without a sigh of complaint, because they have no capacity to bear the expenses of the courts. As regards mental strength, the condition is still worst. The tolerance of insults and tyranny without grudge and complaint has killed the sense of retort and revolt. Confidence, vigour and ambition have been completely vanished from you. All of you have been become helpless, unenergetic and pale. Everywhere, there is an atmosphere of defeatism and pessimism. Even the slight idea, that you can do something does not enter your mind.

Muslim Example:

If, whatever I have described above is correct then you will have to agree with the conclusion that follows. The conclusion is, if you depend only upon your own strength, you will never be able to face the tyranny of the Hindus. I have no doubt that you are oppressed because you have no strength. It is not that you alone are in minority. The Muslims are equally small in number. Like Mahar-Mangs, they too have few houses in the village. But no one dares to trouble the Muslims while you are always a victim of tyranny. Why is this so? Though there may be two houses of Muslims in the village, nobody dares to harm them, while the whole village practices tyranny against you though you have ten houses. Why does this happen? This is a very pertinent question and you will have to find out a suitable answer to this. In my opinion, there is only one answer to this question. The Hindus realise that the strength of the whole of the Muslim population in India stands behind those two houses of Muslims living in a village and, therefore, they do not dare to touch them. Those two houses also enjoy free and fearless life because they are aware that if any Hindu commits aggression against them, the whole Muslim community from Punjab to Madras will rush to their protection at any cost. On the other hand, the Hindus are sure that none will come to your rescue, nobody will help you, no financial help will reach you. Tehsildar and police belong to caste Hindus and in case of disputes between Hindus and Untouchables, they are more faithful to their caste than to their duty. The Hindus practice injustice and tyranny against you only because you are helpless.

Outside Support:

From the above discussion, two facts are very clear. Firstly, you can not face tyranny without strength. And secondly, you do not possess enough strength to face the tyranny. With these two conclusions, a third one automatically follows. That is, the strength required to face this tyranny needs to be secured from outside. How are you to gain this strength is really an important question? And you will have to think over this with an unbiased mind.

From this, you will realise one thing, that unless you establish close relations with some other society, unless you join some other religion, you cannot get the strength from outside. It clearly means, you must leave your present religion and assimilate yourselves with some other society. Without that, you cannot gain the strength of that society. So long as you do not have strength, you and your future generations will have to lead your lives in the same pitiable condition.

Spiritual Aspect of Conversion:

Uptil now, we have discussed why conversion is necessary for material gains. Now, I propose to put forth my thoughts as to why conversion is as much necessary for spiritual wellbeing. What is Religion? Why is it necessary? ... 'That which govern people is religion'. That is the true definition of Religion. There is no place for an individual in Hindu society. The Hindu religion is constituted on a class-concept. Hindu religion does not teach how an individual should behave with another individual. A religion, which does not recognise the individual, is not personally acceptable to me.

Three factors are required for the uplift of an individual. They are: Sympathy, Equality and Liberty.

Can you say by experience that any of these factors exist for you in Hinduism?

No Equality in Hinduism:

Such a living example of inequality is not to be found anywhere in the world. Not at any time in the history of mankind can we find such inequality, which is more intense than untouchability... I think, you have been thrust into this condition because you have continued to be Hindus. Those of you who have become Muslims, are treated by the Hindus neither as Untouchables nor as unequals. The same can be said of those who have become Christians...

That God is all pervading is a principle of science and not of religion, because religion has a direct relation with the behaviour of man. Hindus can be ranked among those cruel people whose utterances and acts are two poles apart. They have this Ram on their tongues and a knife under their armpits. They speak like saints but act like butchers...

Thus, we are not low in the eyes of the Hindus alone, but we are the lowest in the whole of India, because of the treatment given to us by the Hindus.

If you have to get rid of this same shameful condition, if you have to cleanse this filth and make use of this precious life; there is only one way and that is to throw off the shackles of Hindu religion and the Hindu society in which you are bound.

The taste of a thing can be changed. But the poison cannot be made amrit. To talk of annihilating castes is like talking of changing the poison into amrit. In short, so long as we remain in a religion, which teaches a man to treat another man like a leper, the sense of discrimination on account of caste, which is deeply rooted in our minds, can not go. For annihilating caste and untouchables, change of religion is the only antidote.

Untouchables are not Hindus:

What is there in conversion, which can be called novel? Really speaking what sort of social relations have you with the caste Hindus at present? You are as separate from the Hindus as Muslims and Christians are. So is their relation with you. Your society and that of the Hindus are two distinct groups. By conversion, nobody can say or feel that one society has been split up. You will remain as separate from the Hindus as you are today. Nothing new will happen on account of this conversion. If this is true, then why should people be afraid of conversion? At least, I do not find any reason for such a fear...

Revolution — Not Reform:

Changing a religion is like changing a name. Change of religion followed by the change of name will be more beneficial to you. To call oneself a Muslim, a Christian, a Buddhist or a Sikh is not merely a change of religion but also a change of name.. Since the beginning of this movement of conversion, various people have raised various objections to it. Let us now examine the truth, if any, in such objections...

A congenital idiot alone will say that one has to adhere to one's religion because it is that of our ancestors. No sane man will accept such a proposition. Those who advocate such an argument, seem not to have read the history at all. The ancient Aryan religion was called Vedic religion. It has three distinct characteristic (features). Beef-eating, drinking and merry-making was part of the religion of the day. Thousands of people followed it in India and even now some people dream of going back to it. If the ancient religion alone is to be adhered to why did the people of India leave Hinduism and accept Buddhism? Why did they divorce themselves from the Vedic religion?... Thus, this Hindu religion is not the religion of our ancestors, but it was a slavery forced upon them...

To reform the Hindu society is neither our aim nor our field of action. Our aim is to gain freedom. We have nothing to do with anything else.

If we can gain freedom by conversion, why should we shoulder the responsibility of reforming the Hindu religion? And why should we sacrifice our strength and property for that? None should misunderstand the object of our movement as being Hindu social reform. The object of our movement is to achieve social freedom for the untouchables. It is equally true that this freedom cannot be secured without conversion.

Caste Can't be Destroyed:

I do accept that the untouchables need equality as well. And to secure equality is also one of our objectives. But nobody can say that this equality can be achieved only by remaining as Hindu and not otherwise. There are two ways of achieving equality. One, by remaining in the Hindu fold and another by leaving it by conversion. If equality is to be achieved by remaining in the Hindu fold, mere removal of the sense of being a touchable or an untouchable will not serve the purpose. Equality can be achieved only when inter-caste dinners and marriages take place. This means that the Chaturvarnya must be abolished and the Brahminic religion must be uprooted. Is it possible? And if not, will it be wise to expect equality of treatment by remaining in the Hindu religion? And can you be successful in your efforts to bring equality? Of course not. The path of conversion is far simpler than this. The Hindu society does not give equality of treatment, but the same is easily achieved by conversion. If this is true, then why should you not adopt this simple path of conversion?

Conversion is a Simplest Path:

According to me, this conversion of religion will bring happiness to both the Untouchables as well as the Hindus. So long as you remain Hindus, you will have to struggle for social intercourse, for food and water, and for inter-caste marriages. And so long as this quarrel continues, relations between you and the

Hindus will be of perpetual enemies. By conversion, the roots of all the quarrels will vanish... thus by conversion, if equality of treatment can be achieved and the affinity between the Hindus and the Untouchables can be brought about then why should the Untouchables not adopt the simple and happy path of securing equality? Looking at this problem through this angle, it will be seen that this path of conversion is the only right path of freedom, which ultimately leads to equality. It is neither cowardice nor escapism.

Sanctified Racism:

Although the castes exist in Muslims and the Christians alike, it will be meanness to liken it to that of the Hindus. There is a great distinction between the caste-system of the Hindus and that of the Muslims and Christians. Firstly, it must be noted that though the castes exist amongst the Christians and the Muslims, it is not the chief characteristic of their body social.

There is one more difference between the caste system of the Hindus and that of the Muslims and Christians. The caste system in the Hindus has the foundation of religion. The castes in other religions have no sanction in their religion ...Hindus cannot destroy their castes without destroying their religion. Muslims and Christians need not destroy their religions for eradication of their castes. Rather their religion will support such movements to a great extent.

Conversion Alone Liberates Us:

I am simply surprised by the question, which some Hindus ask us as to what can be achieved by conversion alone? Most of the present day Sikhs, Muslims and Christians were formerly Hindus, majority of them being from the Shudras and Untouchables. Do these critics mean to say that those, who left the Hindu fold and embraced Sikhism or Christianity, have made no progress at all? And if this is not true, and if it is admitted that the conversion has brought a distinct improvement in their condition, then to say that the untouchables will not be benefited by conversion, carries no meaning...

After giving deep thought to the problem, everybody will have to admit that conversion is necessary to the Untouchables as self-government is to India. The ultimate object of both is the same. There is not the slightest difference in their ultimate goal. This ultimate aim is to attain freedom. And if the freedom is necessary for the life of mankind, conversion of Untouchables which brings them complete freedom cannot be called worthless by any stretch of imagination...

Economic Progress or Social Changes?:

I think it necessary here to discuss the question as to what should be initiated first, whether economic progress or conversion? I do not agree with the view that economic progress should precede...

Untouchability is a permanent handicap on your path of progress. And unless you remove it, your path cannot be safe. Without conversion, this hurdle cannot be removed...

So, if you sincerely desire that your qualifications should be valued, your education should be of some use to you, you must throw away the shackles of untouchability, which means that you must change your religion...

However, for those who need this Mahar Watan, I can assure them that their Mahar Watan will not be jeopardised by their conversion. In this regard, the Act of 1850 can be referred. Under the provisions of this Act, no rights of person or his successors with respect to his property are affected by virtue of his conversion...

Poona Pact:

A second doubt is about political rights. Some people express fear as to what will happen to our political safeguards if we convert...

But I feel, it is not proper to depend solely on political rights. These political safeguards are not granted on the condition that they shall be ever lasting. They are bound to cease sometime. According to the communal Award of the British Government, our political safeguards were limited for 20 years. Although no such limitation has been fixed by the Poona Pact, nobody can say that they are everlasting. Those, who depend upon the political safeguards, must think as to what will happen after these safeguards are withdrawn on the day on which our rights cease to exist. We will have to depend on our social strength. I have already told you that this social strength is wanting in us. So also I have proved in the beginning that this strength cannot be achieved without conversion...

Political Rights:

Under these circumstances, one must think of what is permanently beneficial.

In my opinion, conversion is the only way to eternal bliss. Nobody should hesitate even if the political rights are required to be sacrificed for this purpose. Conversion brings no harm to the political safeguards. I do not understand why the political safeguards should at all be jeopardised by conversion. Wherever you may go, your political rights and safeguards will accompany you. I have no doubt about it.

If you become Muslims, you will get the political rights as Muslims. If you become Christians, you will get the political rights as Christians, if you become Sikhs, you will have your political rights as Sikhs. In short, our political rights will accompany us.

So nobody should be afraid of it. On the other hand, if we remain Hindus and do not convert, will our rights be safe? You must think carefully on this. Suppose the Hindus pass a law whereby the untouchability is prohibited and its practice is made punishable, then they may ask you, 'We have abolished untouchability by law and you are no longer untouchables...

Looking through this perspective, conversion becomes a path for strengthening the political safeguards rather than becoming a hindrance. If you remain Hindus, you are sure to lose your political safeguards. If you want to save them, leave this religion. The political safeguards will be permanent only by conversion.

The Hindu religion does not appeal to my conscience. It does not appeal to my self-respect. However, your conversion will be for material as well as for spiritual gains. Some persons mock and laugh at the idea of conversion for material gains. I do not feel hesitant in calling such persons as stupid.

Conversion Brings Happiness:

I tell you all very specifically, religion is for man and not man for religion. To get human treatment, convert yourselves.

Convert — For getting organised.

Convert — For becoming strong.

Convert — For securing equality.

Convert — For getting liberty.

Convert — For that your domestic life may be happy.

I consider him as leader who without fear or favour tells the people what is good and what is bad for them. It is my duty to tell you, what is good for you, even if you don't like it, I must do my duty. And now I have done it.

It is now for you to decide and discharge your responsibility.

3

Dalit-Buddhist Movement

The Dalit-Buddhist movement or *Navayana* in India began with the support of Sri Lankan Buddhist monks. It received an impetus with B. R. Ambedkar's call for conversion of Dalits to Buddhism in the context of a caste based society that considered them to be at the lower end of the hierarchy.

The Origin

Buddhism was once dominant through much of India, it had however begun to decline by the 12th century. The Buddhist revival began in India in 1891, when the Sri Lankan Buddhist leader Anagarika Dharmapala founded the Maha Bodhi Society. The Maha Bodhi Society mainly attracted upper-caste people.

South India

In 1890 Pandit C. Ayodhya Dasa (1845-1914), better known as Iyothee Thass, founded the Sakya Buddhist Society (also known as the Indian Buddhist Association). The first president of the Indian Buddhist Association was the German born American Paul Carus, the author of *The Gospel of Buddha* (1894).

Thass, a Tamil Siddha physician, was the pioneer of the Tamil Dalit movement. He argued that Tamil Dalits were originally Buddhists. He led a delegation of prominent Dalits to Henry Steel

Olcott and asked for his help in the re-establishment of "Tamil Buddhism." Olcott helped Thass to visit Sri Lanka, where he received *diksha* from Bhikkhu Sumangala Nayake. After returning to India, Thass established the *Sakya Buddhist Society* in Madras with branches in many places including Karnataka. Thass established a weekly magazine called *Oru Paisa Tamizhan* (One Paisa Tamilian) in Chennai in 1907, which served as a newsletter linking all the new branches of the Sakya Buddhist Society. The magazine discussed traditions and practices of Tamil Buddhism, new developments in the Buddhist world, and the Indian subcontinent's history from the Buddhist point of view.

Brahmananda Reddy, a Dalit leader of Andhra Pradesh, was also fascinated by Buddhism.

Uttar Pradesh

In the early-20th century, the Barua Buddhists of Bengal under the leadership of Kripasaran Mahasthavir (1865-1926), founder of the Bengal Buddhist Association, Calcutta (1892) established viharas in cities such as Lucknow, Hyderabad, Shillong and Jamshedpur.

In Lucknow, Bodhanand Mahastavir (1874-1952) advocated Buddhism for Dalits. Born Mukund Prakash in a Bengali Brahmin family, he was orphaned at a young age, and was then raised in Benaras by an aunt. He was initially attracted to Christianity, but became a Buddhist after a meeting with Buddhists monks from Ceylon at a Theosophical Conference in Benares. He later lived in Lucknow where he came in contact with Barua Buddhists, many of whom were employed as cooks by the British. In 1914, Prakash was ordained Bodhanand Mahastavir in Calcutta in the presence of Kripasaran Mahasthvir. He began preaching Buddhism in Lucknow. He founded the *Bharatiye Buddh Samiti* in 1916, and set up a vihara in 1928. In his book *Mula Bharatavasi Aur Arya* (Original Inhabitants and Aryans), Mahastavir stated that the shudras were the original inhabitants of India, who were enslaved by the Aryans.

Bodhanand Mahastavir wrote another book on Buddhist rituals called *Baudha Dvicharya*. His associate, Chandrika Prasad Jigyasu, founded the *Bahujan Kalyan Prakashan*. The two co-authored a book on the life and teaching of the Buddha.

Acharya Ishvardatt Medharthi (1900-71) of Kanpur also supported the cause of the Dalits. He had studied Pali at Gurukul Kangri and Buddhist scripture was well known to him. He was initiated into Buddhism by Gyan Keto and the Lokanatha in 1937. Gyan Keto (1906-84), born Peter Schoenfeldt was a German who arrived to Ceylon in 1936 and became a Buddhist. Although Medharthi heavily criticized the Indian caste system, he didn't criticize Hinduism. He claimed that the Dalits (Adi Hindus) were the ancient rulers of India and had been trapped into slavery by the Aryan invaders. He also claimed that the sanatana dharma was the religion of "Adi Hindus", and tried to reconcile Buddhism with the Sant Mat.

Another Bhikkhu of Kanpur, Bhikshu Uttam, was a strong supporter of the Arya Samaj and the *Jat Pat Todak Mandal,* the anti-caste wing of the Arya Samaj.

Ambedkar's Declaration

At the Yeola conference in 1935, prominent Dalit leader B. R. Ambedkar declared that he would not die a Hindu, saying that it perpetuates caste injustices. Ambedkar was approached by various leaders of different denominations and faiths. Meetings were held to discuss the question of Dalit religion and the pros and cons of conversion. On May 22, 1936, an "All Religious Conference" was held at Lucknow. It was attended by prominent Dalit leaders including Jagjivan Ram, though Ambedkar could not attend it. At the conference, Muslim, Christian, Sikh, and Buddhist representatives presented the tenets of their respective religions in an effort to win over Dalits.

Buddhist monk Lokanatha visited Ambedkar's residence at Dadar on June 10, 1936 and tried to persuade him to embrace Buddhism. Later in an interview to the Press, Lokanatha said that Ambedkar was impressed with Buddhism and that his own ambition was to convert all Dalits to Buddhism. In 1937, Lokanatha published a pamphlet *Buddhism Will Make You Free,* dedicated to the Depressed Classes of India from his press in Ceylon.

In early-1940s, Ambedkar visited Acharya Ishvardatt Medharthi's Buddhpuri school in Kanpur. Medharthi had earlier been initiated into Buddhism by Lokanatha, and by the mid-1940s, he had close contacts with Ambedkar. For a short while, Ambedkar also took Pali classes from Medharthi in Delhi.

Bodhananda Mahastvir and B. R. Ambedkar first met in 1926, at the "Indian Non-Brahmin Conference" convened by Shahu IV of Kolhapur. They met on two more occasions and for a short while in the 1940s, where they discussed dhamma. Mahastavir objected to Dr. Ambedkar's second marriage because his bride was a Brahmin. Later, his followers actively participated in Ambedkar's Republican Party of India.

Ambedkar's Conversion

After publishing a series of books and articles arguing that Buddhism was the only way for the Untouchables to gain equality, Ambedkar publicly converted on October 14, 1956 at Deekshabhoomi, Nagpur. He took the three refuges and the Five Precepts from a Buddhist monk, Bhadant U. Chandramani, in the traditional manner and then in his turn administered them to the 380,000 of his followers that were present. The conversion ceremony was attended by Medharthi, his main disciple Bhoj Dev Mudit, and Mahastvir Bodhanand's Sri Lankan successor, Bhànte Pragyanand. Ambedkar would die less than two months later, just after finishing his definitive work on Buddhism.

Many Dalits employ the term "Ambedkar(ite) Buddhism" to designate the Buddhist movement, which started with Ambedkar's conversion and many converted people called themselves as "Nava-Bauddha", i.e. New Buddhists.

Post-Ambedkar Movement

The Buddhist movement was somewhat hindered by Dr. Ambedkar's death so shortly after his conversion. It did not receive the immediate mass support from the Untouchable population that Ambedkar had hoped for. Division and lack of direction among the leaders of the Ambedkarite movement have been an additional impediment. According to the 2001 census, there are currently 7.95 million Buddhists in India, at least 5.83 million of whom are Buddhists in Maharashtra. This makes Buddhism the fifth-largest religion in India and 6 per cent of the population of Maharashtra, but less than 1 per cent of the overall population of India.

The Buddhist revival remains concentrated in two states: Ambedkar's native Maharashtra, and Uttar Pradesh — the land of Bodhanand Mahastavir, Acharya Medharthi and their associates.

Developments in Uttar Pradesh

Acharya Medharthi retired from his Buddhapuri school in 1960, and shifted to an ashram in Haridwar. He turned to the Arya Samaj and conducted vedic yajnas all over India. After his death, he was cremated according to Arya Samaj rites. His Buddhpuri school became embroiled in property disputes. His follower, Bhoj Dev Mudit, converted to Buddhism in 1968 and set up a school of his own.

Rajendranath Aherwar appeared as an important Dalit leader in Kanpur. He joined the Republican Party of India and converted to Buddhism along with his whole family in 1961. In 1967, he founded the Kanpur branch of "Bharatiya Buddh Mahasabha". He held regular meetings where he preached Buddhism, officiated at Buddhist weddings and life cycle ceremonies, and organised festivals on Dr. Ambedkar's Jayanti (birth day), Buddha Jayanti, Diksha Divas (the day Ambedkar converted), and Dr. Ambedkar Paranirvan Divas (the day Ambedkar died).

The Dalit Buddhist movement in Kanpur gained impetus with the arrival of Dipankar, a Chamar bhikkhu, in 1980. Dipankar had come to Kanpur on a Buddhist mission and his first public appearance was scheduled at a mass conversion drive in 1981. The event was organised by Rahulan Ambawadekar, an RPI Dalit leader. In April 1981, Ambawadekar founded the Dalit Panthers (UP Branch) inspired by the Maharashtrian Dalit Panthers. The event met with severe criticism and opposition from Vishwa Hindu Parishad and was banned.

In 2002, Kanshi Ram, a popular out-caste political leader from a Sikh religious background, announced his intention to convert to Buddhism on October 14, 2006, the fiftieth anniversary of Ambedkar's conversion. He intended for 20,000,000 of his supporters to convert at the same time. Part of the significance of this plan was that Ram's followers include not only Untouchables, but persons from a variety of castes, who could significantly broaden Buddhism's support. However, he died October 9, 2006 after a lengthy illness; he was cremated as per Buddhist rituals.

Another popular Dalit leader, Bahujan Samaj Party chief Mayawati, has said that she and her followers will embrace Buddhism after the BSP gains control of the government.

Maharashtra

Japanese-born Bhadant Nagarjun Surai Sasai is an important Buddhist leader in India. Sasai came to India in 1966 and met Nichidatsu Fuji, whom he helped with the Peace Pagoda at Rajgir. He fell out with Fuji, however, and started home, but, by his own account, was stopped by a dream in which a figure resembling Nagarjuna appeared and said, "Go to Nagpur".

In Nagpur, he met Wamanrao Godbole, the person who had organised the conversion ceremony for Dr. Ambedkar in 1956. Sasai claims that when he saw a photograph of Dr. Ambedkar at Godbole's home, he realised that it was Ambedkar who had appeared in his dream. At first, Nagpur folk considered Surai Sasai very strange. Then he began to greet them with "Jai Bhim" (victory to Ambedkar) and to build viharas. In 1987 a court case to deport him on the grounds that he had overstayed his visa was dismissed, and he was granted Indian citizenship. Sasai is one of the main leaders of the campaign to free the Mahabodhi Temple at Bodh Gaya from Hindu control.

Mass Conversions

Since Ambedkar's conversion, several thousand people from different castes have converted to Buddhism in ceremonies including the twenty-two vows. The Tamil Nadu and Gujarat governments passed new laws in 2003 to ban "forced" religious conversions. These laws were later withdrawn due to heavy opposition.

1957: In 1957, Mahastvir Bodhanand's Sri Lankan successor, Bhante Pragyanand, held a mass conversion drive for 15,000 people in Lucknow.

2001: A prominent Indian Dalit Buddhist leader and political activist, Udit Raj, organised a large mass conversion on November 4, 2001 where he gave the 22 vows, but the event met with active opposition from the government.

2006, Hyderabad: A report from the UK daily *The Guardian* said that some Hindus have converted to Buddhism. Buddhist monks from the UK and the US attended the conversion ceremonies in India. In response, Hindu nationalists asserted that Dalits should concentrate on illiteracy and poverty rather than looking for new religions.

2006, Gulbarga: On October 14, 2006 hundreds of people converted from Hinduism to Buddhism in Gulburga (Karnataka).

2006: A Buddhist source claimed that "300,000 Dalits are estimated" to have converted to Buddhism as part of 50th year celebrations of Ambedkar's deeksha in 2006. Non-Partisan sources put the number of attendees (not converts) at 30,000. The move was criticised by Hindu groups as "unhelpful" and has been criticised as a "political stunt."

2007, Mumbai: On May 27, 2007 tens of thousands of Dalits from Maharashtra gathered at the Mahalakshmi racecourse in Mumbai to mark the 50th anniversary of the conversion of Ambedkar. The number of people who actually converted, however, versus the number of people in attendance was not clear. The event was organised by the Republican Party of India leader Ramdas Athvale.

Criticism of Conversions

Hindu critics have argued that efforts to convert Hindus to Ambedkarite Buddhism are political stunts rather than sincere commitments to social reform. In addition, several Dalit leaders have stated that they are not against the upper castes *per se.* Leaders of the Dalit Bahujan Samaj Party have said that their being branded as "anti-Hindu" because of the publicity associated with the conversions is largely the work of partisan and politically motivated groups within the Dalit movement and that they are only interested in peaceful dialogue with the Brahmins.

The critics also note that Gautama Buddha, the founder of Buddhism, himself was a Kshatriya of the Uakya clan. Buddha is also said to be a descendant of Sage Angirasa in many Buddhist texts. Scholars like Dr. Eitel connects it to the Rishi Gautama. Buddha declares in the *Vasalsutta,* "Whosoever by falsehood deceives either a Brahman or a Sraman or any other mendicant, let him be an outcast." He again declares in the text, "Whosoever annoys either a Brahman or a Sraman when meal-time has come and does not give him anything, let one know him as an outcast."

Distinctive Interpretation

According to controversial academic Gail Omvedt:

> "Ambedkar's Buddhism seemingly differs from that of those who accepted by faith, who 'go for refuge'

> and accept the canon. This much is clear from its basis: it does not accept in totality the scriptures of the Theravada, the Mahayana, or the Vajrayana. The question that is then clearly put forth: is a fourth yana, a Navayana, a kind of modernistic Enlightenment version of the Dhamma really possible within the framework of Buddhism?"

Most Dalit Indian Buddhists espouse an eclectic version of Buddhism, primarily based on Theravada, but with additional influences from Mahayana and Vajrayana. On many subjects, they give Buddhism a distinctive interpretation. Of particular note is their emphasis on Shakyamuni Buddha as a political and social reformer, rather than merely as a spiritual leader. They point out that the Buddha required his monastic followers to ignore caste distinctions, and that he was critical of the social inequality that existed in his own time. Ambedkar's followers do not believe that a person's unfortunate conditions at birth are the result of previous karma.

They also point out that Ormvedt's idea of an 'Enlightenment version of the dharma' opposed to a traditional 'acceptance by faith' is a misapplication of Western categories, since the Buddha encouraged people to put all teachings — including his own — to critical test and not to accept anything on the basis of tradition.

4

Redefining Ambedkar

Ambedkar's thoughts are variously presented by scholars. Some tend to put them in familiar academic slots, viz.: social, political, economic, religious, etc. The other method may be bracketed as biographical. The problem with the former is that it tends to discretise his thoughts within the artificial compartments of academic disciplines. The latter tends to be narrational, eulogical and scarcely analytical. Both of them are likely to miss out the underscoring vision and more so the futuristic dimension, which are essentially the attributes of the holistic conception.

Visions and Icons of the Great Man

Every great person has a vision that impels all her/his works. Its discernibility may vary from case to case, generally being the function of the degree of turbulence around her/him, her/his relative position within the power structure in the given environment, her/his own equipment and conception of self-role. Marx, for instance, offers an articulate vision in clearest terms as he assumed the primary role of a philosopher to bring about revolutionary change, whereas Ambedkar had donned the mantle of mass-leadership in his primary role to spearhead the change; the degree of turbulence in the work domain of Marx had been minimal as he basically struggled in the realm of thought spanning complete human history whereas Ambedkar situated himself in the political turbulence that obtained in India as his strategy; Ambedkar's position in the power structure that bounded his work domain was certainly weak relative to Marx's. This is neither to undermine the role of Marx as the activist constantly trying out his philosophy in the realm of practice nor to belittle the problems he suffered in life. With regard to personal equipment, both Ambedkar as well as Marx, could be taken to be equally equipped to undertake their respective tasks that they had undertaken. Marx had started off with philosophy and adopted the class-consciousness of the proletariat quite unlike Ambedkar, in whose case it was his own consciousness — the consciousness of an untouchable built up through concrete experience that had propelled his philosophical search. Marx was well aware of his role in the revolutionary project, that he had to provide requisite tools and tackles for the working class for bringing about a change in the overall interest of humanity. But, Ambedkar was always loaded with anxiety as he had to strategise his way through the political maze around him, winning for dalits the maximum he could in a short span of time. In process, his role also underwent transformation with the expanse of the battleground. Inevitably, his thoughts and action always remained context-laden, polemical and pragmatically purposeful. It is therefore a relatively difficult task to discern a coherent vision underscoring the life work of Babasaheb Ambedkar.

It is a moot point as to what extent a great person, who is essentially anchored in her/his space and time, could transcend these barriers and be equally effective in a different situation. A great person basically is the product of prevailing social relations. It is a particular moment in history that reflects an acute demand for such a person. Depending upon her/his location in the social setting, s/he imparts her/his individual feature to the historical moments and movements in terms of working out specific means for resolving contradictions that engender them and releasing the forces of history in a specific direction. The masses whose cause she/he espouses throng around her/him in this process, depending upon the level of their collective consciousness. The longevity of the ideas a great person propounds in a historical setting depends upon the nature of contradictions, the size and expanse of problems and the time domain in which they are situated. Generally, the classes that share the vision and ideology of such persons tend to iconise them with specific attributes of their class choice, in an attempt to institutionalise the latter. In this process, they would decontextise some of the ideas and proffer them as universal theorems, if they perceive a pay-off for themselves in the sphere hegemonised by them. This phenomenon becomes clear only over a long time horizon. For instance, the religious principles that were sprouted in the soil of certain specific social relations have basically blossomed in an alien soil with the help of the nutrients of class interests. Very broadly speaking, the trend of iconisation of great persons and the attempt of institutionalising their ideas is a gauge to assess the forces of *status quo* in the society.

Ambedkar's: Commitment and Constraints

In the case of Babasaheb Ambedkar, iconisation was inevitable. The combination of factors like his high stature, his devotion to the cause of his people; the historical setting in which he lived, the low level of literacy and political consciousness in masses; and the vested interests of internal as well as external people have been its cause. The problem is not with iconisation as it is with its multiplicity. A question may be pertinently asked can Ambedkar be uniquely represented by a single icon? As Prof. Upendra Bakshi had outlined in one of his articles during the centenary year of his birth anniversary that there were many Ambedkars and had questioned as to which Ambedkar do we commemorate? When he said so, Prof. Bakshi was referring to different facets of Ambedkar's personality that could be virtually segregated. One can even periodise some of them. For example, the pre-1942 Ambedkar as a young, untouchable man endowed with highest scholastic distinctions, struggling within and without for the emancipation of his people is a grossly different personality than the Ambedkar as a member of the viceroy's Executive Council or the Ambedkar as the law minister in the Nehru Cabinet in the post-independence India or the Ambedkar as the chairman of the drafting committee for the Indian Constitution or even the Ambedkar of still later years who had completely identified himself with Buddhism and in a way completely spiritualised himself.

What comes clearly however, from this review is that the changes in his outlook and role were essentially driven by his unstilted commitment to the cause of emancipation of oppressed humanity in general and dalits in particular. He might not have had appropriate methodological tools to deal with the problem at hand. With the equipment that basically belonged to a school of social engineers, he tried to dissect history. Paradoxically, he attempted to demolish the establishment with the very tools that were forged to serve the ruling classes. By training he did not have the facility to look at history as the continuum of human struggle with a certain inherent logic. He did use history as a repertoire of human episodes and attributed even logic to it but its source was externalised.

Non-Dialectical Solution: State and Religion

It appears that Babasaheb Ambedkar had really internalised the doctrine of momentariness (*Anityatawad* and later *Kshanikwad*) of Buddha and therefore even refused to care for consistency in his views and opinions. This doctrine states that every thing changes every moment, that things are constantly becoming. It follows that in this situation of flux not even mental processes could be static, they had essentially to match the dynamicity of the material world. He thus never hesitated in changing his thoughts or strategy as per the unfolding situation. Viewed another way, these changes can be understood in relation to foci of control. The degree of consistency in thought and action is generally inversely proportional to the distance of the subject from the foci of control of its surrounding. Ambedkar had nil or little control over his situation. He had to consistently create space for himself and strategise to influence the situation to his advantage. (The dynamics of the situation was propelled by the forces that were variously placed in the adversary camps). The framework within which he conceived his struggle had exposed him to his lot to respond to this dynamics. The hallmark of Ambedkar's thoughts is the dynamic rationale, which he has consistently employed to comprehend situations and to strategise his response thereto. 'Ambedkar' therefore cannot be captured in static terms. His icon will have to represent the dynamism that he lived. Since, this is an infeasible proposition; we will have to discern the underscoring vision behind his works, the intransient essence of his entire mission to create a suitable icon. This icon, even if it does not resemble the familiar Ambedkar, alone could be the beacon of the dalit movement.

The concept of *Anityawad* in Buddhism essentially belongs to dialectics that has made Buddha an early dialectician philosopher.

The dichotomy that creeps in can only be resolved by dialectical method. It may be questioned whether Ambedkar's method was dialectical. It appears that while he accepts constant becoming of things as the principle underscoring the universe, he faces a dilemma with respect to the conception of order in this State. It could be resolved dialectically in terms of systemic attribute of self-regulation — a characteristic of internal control. But the conventional conception of order, essentially a non-dialectical conception, leads to externalisation of control.

Ambedkar, having experienced the brutal aspects of history and unbridled exploitation of man by man, appears in need of a control mechanism operating at two levels, viz. internal and external, so as to maintain the societal order in the desired State. His internal control mechanism is the moral code provided by the religion and the one for external control is the State. If this moral code is internalised by all individuals and in turn by society as the summation of the latter (as the liberal tradition held), society is expected to have an internal order. If however the baser instincts of some people or group of people defy this order, either as a result of conflicting codes they follow or for any other reason, then in such case the State will step in and restore the order. The will of the collective is supposed to be embodied in the State by the Constitution. It is therefore that Ambedkar has reservation in agreeing with Marx that 'religion was the opium of masses' or the 'State shall eventually wither away'. Ambedkar certainly did not know that the order could be the attribute of the system itself. It is only in the sixties that Cybernetics principles came to lime light that the complex probabilistic systems, which the social systems certainly are, do have the inherent capability of self-regulating and self-organising control.

Liberalism and Reformism

By upbringing and training Ambedkar was influenced by western liberalism. The openness and liberal values of the western society had struck him with pleasant surprise by his own admission. There is a reason to believe that he had studied Marxism. His first essay on caste reflects some amount of analytical orientation of Marxism. One of the subjects in his curriculum also happened to be related to Marxian socialism and his guide Prof. Seligman was well versed with the economic interpretation of history. However, as his later work reveals, Ambedkar reflected more closeness with the liberal tradition than Marxism. However, consciously he never identified himself with the Liberalism. Being aware of its pitfalls, he needed to declare that he was not a liberal reformist, although while having reservations with the postulations of Marxism he could never hide his attraction towards it.

The pitfall of his thinking emanates from his conception of the moral force of religion divorced from the material reality. He therefore hopes that without any bloodshed, the society based on liberty, equality and fraternity could be created. Of course as hypothesised above, he conceptualises the constitutional State based on these principles. With this wishful thinking, he tends to ignore the fact that regardless of the pretensions of ruling classes, the impact of liberal governance in the multi-centric iniquitous society is bound to result in sustaining multi-centricity and inequality. This liberalism rather promotes politics of casteism and communalism, schism among dalits, their use in political power games, subversion of their real problems and protects the interests of the few rich. It was a kind of contradiction in terms to assume that liberal democracy, which is actually the manifestation of the political power of the bourgeois, will do justice to the paupers. It might appear to extend certain concessions to the weaker sections, but its real motive is to maintain the existing rule of the ruling classes. Liberal democracy might appear better than the decadent Hindu caste system but it is incapable of bringing any real change in favour of dalits. It muffles the tension of the exploitative system and kills the revolutionary motivation of its victims.

Redefinition Project

Many of the constructs employed by Babasaheb Ambedkar in his working have a qualified meaning. Firstly, they are not absolute as they appear. They are the derivatives of his thought process, the source of which could be traced to his basic objective of annihilation of castes and creating a society based on equality, liberty and fraternity. Even these three principles that he held so dear to his heart, bear very different meaning from the familiar ones associated with the French Revolution. He said he had them from Buddha. What Buddha said also is to be understood from his interpretation, which could be as different from the accepted version as to be disproved by the Buddhist church. His Buddha and His Dhamma, for instance, had faced this kind of disapproval initially from many Buddhists. Understanding Ambedkar thus essentially demands extra consideration and care about the specific meanings of the constructs and concepts he uses.

The lack of it has already caused much misunderstanding among many people. It is one thing to have a clear understanding of what he said or meant but quite another to extrapolate it to something congruent to his basic objective or vision that may be useable in shaping the future movement. Quite like Marx had said of philosophy, it could be said that the issue is not to understand Ambedkar as he is but to possibly think of him as a weapon in the struggle to which he devoted his life.

The redefinition referred to here will have to essentially address both these issues. From the viewpoint of one seeking a revolutionary change, there are indeed many dimensions on which Ambedkar calls for critical interpretation. Many of the concepts that seem to act as the props for his formulations are rooted in the reactionary camp. Paradoxically, he brings them to work for his emancipatory project, which potentially is no less than a revolution. Predominant among these concepts are identified as State, religion, liberal democracy, constitutionalism, revolution, socialism, violence and Marxism, that some way or the other have been the cause of misunderstandings about him.

It is important to appreciate that Ambedkar employed the search process that is essentially rational and the underlying objective undoubtedly radical. There could be flaws in the specific design or the application of the search process, depending upon the State of his knowledge and complexity of the situation to which it is applied. Besides this, the end result depends upon the repertoire of alternatives used for the search. What it means is that the specific method, thought or action of Ambedkar may constitute the historical facts but they cannot be taken in their face value if one wants to comprehend the ideological aspects of Ambedkar.

In his usage of the above concepts for instance he does not always exercise the academic rigour. Besides the reason that much of his usage was addressed to the unacademic lot, most of the times he tended to impart his own meanings to the terms he used. With the changed contexts or with the change in information, he readily changed his opinions. For, hypothetically speaking, if Ambedkar had lived longer he would have certainly changed his views, looking at more information available or experiencing the undesired aftermath of some of his own beliefs and opinions. Had he not disowned the Constitution, which he had so laboriously written and so forcefully defended, saying that he was used as the hack to write it? Whatever he had done had several limitations. He never hesitated to change his opinion or stand if he was convinced that it was right. The redefinition project proposed here, in a way, is something, which he has done himself, all his life and would have continued doing if he had been alive. It is essentially something in the nature of continuing his unfinished task.

The methodological aspects of this exercise consists in the process of conceptualisation of the core vision and ideological proclivities of Ambedkar through the analytical study of his life within its contextual parameters, oriented towards capturing its intransient content. It should reflect the basic purpose, that is, to see whether and how he could catalyse the emancipatory movement of dalits and in turn democratise the Indian society. This process may not be free from bias. The bias could be in favour of the change craved for by the have-nots, not of the ruling classes that has necessarily been colouring the history so far. It cannot escape the viewpoint of the latter. The viewpoint is rather embodied in the basic intention to forge Ambedkar as the weapon for the future struggles of dalits. The process of conceptualisation may be formalised by drawing out multiple ideological patterns based upon the constituent parameters of the hypothesised vision and testing them with the facts in their macro and micro settings. The test results could be used to refine the definition of the parameters and repeating the exercise until they can no more be improved. The iterative process will eliminate the tactic-based episodes and increasingly highlight the intransient dimensions. The radicalisation consists in derivation of the programme from these dimensions with any scientific methodology.

'Ambedkar' for the Movement of Dalits

'Ambedkar' for the dalit movement, first of all, should be shorn of all the sectarian outlook that unfortunately came to be associated with him. He was an iconoclast and therefore should inspire us to break such icons that are imbued with this outlook.

Dalits have to demolish all the handiwork of the reactionaries and vested interests. The project of redefinition of Ambedkar should liberate him from the dens of the ruling class and bring him back to the huts in slums and villages where he rightly belongs.

The greatest thing about Ambedkar is his consistent anti-dogmatic stance. He never accepted any thing in name of authority. He hated humbug of every kind. He always approached problems with a student's sincerity and researcher's intellectual honesty. He gave a vision that even the ideologies are bound by the tenet of impermanence and no body should claim them validity beyond their times. His followers therefore can assume absolute liberty to think through things as per their own experience in changing times.

'Ambedkar' against Exploitation

The underscoring vision in Ambedkar's thought and action is to be found in his yearning for the end of all kinds of exploitation. Whenever and wherever he smelt exploitation, he raised his voice against it. The caste system that subjugated more than one fifth of the population to levels worse than animals' for more than two millennia and which represented institutionalisation of the most heinous inequality by the Hindu religion as ordained by its gods, became the prime target of his life. He attacked it from the standpoint of its victims — the untouchables. He waged many battles; initially targeting the citadels of Brahminism — the custodian of the Hindu religious code, and later politicised the battle, realising the ineffectiveness of the former. He did not let this objective out of sight even for a moment and worked incessantly for its achievement. This Herculean task almost completely overshadows the fact that his struggles extend well beyond the caste struggles and rather encompass all other forms of exploitation.

Even the credit for struggling against untouchability was reluctantly granted to him by the establishment which had belittled him initially as merely a leader of his own caste — Mahar. This prejudicial treatment of Ambedkar could itself be taken as a measure of the severity of the problematic of caste. The facts are clear today that not only was his struggle directed towards the emancipation of all the untouchables but also towards annihilation of the entire caste system. It was basically against the systemic exploitation that ran unabated for centuries. The protest against this inhuman system could be articulated only in a concrete situation, not in a vacuum. He did not theorise the struggle on a hypothetical plane. He built it on the basis of real problems in a concrete situation. Unlike many cases, the motive force for his life mission was provided by his experience itself. Although he pitched his tents against Brahminism, he never bore any enmity against the Brahmins or identified any one for his friend or foe by caste. The Bahishkrit Hitkarini Sabha that was the launch vehicle of his movement had majority from the forward caste people in its executive body. Even later, this intention of having a non-caste base for the organisation could be consistently seen in his movement, be it the Mahad struggle or the Indian Labour Party. He was perceptive enough to say that the Brahminism could exist in all the castes including the untouchables, for that was the essence of the casteism. It is tragic to find his legacy being monopolised today by only the scheduled castes.

Although, he considered the magnitude of the problem of emancipation of dalits is such as to warrant his sole attention, he did take cudgels for other oppressed entities like workers, peasants and women. At one occasion in response to the accusation that he did not care for the tribals, he had to squarely admit the fact that he considered the problem at hand big enough to outlast his life and provokedly put that he never claimed to fight for whole humanity. Such instances though disturbing enough could be understood within their specific context. While dealing with the socio-economic depravation of dalits, he comprehensively exposed certain systemic dimensions that help perpetuate exploitation. For instance, he was well aware of the capitalist and imperialist oppression besides the decadent feudalism within which domain his problem lay.

Capitalism

During the colonial British regime, capitalism started taking root in India with the collaboration of Indian mercantile capital and British capital. Unlike Europe, it did not have to battle against feudalism; rather it was implanted on the trunk of the latter in India. As a result, even in the capitalist institutions in the cities, caste discrimination simultaneously existed. Ambedkar was quite aware of the exploitative potential of capital and hence he had declared capitalism and Brahminism as the twin enemy of his movement. Capitalism was in an infantile stage then but Brahminism encompassed the phases of slavery, feudalism and extended its tentacles as we see to the phase of imperialism. Moreover, he noted the reactionary compradore character of rising capitalism in the contemporary sectors of the economy and the inhuman exploitation of workers that it unleashed. His, Indian Labour Party (ILP) was an attempt to take up the question of capitalist exploitation, as well as to combine the struggle on both caste and class basis. Various workers' problems were taken up by the ILP, the leadership of combined strike of the mill workers, parliamentary fight for the workers' interest in relation to the Industrial Disputes Act, and various legal reforms that were brought about while he was in the Executive Council of the Viceroy, can be the examples of his concern for workers' exploitation.

It cannot be denied that his approach to these contemporary problems was closer to that of the Fabian socialists with whom he was more familiar. But, it was a model adopted out of familiarity and pragmatism, a matter of strategy, never thought out on an ideological plane to be a theoretical plank. Although, there cannot be any doubt that he stood against capitalism, he could not articulate a sound theoretical basis for doing so. Resultantly, his efforts remained constricted with a short view of workers' welfare but could not provide them a vision of their liberation.

Imperialism

Ambedkar's attitude towards imperialism has been projected in a distorted manner right from the beginning, mainly because he refused to take part in the freedom struggle or opposed Gandhi who for certain category of ignoramuses was the anti-imperialism personified. He strategically sought to maintain neutrality vis-a-vis the colonial State. As per him, it would not be possible for the resourceless dalits to fight its mighty foes all together. He did not want to dissipate and squander his extremely limited resources on several fronts. He however knew the basic exploitative character of the colonial regime. At several occasions, he burst out saying that British imperialism and Indian feudalism were the two leaches that clung to Indian people. However, there was a fundamental difference between his and others' viewpoint. For instance, he did not approve equating opposition to imperialism with opposing the British. He noted that the opposition to imperialism couldn't be effective until its supporters within the country are left untouched. The then leader of the Communist Party of India — Manabendranath Roy once met him at his residence and during discussions insisted that destruction of imperialism had to be the first and foremost objective of Indian politics. Ambedkar's response to him summarised his outlook towards this problem. He replied to Roy in explicit terms that without struggling against the landlords, mill owners, moneylenders — the friends of imperialism within the country, it was not possible to wage an effective fight against imperialism. It may be a matter of research but a priori his anti-imperialist attitude pervades even his writings as a student.

The validation of his stand comes from an entirely unrelated corner and nearly half a century later. Suniti Kumar Ghosh, (1985 and 1995) in his books has shown in great detail how the Congress representing landlords and capitalists had played a compradore role to serve the interest of imperialism during the so-called freedom struggle and how even after the transfer of power in 1947 the grip of imperialism instead of weakening became stronger. Does it not indicate that he was more correct than any of his contemporary politicians? The ones who biasedly wish to pronounce their half baked verdict that Ambedkar was a stooge of British merely on the basis of his acceptance of membership of Viceroy's Executive Council or talking to the Simon Commission, not only display their ignorance of history but also their casteist fangs. They ought to rethink the comparison between Ambedkar who, even being apparently a part of the imperialist apparatus was perhaps striking at its roots by empowering the people and many others, so-called nationalists, who after wearing the mask of anti-imperialism were indirectly strengthening its pillars.

In relation to British rule, Ambedkar basically makes two points. The first is that he questions the so-called freedom struggle launched under the leadership of Congress as an anti-imperialist struggle. He contended that the Congress basically represented the class of feudal lords and the urban capitalists — the twosome exploiters of Indian masses. Although, it succeeded through the charismatic leadership of Gandhi in galvanising masses in its support, it essentially relied on bargaining with the colonial rulers for securing itself more share of power. It always throttled the mass spontaneity as in the case of 1942-uprisings and actively opposed the genuine anti-imperialist struggles of the revolutionaries like Bhagat Singh. Ambedkar reflects the understanding of true character of the Congress in his own way, when he says that if Congress was fighting a real anti-imperialist war, he would whole heartedly support it. The rhetoric of such statement apart, for he never appears to even take a note of other truly anti-imperialist struggles like the one referred to above, it is enough to reveal his attitude towards imperialism and understanding of the class character of the Congress. He knew that the class character of the Congress would not permit it to don this role in reality.

Ambedkar could see through the anti-imperialist masks the real fangs of an exploiter of masses. He thus not only saw no point in siding with this more real exploiter of people than perhaps the colonial rulers, but also did not hesitate to openly oppose it when it came in the way of dalit liberation. He smelt rot in all such struggles that refused to notice existence of inhuman exploitation of some of their own people within their precincts and tended to over-externalise their woes. Here lay his second point when he raised a question of Hindu imperialism perpetrated through its caste system that was certainly seen as more vicious by its victims than the British rule. It may be pertinent to ask of those who raise the issue of Ambedkar's attitude and conduct towards imperialism, to answer as to why the problem of untouchability or caste system that reduced its one-fifth of the population to subhuman levels did not find a mere mention in the lofty discussions of freedom struggle that pre-dated Ambedkar's raising it.

The anti-imperialist aspiration also could be seen in the context of the class/caste division in the society. The battle for the lost kingdom waged by the vanquished lords also could be camouflaged as an anti-imperialist struggle and at the same time the genuine peoples' anti-imperialist aspiration manifested in the form of say anti-feudal struggle could be condemned as the pro-imperialism, merely because it directed its gun towards the props of the imperialism. The real anti-imperialist aspirations belong to the masses of people the manifestation of which is possible only through the peoples' war. Whatever anti-imperialist struggle people waged were soon hijacked by the phoney war whose real intent was to extract political power to native ruling classes. While the scenes of anti-British struggles were being enacted for the 'mother' India of exploiters, Ambedkar busied himself to liberate the other India- the India of the exploited and oppressed.

Against Oppression of Women

Besides these mainstream forms of exploitation even the subaltern forms like women's exploitation, could not escape his agenda. He viewed them as the most oppressed of all. His approach to the problems was typically that of a liberal democrat constitutionalist. This certainly constrained his articulation of this problem as in many others. This issue will have to be seriously rethought by dalits under the redefinition project. But suffice here to say that at any opportunity, he raised his voice against women's discriminatory situation in the society. His basic law of social engineering was that the social revolutions must always begin from the standpoint of the most oppressed or the ones on the lowest rung of the society. Right from the days of Mook Nayak and Bahiskrit Bharat, he appears to take cudgels for women. He always involved women in his struggles and tended to give them vanguard positions.

For example, about 500 women had marched at the head of the historical procession at Mahad to assert the untouchables' right to drink water from the public tank. He was immensely pained to see the permanent denial of education and religious rights to women ordained in the Shastras of the Hinduism (e.g. Manusmriti). His democratic consciousness never reconciled with any thing lesser than the equality of men and women though its expression was acutely constrained perhaps by his anxieties about the possibilities, so much so that it might even be mistaken as the male centric tactic. While he asked women to be good mothers so as to shape up their son or to be good wives to their husbands or be a carrier of community's cultural baggage, he did struggle for their equal rights as in the case of Hindu Code Bill. He described sacramental marriages as polygamy for men and perpetual slavery for women because under no circumstances within that system the latter would get liberty from their husbands, however bad or undesirable they may be. He insisted that women should have the freedom to break this contract.

Constitution: an Exercise in Liberal Democracy

Although, Ambedkar was conscious of the limitations of liberal democracy in the emancipatory project he had undertaken and at times had even declared that he was not a liberal democrat, for many reasons he could not escape its clutches completely. He could not be unaware that liberal democracy basically was born as the ruling class ideology in 19th century Europe. It takes individuals and their groups as basically selfish units as its premise. It holds that individuals and social groups progress only through competition. It had however to take cognizance of weaker sections in the society, paradoxically in a large number, who cannot enter this competition openly and hence could be potentially be spoilers of the game. The French Revolution had demonstrated this potential in ample measure. As the Whigs in the English Liberal party had thought "the best way to ward off revolution was to adopt a liberal generous attitude towards the lower classes.

The upper classes should make concessions gracefully and in good time, and not wait until the lower classes are roused to exact them. If a revolution happens, it doesn't show that the people are bad and should have been repressed more thoroughly... repression is self-defeating. What it shows is that the upper classes were not wise enough and self-confident enough to make reasonable concessions in good time." It accommodates the relatively weaker sections by extending them some concessions or aids for some time, basically to equip them for this universal competition. The State performs the role of a referee in this competition. This State is supposed to be run by the representatives of all the social groups. Notwithstanding his awareness of the above facts, Ambedkar's schema does reflect the expectation that the State would perform the role of independent referee.

The influence of liberalism on Ambedkar is more pronounced after he accepted the role of the chairman of the drafting committee for the Indian Constitution in collaboration with the Congress. In the light of his own proposals of State socialism submitted to the Constituent Assembly on behalf of the Scheduled Caste Federation, this ideological somersault could only be understood as the situational compulsions acting upon him. Just before entering the Constituent Assembly he had experienced the bitter phase of political oblivion and had seen from closer angles the prospect of his life's mission ending without any result. He had a dire need to enter the Constituent Assembly and include certain provisions for his people in the future Constitution. When Congress offered him this role, he had to perform it within bounds in exchange for his life's ambition to provide for his people. The compulsions are too obvious to be ignored. His States and Minorities envisages most of the productive assets to be the State property. This was against the principle of liberal democracy. The liberal theory of property right from the days of John Locke and Thomas Hobbes in the 17th century stressed on private property and on the duty of the government to protect it. It was the Congress liberalism that he had to submit to and had to plead for property rights that were considered pivotal within the Constitution. The same holds true for the centralisation of power and certain basic rights, which were congenial to the capitalist class. He had to accept all such provisions that considered the existing power structure from *status quo* viewpoint instead of transformation. He was compelled to accommodate the principles of social democracy, which he has been regarding as the basic soul into the ineffective chapter of the directive principles of the Constitution. He himself had to accept the same parliamentary executive that he had always misgivings about as being dangerous to the life and freedom of ex-untouchables.

He could not be unaware of the fact that from the viewpoint of the oppressed and dalits, except for the reservations, the Constitution was not making any material difference. On the contrary, it had made all the arrangements for letting all the benefits of power stay with the wealthy and traditional elite classes while dangling the carrot of Constitutional safeguards and reservations for dalits and the oppressed people. The existing socio-economic structure was kept in tact in the Constitution underneath the western democracy which proclaimed the principle of 'one vote, one value' in political arena.

Ambedkar could not hide his discomfort at this dichotomy and had to burst out in his famous warning that if equality in the socio-economic sphere is not achieved within a reasonable time, the disadvantaged people would blast off the structure of the political democracy. He was aware of the fallacy in the assumption that political democracy would catalyse the social revolution through universal franchise and periodic elections. He had himself tested the bitter fruits of this process through the electoral defeats. Politics run on the principles of free market economy can never entail equality. The slogans like socialism, social justice, equality, etc. were merely masks to fool the people. The grammar of the game of electoral politics foreordained the politicians serving the interests of big landlords, capitalists and compradore bourgeoisie.

They could not survive free political competition without the latter's blessings. Ambedkar should have been aware that liberal values and liberal institutions are incapable of arresting the monopolistic hold of the moneyed classes on political power.

On Revolution

Revolution, on the face of it, appears to be an anathema to Ambedkar who seems to dread it and instead advocates reforms. But it would be disaster to take it at face value. For, like many other terms, his usage of the term 'revolution' does not bear the same meaning as is in vogue, particularly in Marxist circles. What Ambedkar seems to detest in revolution is the violence. At many places he tends to equate rebellion, revolution and revolt with violence. He also seems to disagree with the method of insurrection. He thought that without mass consciousness being ripe enough for revolutionary change, insurrectionary methods would not succeed. Moreover, he appears to be sceptical of the justness of revolutions as they invariably represent the triumph of the collective over the individual. It may be attributed to the influence of liberal democracy in which he got his indoctrination in his formative days. Liberal democracy always put an individual on a high pedestal and considered it precious. His concern for the individual is not again doctrinaire but emanates from the value that any and every human being is precious and the belief that alone can act as the best guarantee against the collective tyranny and totalitarian excesses any time.

In the context of the collapse of erstwhile Soviet block, where the totalitarian states that came into being in the name of dictatorship of proletariat and played havoc with people, this human-centric value assumes importance. One needs to be however reminded that even the values do need to have some material bases. They do not fall from sky. The contradiction between collective and individual has thus to be resolved in the concrete situation. As for Ambedkar, apart from this scepticism, he does not seem to have any dispute with the general aim and object of revolution.

Revolution, inasmuch as it seeks to bring about a fundamental change in the social relations in the society, will always be opposed by the forces of *status quo*, whose material interests are directly threatened by this change. In corollary, it becomes imperative for the forces of revolution to overcome this resistance whatever be the means. Whereas, the antagonist camp will always project codes of ethics and morality for their tactical defence in face of the onslaught of revolution, the revolutionaries discard them as decadent; for them revolution itself represents the highest value. Being the upsurge of the suppressed ones, revolutions do have a tendency to be bloody, but it is always in response to the resistance of its opponents.

Therefore, it is a representation only by the vested interest to associate violence or moral turpitude with revolutions. On the contrary, it would be more logical to say about the revolutionaries that being propelled by an external motivation to deliver mankind from the existing traps at the risk of their own lives; they cannot be bloodthirsty people. The revolutionary violence is almost an inevitability that arises at the instance of the oppressors. In that sense Marx called "violence as the midwife of history", emphasising its inevitability. It is the inevitability that marks the compulsion of the vast majority of people to resist the anti-revolutionary violence of the minority. The pre-requisite here is that the revolution truly represents the majority consciousness. If it does not, then the violence of the few exercised with howsoever a lofty objective could transform into its anti-thesis, fortifying itself against the majority will. In this sense and insofar as the recent history showed the scepticism that revolutions trample upon individual's rights therefore cannot be dismissed as baseless.

Historically, revolution is the process of identifying and destroying the obstacles in the existing order to take productive forces to the qualitatively next higher level, for the overall progress of human race. The progress achieved by mankind so far is basically due to the qualitative transformation from quantitative continuum that characterises revolutions. The qualitative transformations always need concentrated inputs, akin to latent heat in the case of phase transformation of water. In social transformation it takes the form of revolutionary energy that in turn may manifest into violence. Ambedkar does not neglect the necessity of violence. As he himself said that if dalits wanted to be effective they would need the canons. It is erroneous to construe that his opposition to violence was idealistic or doctrinaire. Violence was not a taboo for him; it could be practised when it was absolutely necessary.

Even his mentor Buddha, who is respected as the greatest apostle of non-violence had the same pragmatic approach towards violence. Ambedkar was not obsessed either with the idea of non-violence or the value of individualism professed by the classical school of liberal democracy. His reservations were against the possibility of the cunning of a few over-riding the will of majority as had happened in the case of caste institution. He would hate to see any thing like caste getting institutionalised again. In his scheme of things he therefore was not ready to compromise the value of democracy, the will of majority of people, whatever may be the end.

Ambedkar did not juxtapose reform against revolution, as many people tend to do. He does not reflect comprehension of technicality of dialectical materialism in his usage of these terms. Often his revolution is the violent overthrow of the existing rule and establishment of the new rule. Likewise, he does not seem to mean that reforms will not entail a qualitative transformation. What he certainly means by revolution is the change brought about in a 'big bang' manner.

Notwithstanding what Ambedkar said about his own work, revolution does not always entail a 'big bang'; it is not a point concept as mistakenly regarded in common parlance, but a line concept. Mao's Great Proletarian Cultural Revolution may be a good example of this. There could be many bits of work, which contributes to taking society to a qualitatively higher rung in the ladder of progress that qualify to be the revolutionary work. The qualitative change itself occurs over a discrete time horizon and not a moment. The moment that marks out transformation of power and looks like a 'big bang', alone is not the revolution. The particular phase of history puts constraints on the kind of changes that can be conceived in its womb. Some one dreaming of a socialist revolution in the slave society would only at best be a daydreamer; a romanticist but he cannot be a revolutionary. Likewise, certain phase of history demands a lot of quantitative preparation before a revolutionary change can be planned for. Ambedkar largely reflects these kinds of concerns while dealing with the issue of revolution. He did not see Indian situation ripe enough for any revolutionary change. Any change without resolution of the caste question, according to him, would not only be detrimental to dalits but also be an extremely short-lived.

The importance of Ambedkar's work can be gauged in relation to contemporary social situation and its transitional social context. Indian society was ridden with a peculiar brand of feudalism, the most prominent feature of which was caste. Caste had incapacitated over 15 per cent of its population and maintained them at the subhuman level. The large part of the balance population also suffered the degradation in a varying degree. This decadent institution had far outlived its minimal utility and as a result for centuries kept Indian society in a fossilised form. It served the material needs of a handful of people but all perceived varying stakes in the system on account of its hierarchical structure and faithfully practised it because they internalised it as their *Dharma* ordained by none other than God.

The possible exception in generic terms were dalits who were placed at the lowest rung of the caste ladder and had hardly anything to their share. However, in particular terms only a few castes from the dalit castes, who did not have any specific caste profession and hence little stake in the system and consequently who as the general workmen of villages had better exposure to the changing urban life than any one else came out of the hegemony of Brahmins to articulate the challenge to the system. The hierarchy among dalits however prevented them to come together and consequently this challenge had to be articulated caste by caste. Capitalism that took root in India in big cities also had struck compromise with the caste institution like its harbingers, the British imperialism. It was an arduous task, as it still is, to conceive a model for this struggle and still more difficult to build.

During the colonial times for various reasons these struggles had germinated largely in Maharashtra and Southern states where the social structure reflected sharper polarisation between dalits and balance society. Ambedkar's advent in the Indian socio-political scene marked their zenith. It articulated its attack on Brahminism and capitalism that accepted its alliance, focused its organisation on dalits and gave a clarion call for annihilation of castes for achieving the ultimate aim of society based on Liberty, Equality and Fraternity to provide wider umbrella for all progressive forces to work. It reflects the distinct historical need to democratise Indian society without which it was bound to suffer constriction of its productive forces. This work had to have large content in the socio-cultural realm; it is a credit to Ambedkar's acumen that he gave it a political dimension. It had to be approached as reform. Ambedkar clearly found the talks of communist revolution as out of phase with the history although he never fully accepted the tenets of historical materialism as he thought it negatived human ingenuity and carried it through a predetermined channel. He insisted that India did not provide congenial soil for germination of class-consciousness because of castes. Their annihilation therefore constituted the first task in the revolutionary agenda.

It is unfortunate that many communist revolutionaries still parrot the same characterisation of his work as in years back their predecessors proclaimed using the spoon fed theories from the West. One day it is hoped that the contributions of all the caste struggles to democratisation of Indian society would be restored as a native revolutionary heritage by these well meaning people. Till then it will always sound puerile to pigeonhole the historical work as reform or revolution merely on the basis of syntax and not the content. However, it is much more unfortunate for Ambedkarite dalits to deny themselves the credit for this historical contributions by dissociating from the revolutionary agenda, mistakenly thinking that it something alien to them. Effectively, not only they are denying themselves a historical opportunity to contribute to revolution but also delaying their own emancipation.

Dalits have to rethink their position vis a vis revolution. Ambedkar's dream of a society based on liberty, equality and fraternity cannot be realised except through revolution. They will have to understand Ambedkar's life and mission only from this perspective. His contribution to Indian revolution lies in the fact that he tried to comprehend Indian reality independently and tried to contribute to the resolution of its contradictions in his own way. Indian history held out the gauntlet of fossilised Indian feudalism for so long to the Indian revolutionaries but every one conveniently wished it away, initially as a superstructural matter that would disappear automatically when the material base is revolutionised and now after seven decades as a problem belonging to both structure and superstructure, that could be solved through revolutionary practice. It still lacks the clarity and courage to hold the bull by horn. Ambedkar did not confuse issues, he saw clearly that the annihilation of caste will have to be consciously worked for before taking up any revolutionary project. He went beyond and found out the institutional base of castes in the Indian village whose economic support lay in the land-relations and caste division of labour. But, unlike many communists who still use the stereotype of land reform - a slogan of land to the tiller as the only revolutionary programme, he did not hamper on it because he knew that firstly it was economically impossible to satisfy the land hunger of the landless in the country, secondly the likely transformation of landless to a marginal farmer through land reforms was unlikely to solve the problems of dalits and thirdly, as the later empirical data showed, contrary to expectations the land reforms could aggravate the problem of caste.

Instead, he proposed nationalisation of land and cooperativisation of farming. He realised the necessity of detaching substantial village population from land and absorbing it into the industrial sector that was to be mainly under State sector. Even in retrospect, these points could have constituted a viable agenda for democratic revolution. As one naxalite scholar perceptively puts it, for having independently seen the question of annihilation of castes linked with the question of land one could unhesitatingly call Ambedkar as the torchbearer of the people's democratic revolution.

Ambedkar as the Radical Thinker

Dalits are never tired of projecting Ambedkar as the greatest of all the leaders. That unfortunately smacks of sectarian attitude and of their blind devotion to him. They need to understand that the measure of greatness of any person could only be her/his contribution to better the human situation, in terms of correct understanding of its ailment and contribution to cure it. What Ambedkar did could be seen in relation to the broad five currents in Indian politics of his times:

- The Reformists current that wanted to bring about development on the western pattern, possibly with the support of British imperialism,
- Congress, that represented Indian capital and which demanded self-rule under the domination of British imperialism,
- The Terrorist Nationalists who had taken up arms in their fight for freedom against British imperialism,

- The Communists who were trying to implant Bolshevik revolution in India, and
- The Muslim League which opened up a separatist front of Muslims.

All of them scarcely reflected an understanding of the Indian situation. For instance, none showed even a cursory concern about the problems of one fourth of their countrymen who were forced to live worse than animals as ordained by their decadent religion. It was indeed surprising that although all craved for self-rule from the British, none concerned with the caste-system which basically was responsible in pushing the country repeatedly into slavery. None seemed to attempt an objective analysis of either the history or the present of this country.

It could circumstantially be said that their motivations came from their narrow class-caste interests. These movements were motivated by the desire of an abstract freedom for country and a refusal to see the concrete slavery of their own people. Granted that the problems before the country were really intricate, still no one would dare say that the need for democratisation was in anyway subordinate.

The real people's movement in the country was required to wage simultaneous war against imperialism, internal compradore bourgeoisie, landlords and Brahminism. It was only Ambedkar who clearly indicated this requirement. In this light, he was certainly ahead of all others. His own bitter experiences with untouchability had stood him in good stead in seeing this more clearly than any other. He strove to build his movement along this understanding but unfortunately it was neither in his power to deal comprehensively with all the issues, nor was there an ideological and programmatic clarity required therefore. He inevitably had to focus his attention on dalits who were the worst victims of this multi-faceted oppression. It was the misfortune of Indian history that this struggle progressed in a constricted manner and eventually got dissolved into regressive statist politics. It reflected both the limitation of Ambedkar as well the situational compulsion on him.

The anti-caste movements before Ambedkar were mainly welfare oriented. Some wanted a higher rank for their own caste in the caste hierarchy and some taking the inferior culture of their caste to be the reason for their suffering, aimed at improving the same. Mahatma Phuley's movement was an exception to this trend insofar as it attempted to unite the Shudra and Ati-Shudra castes against the exploitation by the parasitic castes of Shetjis (capitalists) and Bhatjis (priests). While Ambedkar accepted the lineage/inheritance of this movement and held Phuley in greatest esteem as his one of the three *Gurus,* he went beyond to declare annihilation of caste to be the object of his movement in the direction of the goal of 'liberty, equality and fraternity'.

In the historical context it certainly was a radical step. He rightly diagnosed that the caste system is basically sustained by the peculiar economic Constitution of the Indian village of which the land relations were the main features. Towards breaking this link he toyed with an idea of separate settlement for dalits at one time and at another exhorted them to leave villages for cities. He had clearly understood that castes stood on multiple props, viz. the religio-cultural relations, feudal relations in village setting of which land relations constituted the crux and the socio-political nexus with the State.

Annihilation of castes thus needed destruction of all of them. He soon realised the necessity of political power for this multi-fronged attack. Even to bring about the residual change in the belief system either through the cultural or religious route, he stressed the necessity of political power. In this way, for the first time he brought the problem of untouchability and caste out of the confines of culture to the political agenda.

Unfortunately, this political agenda got lost into the maze of parliamentary politics that soon became be-all-end-all with dalit leaders. Even during Ambedkar's times the economic aspects of the problem remained largely untouched giving the impression to his followers as though they did not count. In the overall context it can be seen that they could not be as easily dealt with as the religio-cultural and political aspects of the problem. Moreover, it meant direct confrontation with the State for which Ambedkar was certainly not prepared. Alternately, the feudal relations in villages could be destroyed only if the private ownership of land is abolished and cooperativisation of farming is introduced. He thought, this structural change could be effected through the Constitution. It was a folly that he would soon realise when even as the 'chief architect' of the Constitution he failed so much as to bring this point on the agenda of the Constituent Assembly.

Conception of an Ideal

Babasaheb Ambedkar envisioned his ideal in the famous three principles: liberty, equality and fraternity. They were the basis for the ideal society of his conception. He denied that he had adopted them from the French Revolution. He said he had derived them from the teachings of Buddha. These principles were the clarion call of the French Revolution but later became the ideological props of the liberal bourgeoisie in Europe. Since Marx had ridiculed these principles as the fantasy of the bourgeois society, many people tended to stereotype Ambedkar as the petty-bourgeois liberal democrat. As according to Ambedkar the source of these principles is different from the French Revolution, familiar to Marx, there is a prima facie scope to argue that Marx's ridicule does not apply to him. His conception of these principles is indeed substantially different from that associated with the liberal bourgeoisie. Actually, what Marx refers to are the slogans of liberty and equality of the bourgeois parliamentary democracy. There, 'liberty' is the liberty to contract and 'equality' refers to equality in market.

Ambedkar insists that the conception of the ideal society ought to have them all the three together. Absence of any would not be acceptable to him. The ideal society of his dream could only be seen within a kind of spiritual frame. It would be interesting to compare this society with the communist society of Marx's conception. Marx reached his inference following the dialectical track of historical materialism. In Ambedkar' case it was just his vision. Inevitably, he had to attribute the origin of them to some spiritual source. For Ambedkar they meant to denote the State of society sans exploitation and with an emotive ambience of fellow feeling. It was beyond him to describe this State further in concrete terms and much so to indicate the forms of struggle to reach it. Known for his obsession with pragmatism and belief that any definitive laws could not bind the flow of human history, he would avoid the speculative construction of this distant stage of human society. Not even Marx could describe what his dream communist society would be like beyond that it would be freed of the familiar contradictions. It essentially reflected a contradiction between human desire and material reality. It would be disaster to derive the meaning of this ideal State of Ambedkar's conception from what he did. He left that to posterity to decide as per their circumstances. But, rationally there could be little doubt that the vision of Ambedkar can only be realised in the communist society of Marx's conception where most (not all) of the contradictions in human society would have been resolved.

Dalits ought to internalise this vision and strive for its realisation. Ambedkar had a radical enough interpretation of his principles of liberty, equality and fraternity so as to feel inadequacy even in Marxism. He said that Marxism supported only equality. He was in need of a body of thought that would give equal importance to all these three principles. He met it with a convenient conceptualisation of religion. It is paradoxical that a person who is rational enough not to bind the posterity with his vision volitionally binds himself with what is said more than 25 centuries before. It is natural to find ideals better articulated in spiritual spheres but it is equally true that these dream worlds are incapable to provide any clue for their realisation on the earth except for their pet prescription to ignore the material reality and imagine it happened in the mind. They run away from the fact that the evil humans suffer from are the attributes of the divisions in human society, and their abolition essentially calls for struggles by the sufferers against those who perpetrate sufferings. Howsoever, inherently rational the religion may be or radical its interpretation may be it cannot fully escape these limitations. It can be seen in relation to Buddhism handed down by Babasaheb Ambedkar with his radical interpretation. Notwithstanding the familiar quibbling around the Dhamma and Dhamma among dalits, what remained of Buddhism with them is what would happen to any religion. It is a different question whether Marxism embodied Ambedkar's ideals or not but it is certain that they are neither realisable neither through any kind of constitutional acrobatics nor through any religious practice.

State

Ambedkar's conception of State reflects some amount of autonomy from the hegemony of the ruling classes. It is why he expected it to act as per the constitutional structure and endeavoured to incorporate the pro-dalit bias into the Constitution.

He must have realised the true nature of it, the boundaries of the autonomy and basic class bias of the State, when he actually reached not only the Constituent Assembly but also became the chairman of its Drafting Committee. In his anxiety to secure some provisions in favour of dalits, he accepted to be the 'hack' to write what was acceptable to the ruling caste-class representatives. He must have thought that within the given constraints he had done a good job of making the Constitution responsive to the needs of the downtrodden people.

Indeed, many of the provisions in the directive principles and elsewhere apparently bear clear imprint of his zeal and owe their existence to him. But, even they had to be within the strategic space provided by the rulers. His realisation of the folly was near complete when he had to burst out in utter dejection at its ineffectual implementation, that he would be the first man to burn the Constitution as it was of no good to any one. He was inaccurate, as the Constitution had proved good enough to the upper caste-class combine who had hegemonised complete political space in post-1947 India. He attributed it to the 'devils' in the Congressmen who had occupied the constitutional 'temple' he and others had built. Had he lived little longer, he would have realised that the ones that he considered his co-workers to build the temple were themselves the agents of the very devils.

He hoped to thwart the devil's march by people's power conceived in the form of a parliamentary party called Republican Party of India. It was within the very precincts of the temple inhabited by devils and therefore it soon proved to be the devil's feast.

Ambedkar could not reach the point of understanding that the State is a mere instrument in the hands of the ruling classes to coerce the ruled ones into submission to their interests. Until the downtrodden themselves become the ruling class, they cannot expect the State to do good to them. Whatever good that appears to come to their share, in ultimate balance accrues to the other side in multiple measure.

The post-1947 State, which has never tired of propagandising its concern for dalits and poor, has in fact been singularly instrumental in aggravating the caste problem with its policies. Even the apparently progressive policies in the form of Land Ceiling Act, Green Revolution, Programme of Removal of Poverty,

Reservations to Dalits in Services and Mandal Commission, etc. have resulted against their professed objectives. The effect of the Land Ceiling Act, has been in creating a layer of the middle castes farmers which could be consolidated in caste terms to constitute a formidable constituency. In its new incarnation, this group that has traditionally been the immediate upper caste layer to dalits, assumed virtual custody of Brahminism in order to coerce dalit landless labourers to serve their socio-economic interests and suppress their assertive expression in the bud. The Green Revolution was the main instrument to introduce capitalisation in agrarian sector. It reinforced the innate hunger of the landlords and big farmers for land as this State sponsored revolution produced huge surplus for them. It resulted in creating geographical imbalance and promoting unequal terms of trade in favour of urban areas. Its resultant impact on dalits has been far more excruciating than that of the Land Ceiling Act.

The much publicised programme for Removal of Poverty has aggravated the gap between the heightened hopes and aspirations of dalits on one hand and the feelings of depravation among the poorer sections of non-dalits in the context of the special programmes especially launched for upliftment of dalits. The tension that ensued culminated in increasingly strengthening the caste — based demands and further aggravating the caste — divide. The reservations in services for dalits, notwithstanding its benefits, have caused incalculable damage in political terms. Reservations created hope, notional stake in the system and thus dampened the alienation; those who availed of its benefit got politically emasculated and in course consciously or unconsciously served as the props of the system. The context of scarcity of jobs provided ample opportunity to reactionary forces to divide the youth along caste lines. Mandal Commission, that enthused many progressive parties and people to upheld its extension of reservation to the backward castes, has greatly contributed to strengthen the caste identities of people. Inasmuch as it empowers the backward castes, actually their richer sections, it is bound to worsen the relative standing of dalits in villages.

Thus, the State, its welfare mask notwithstanding, has viciously and consistently acted against dalits and poor people. It is a complete contra-evidence to hopes of Ambedkar who strove to maximise and make use of the autonomous space of the State for the benefits of the have-nots, particularly dalits. It is one thing to assume autonomous space but quite another to equate it with caste-class neutrality. Unfortunately, the dalit political behaviour always reflected this erroneous notion of caste-class neutrality of the State. It has already caused great damage to the dalit interests. The radical Ambedkar might have strategy to use State for dalit cause but would never see it as caste-class neutral.

Socialism

Despite his ambivalence and reservations about the emphasis on the economic dimension in socialism, Ambedkar broadly remained a socialist. Some scholars do find little scope for suspecting his socialist credentials because of his disapproval of Russell's criticism of property, his non-acceptance of Marxian formulations and his placement of social issues higher than the economic and political issues. He called the complaint against love of money as 'philosophy of sour grapes' and ridiculed materialism as 'the ideology of pigs'. This impression is moreover strengthened by his reservations to accept the economic interpretation of history. But, in all fairness it may be said that what he appears to mean is the integrative consideration of all the factors that are needed for any society to be based on liberty, equality and fraternity.

Notwithstanding his variant conception, there should not be any doubt about his socialistic antecedents. His conception of socialism also underwent evolution. Once he had stated that there was hardly any difference between his socialism and communism. As such, his disagreement with the communists was about the means and not about the aim. He warns the communists that the classless society can emerge only after the emergence of a casteless society. It implies that his quarrel with the then communists was over the stages of revolution. In the 1920s and 30s, these people had borrowed the communist dogma and parroted class struggle in utter disregard of the reality. Ambedkar, on the contrary, was firmly rooted in it. They believed that the soviet Russian model of revolution was importable for bringing about a socialist revolution into India whereas Ambedkar realistically postulated that unless the consciousness of the working class was congenial for revolution, there was no question of it materialising. And, unless the caste system is destroyed, creation of the pro-revolution consciousness was out of question. His annoyance with the Bombay communists was largely because of their dogmatic behaviour. It is unfortunate that the ideal of classlessness that was latent in his agenda never really surfaced during his lifetime.

Ambedkar relies on the concept of 'State' for materialisation of his conception of socialism. His conception of State is largely idealist. He wanted the State to intervene in the economic structure and its monitoring. He wanted to constitutionalise this State intervention so that it would not be subject to change any time with the whims of simple majority vote in the legislation. Ambedkar who taught, "The lost rights cannot be regained by making appeals or requests to the robbers; it needs struggles"; did not say anything on how the oppressed people will get such strength as to create the constitutional provisions, that would put the class structure upside down. On behalf of his party — Scheduled Caste Federation, he had submitted a draft for the future Constitution to the Constituent Assembly for the independent India. It was published later as "States and Minorities". This book has really aided students in understanding some aspects of his conception of socialism. Nevertheless, one cannot afford to forget the constraints placed by the context in which it was written. The context was that he had failed to get into the Constituent Assembly and was therefore anxious to strike a feasible and still radical note that could find the support of the vast majority of the have-nots which might then create some pressure either for its inclusion in the Constitution or for his entry into the Constituent Assembly. For some years, during the preceding turbulence of negotiations for transfer of power, he found himself totally marginalised. Notwithstanding the probable limitations of this draft, its provisions in operational terms were still very radical. The main provisions are:

- All important industries and services shall belong to the nation.
- Insurance industry shall be in public sector and insurance will be compulsory for every citizen.
- Private sector and entrepreneurs shall have a role in the economy but it shall not be dominating.
- Nationalisation of land and promotion of cooperative farming on a collective principle.

These provisions, if implemented, would have gone a long way towards supporting democratic revolution in the country. It would have limited inequality and exploitation in the economic and political sphere. Politically, it would have had far-reaching impact.

Ambedkar till the end could not completely remove the Fabian influence (which he might have gathered while in England) on him. In his times, particularly before World War II, few people in India were well versed in Marxist philosophy. The knowledge of Marxism seldom exceeded some broad principles and 'Stalin's dictatorship' painted by imperialists or the 'revolt of the workers, the insurgency of the poor. Ambedkar also does not seem to have gone very far from this point. Without indulging into the debate of ifs and buts, there should not be any iota of doubt that the ideal society of his conception could materialise only through socialism.

Democracy

Ambedkar had unshakeable faith in democracy. In his conception of an exploitation-less society, democracy has an extraordinary role. Democracy means 'one person, one vote'; and 'one vote, one value'. Democracy means empowerment of any person for participating in the process of decision-making relating to her/him, democracy means liberty, equality and fraternity — Ambedkar's definition of democracy had such a tone. Because he presided over making of the Constitution and is being projected as its chief architect, there is a misunderstanding that parliamentary democracy is what he wanted. But nothing could be farther from the truth than this. He himself spoke against parliamentary democracy. For instance, he defined parliamentary democracy as "voting by the people in favour of their owners and handing over the rights of ruling over themselves". This provides a glimpse of the expanse of his ideal, which certainly was much beyond the Indian Constitution or any common place understanding about him.

His conception of democracy appears to be purely people oriented. He showed that the bookish concepts of equality are detrimental to the disabled sections of society in the prevailing social setting and proposed a fundamental change in the concept of equality. It envisaged complete abolition of inequality. His principle of positive discrimination is based on this very concept of equality. But the operational aspects of this concept involved the need for some kind of autonomous institution, which was met by 'State' and 'religion'. It is necessary to stress that his greatness lies in the radicality of his conceptions, his vision of a human society sans any kind of exploitation; not in the remedies or apparatus he proposed in the circumstances prevailing in his time.

Buddhism

Religion was the institution envisaged to control the organisation at the level of an individual and society to curb their latent exploitative instincts. It was a philosophical device that would regulate their lives, including the interface between them at the most primary level. Ambedkar viewed it as a code of behaviour, a way of life that is upheld by the multitude. He insisted that this code should be based on and be compatible with the precepts of modern science.

The religion as normally defined or that became a pill of opium for Marx, was not the religion of his concept either. When ultimately he embraced Buddhism he claimed to have used the criteria of modern science. Buddhism, as it was propounded by Gautama the Buddha hardly qualified to be called religion in so far as it did not have even a single of the three necessary features of religion —, viz.: belief in God, permanent entity and a set of rituals. But it is a matter of opinion whether its institutionalised form that we are familiar with still retains its uniqueness. Shunning the futile debate, it could be definitely said and has been acknowledged that the Buddhism that he embraced was far more radical than its familiar version. His 'Buddha and His Dhamma' is replete with instances where he reconstructs and redefines Buddhism with a near-scientific approach.

Buddhism, in its purer form, puzzled many people with its radical outlook and rational approach. It did not have a place for God, ritual of any kind or for any permanent entity that characterise all other religions. Morality is said to be its basis and surprisingly a pure democratic criterion of 'happiness and welfare of many' (*Bahujan Hitay, Bahujan Sukhay*) as its motto. He exhorted Bhikkus (monks) and Bhikkunis (nuns) to wander all over the world carrying the Dhamma to people and not to rest at one place. Even by this, he did not mean spread of his creed; it was essentially an expression of the compassion and concern he had for suffering humanity. For, he had repeatedly advised people not to take his word for granted but test it on the touchstone of their experience and intellect before accepting or rejecting it. He never claimed any role in their emancipation asking them to be their own light — " *Atta Deep Bhava*". He treated the Sangha (the order of his Bhikkus and Bhikkunis) as a microcosm of the society. The Bhikkus and Bhikkunis were not allowed to have any private property except for the basic eight things for their personal use. In economic and political sphere, he put forth the ideal of service before the monks and nuns. The people who did not observe this ideal are said to be the parasites, consuming national wealth.

In the realm of philosophy, Buddha's contributions were far reaching. Several centuries before Hegel, he presented full-blown dialectics in his philosophy. Hegel had provided the basis for Marxism, in a sense that Marx had just to make the reality in Hegel upside down. Buddha's reality also had shades of Hegel, although he never explicitly accepted, unlike Hegel, the primacy to the consciousness, but he did not get his Marx to resurrect his dialectical non-materialism. The principle of impermanence is the fundamental tenet of Buddhism. For Buddha, any thing that is not permanent does not exist; its application is all pervading. Somewhat as a corollary of this principle, Buddha proposed the tenet of dependent origination (*Pratit Samutpad*). With regard to materialism, and consciousness, Buddhist philosophy goes quite close to materialism, in the sense that it does not regard independent existence of consciousness without the body. Significantly, Buddha's approach reflects his orientation to help people emancipate themselves and not pontificate on things irrelevant. It is quite the same as Marx insisting on 'changing the world' as the object of philosophy. There are many 'unknowables' on which he kept his famous silence. His 'middle path' appears to provide for the grey areas where a definite stand could be erroneous.

Ambedkar's attraction to Buddhism is basically on account of its moral base and absence of irrationality. On this account it has been the subject of admiration and awe of scores of intellectual people. A person like Einstein had opined that it was the only religion suitable for the scientific age. Ambedkar must have had multiple motives behind embracing Buddhism. Basically he was in search of a religion as an instrument of internal control on individuals' instincts and social behaviour. He had a social need of an appropriate cultural identity for his people after they had discarded the chains of Hinduism. He was moreover aware of the aberrations that had crept in Buddhism and had to redefine it to present its rational version. Basically, he included many a rational interpretation presented by scholars like Dharmanand Kosambi, and left a mirror to posterity to have a glimpse of his worldview. This worldview, does take cognisance of the material reality of living, subscribes to law of causation, relies on humane rational to interpret the world and finally embodies a craving for changing it. Although, there is no difficulty in understanding or empathising with his decision, the claim that Buddhism could be the substitute for Marxism or a liberating philosophy for the whole world is not only anachronistic but also grossly magnified idealistic hyperbole.

Another notable feature is his repeated reference to Marxism in relation to Buddhism. Many of his disciples misused it as his opposition and even extended it to enmity to Marxism. It is untrue and unfortunate. Like his claims to have checked the consistency of Buddhist tenets with those of modern science, he claimed that his Buddhism was Marxism plus some thing. It certainly shows that he did not hold Marxism in the same esteem as science, but there is no doubt that he considered Marxism as the near-best and willed that his chosen religion should contain all of it and be superior to it. It is interesting to study what aspects he considers important in Marxism and what methodology he employs to compare them with corresponding contents in Buddhism. What is important is to note that with the amount of information available on Marxism to him, he considered it great enough to serve as a benchmark to assess Buddhism.

On Marx and Communism

Babasaheb Ambedkar thought that the communists while attempting to bring about revolution do not bother about justice or injustice, truth or untruth; atrocities and taboos and if times demand, are prepared for bloodshed to establish the State with soviet methods. It was shocking to his moral philosophy and therefore he always expressed his reservation and even disapproval for these methods. He says "The object of communism is as economic and social as it is political. About social, the revolution in public opinion has not taken place. Moreover, majority of people does not have ability to understand the economic and political aims of communism". Elsewhere, he cites the historical examples in the context of historical materialism of Marx and says that the political revolution has always taken place on the background of social revolutions. Howsoever congenial the objective situation for revolution may be, it should be an axiom that till the revolutionary consciousness in people does not impel them to revolt, revolution cannot take place. He could not agree with the communists of his times who reared a mechanistic belief that revolutionary consciousness would automatically be born out of the material reality around. He wanted to stress the importance of the mediation of the conscientisation process in creating the revolutionary consciousness. He had little difficulty in visualising the communist prospects of a stateless and classless society as many people have. But there cannot be any doubt that he wished materialisation of some such 'utopia' where all kinds of exploitation would be deeply buried in the past and all the people would enjoy liberty, equality, and fraternity in their sublimest part in full measure.

One of the main problems with the prevailing icons of Ambedkar is that they project him uniformly as anti-Marx. It is the single saddest aspect for the moribund state of the dalit movement. Ambedkar often referred to Marx in various ways but never discussed him at the philosophical plane where essentially Marx resides. It is notable that he has not much to disagree with Marx on the ideological level except for the derogatory comments on materialism. Any one knowing even the basics of Marxism would say that these comments do not have anything to do with Marxism. They relate with the mechanical materialism and not with the dialectical materialism of Marx. What prompted these comments perhaps was the practice of the then communists who vulgarised materialism in tending to ignore anything not material and have been spiteful of the movements of dalits. Beyond this nowhere he appears to discuss basics of Marxism, viz. dialectical materialism, historical materialism and scientific socialism. He did express doubt about the uni-linear flow of human history but unfortunately not in any depth to discern the areas of disagreement. Insofar as it implies that the history can develop divergent streams under certain conditions, the validity of the doubt cannot be dismissed.

Ambedkar and Marx share many common spaces. Both were driven by the same goal of reaching the society sans exploitation. Both had a firm commitment to the most oppressed people (technically not so for Marx, though), and saw them in the vanguard role for bringing about the revolutionary change for overall progress of the mankind. Marx arrived at his formulation by scientific study of history and found that in the era of capitalism the working class would be the vanguard of the socialist revolution. Ambedkar did not see working class in India and any probability of its emergence until the castes were annihilated. He therefore saw the necessity of launching the anti-caste movement with its worst victims — the untouchables in the vanguard role. The language and syntax certainly differed because of different frameworks they came to follow. Marx laboured on rigorous philosophical formulation and came out with his own body of thought or a science of revolution. Ambedkar got drowned into the turbulence of present and used philosophy for his reassurance or as a support for practice. A large part of his thoughts have a polemical hue and therefore cannot be used shorn of its context without risk. Ambedkar quite like Marx felt that the object of philosophy was to change the world. His statement that he does not believe in any 'ism' can be considered anti-dogma. It is with the same sense he used to say He was a realist. What a coincidence between this and the statement of Karl Max, when he said, "I am not a Marxist".

Besides these similarities, Marx was always referred to by Ambedkar as a kind of benchmark right up to his last days though unfortunately he never reflected the rigour that is expected in such discussions. It hovered around the superfluous and hearsay features of Marxism. Serious thinkers of Marx are surprised at his conception of Marxism till they are reminded of their location in times. Notwithstanding Ambedkar's claim that he had read more number of books on Marxism than that read by all the communists in India, in those days the philosophical material on Marxism does not seem to be easily available. What was available was the stuff that talked about the Bolshevik revolution and what went in the Soviet Russia. Rarely does one find a purely philosophical discussion even in Marxist circles in those times. The point is that the impression spread by the vested interests that Ambedkar had rejected Marxism after careful consideration is firstly not true. Whatever his understanding of it, his interest in Marxism had never waned. He prophesied that if Buddhism failed to deliver the results, the whole world would go in for Marxism. Secondly, his feeling of inadequacy of Marxism was related to the superfluous picture of Marxism available to him.

Obviously, Marxism did not have what he was looking for, to readily offer. In the realm of practice, the natural possibility of an alliance between him and the communists seems to have been thwarted by the mechanical outlook of the Indian communists who refused even to take cognisance of the problem of castes. Their ostrich like behaviour towards the frozen reality of this land was more unMarxist than anything conceivable. Still, Ambedkar had joined hands with them during the ILP days to protest against the anti-labour bill and had led the historical strike of the workers in Bombay. But this alliance was short-lived. Endowed with the most potent tools for analysing the social phenomena, it was the duty of the communists to understand Ambedkar and not vice versa. They not only failed in that but also went further to antagonistically oppose him. The Brahminical puritanism that they brought in Marxism was totally misfounded as the times proved. On the sheer consideration that dalits as the most oppressed people of this country did constitute their potential base, their strategy should have had a place for them if they were really committed to revolution. But, it is a fact that dalits just did not exist in their scheme of things. If any one were to be held responsible for betrayal of the revolution in India, it would be these mistaken comrades and not Ambedkar.

Unlike the frontline communist leaders in Bombay, Ambedkar did not need to declass himself to internalise the proletarian class-consciousness. Ambedkar belonged to the working class, he lived in the chawl — the mill workers quarters in Bombay. Even during his stay in USA and Europe, he lived the life of utter depravation, not even having enough food to eat. But for his western attire, which was supposed to reflect disgust for humbug prevalent in those days, he continued to identify himself with the masses and working classes in their trials and tribulations. He did not have any necessity to demonstrate this identity by any extraneous means. The overpowering politician in him in the later days certainly eroded this consciousness and consequently led him increasingly after the short solutions shunning the direct struggles.

The communists basically had their base in the Trade Unions (TU) of the textile mill workers of Bombay. These TUs were tight-lipped on the discrimination faced by dalits in not getting the jobs in better remunerative departments like weaving in textile mills. The economic condition of dalits was much worse than their *savarna* counterparts. Ambedkar observed that the communists used these TUs for their political gains rather than for the welfare of the working class. Whenever they took precipitate action to strike the work, the workers tended to suffer differentially, owing to their castewise placements. Ambedkar's objection to this 'irresponsible' TU behaviour was on two counts: (i) they were driven by raw 'economism' to the detriment of prospects of enhancing the political consciousness of the working class, (ii) they were using them as cannon fodder in the promotion of their political interests. Ambedkar's writing on communism or Marxism is heavily imbued with his annoyance with the Bombay-communists. This legacy to identify Marxism with its self-appointed practitioners still appears to be followed by dalits. They cite examples of the parliamentary communist parties to show the lacuna or inapplicability of Marxism. It is necessary for them to understand that Marxism needs criticism but it presupposes its careful study.

One of the greatest barriers the communists pose to others is their unMarxist and puritanical attitude. In India that was naturally likened to Brahminism with which all were familiar and because by default the communist leadership happened to come from Brahmin and other *dwija* castes. Marxist essence presupposes scientific enquiry, a dynamic understanding of the situations and requisite tolerance for divergent views. But the institutionalised Marxism always appeared ready with the glued labels like renegade, reactionary, revisionist, etc. to mark out those who did not toe the official line. These fallen comrades then are treated as the worst class enemies nullifying in one shot their life time contribution to the revolution. This tradition has unconsciously induced a dogmatic behaviour in the Marxist circles. By virtue of the powerful analytical tools of Marxism their analyses still read superior to any one around but it could be generally said that they have not made full use of their potentialities. They are adept at stuffing new facts into the old inferences to demonstrate eternal validity of their dogma. For instance, if they had seen the objective reality in Ambedkar's time as they did now about the problem of castes, the history of this country could have been a bit different! What worries the committed revolutionists is this attitude of the 'official' Marxists. For instance, there does not appear any significant appreciation of the changes in the mode of production under capitalism with the advances in communication and computational (information) technologies.

The capitalist organisations have undergone sea change with adoption of them from the Fordist models that constituted the reference for the Marxist schema. These organisations have re-engineered themselves into delayered, downsized, flexible, decentralised units and are tending to destructure so as to reduce the cycle times with the fullest use of information technology. In place of factories employing huge numbers of workers engaged in monotonous assembly line tasks, alienated from the product of their labour are coming the distributed production units with knowledge workers, fairly autonomous in their work sphere, located in apparently authority neutralised teams, with flexi-times and profit sharing avenues.

The policy package of globalisation that is out to increasingly marginalise and crush the people in poorer countries is just the corollary of this paradigm change. Although, contrary to opinion of many, this so-called flexible capitalism does not any way affect the validity of the theory, one worries to note no influence of these changes in the strategy and tactics of the Marxists. The redefinition project will have to take into account this emergent shape of the world.

One of the problems Ambedkar appears to face in accepting Marxism is its prescription of the 'dictatorship of proletariat' during the post-revolutionary transition period to communism. For him any kind of dictatorship was an anathema. He equates it with monarchy. While it is true that he had not understood the basic rationale behind or rather derivation of this concept, his apprehensions cannot be said to be mis-founded as the later developments in the socialist countries revealed. To overcome this lacuna he devises a via media solution of State socialism without demolishing the parliamentary democracy. To cover up the inherent lacunae in the parliamentary democracy, he proposes to incorporate the structure of the economy in the Constitution and limit the sovereignty of the Parliament. He visualised this solution as bringing in socialism without 'shedding a drop of blood' or resorting to dictatorship. It is unfortunate that instead of understanding the inherent defect of the framework of the political economy, he strove to propose such unrealistic solutions.

The separation of the dalit and communist movements has caused the greatest loss to the revolution in India. The fact that dalit and oppressed people, who constitute the backbone of this movement were kept away from it, restricted its growth. On the other side, on account of discarding the ideology of class struggle, the dalit movement could never come to grips with the real problem of dalits and comprehend the means to solve them. As a result, the condition of this community went on deteriorating, their movement remained revolving around the trifling, temporary and emotional issues thrown in their front by the cunning of ruling classes and their leaders remained entangled with their self interests and politics of *status quo*. The project of redefinition of Ambedkar will consist in systematically examining Ambedkar's conceptions and relocating him in relation to Marxism.

Aspects of the Strategy and Tactics

In the context of strategy, some of Ambedkar's contributions are really noteworthy. He brought the struggle against Brahminism into the political battlefield. He inferred that without political power the social and religious structures will collapse and motivated his followers to capture political power. But his conception of political power being acutely constrained by the parliamentary framework where bargaining is the predominant medium of securing political power, inevitably it made way for all kinds of aberrations and perversities to creep in.

The prevailing politics being the game of possibilities, he was soon sucked into its vortex. Politics came to dominate the other aspects of his personality. Slowly, the impact of politics started becoming visible everywhere. This phase significantly contributed to multiplication of his inconsistencies out of tactical imperatives. Dalits have taken this legacy of parliamentary politics very seriously, almost as the be all and end all of their political being. It may be, interesting to probe how much damage this kind of political orientation inflicted on the dalit movement.

It is altogether a different question whether Ambedkar had any other alternative to parliamentary politics for political practice. It may be argued that in the context of his resources, adversarial environment and to some extent his persona' limitations, he had none. Even if it is taken as correct, it should not be forgotten that it was a matter of strategy and tactic that presuppose contextual variables: it cannot be taken as the lasting value.

The fundamental source of most of Ambedkar's political thoughts and action is his conception of State and religion, that he had adopted as the extraneous instruments to reconcile the state of flux of things and the necessity of order in them. It is necessary to understand that both, the State as well as religion, are the products of the evolutionary process of the human society. There is nothing inevitable about them. Marx took State as the instrument of coercion in the hands of ruling classes and religion as the opium of the masses. Dalits have a long experience of nearly five decades with the so-called welfare State of Ambedkar's design. What does it say? Does the State side with them in their conflict with the landlords? Does it come to their rescue when every day three or four of their daughters are raped? Does it come to save the shame of their women when they are paraded naked in the streets? Does it take their side when they come in conflict with landlords, moneylenders in villages or with management in the modern settings? Does it really ensure they get their dues as provided in the Constitution or punish the defaulting management for non-compliance? To all of such questions the answer could only be in the negative. It is not a matter of 'devils occupying the temples' as Ambedkar lamented seeing the people occupying the Constitutional positions. The State possesses the characteristics of its master class. In India the upper caste capitalists, landlords, top bureaucrats, etc. being the ruling class, the State can never have saints who would favour dalits. It is a fact that even the government by a dalit party like the BSP could not transform it into a dalit State.

Religion, in Ambedkar's conception is necessary to maintain the moral order of the society. It may be interesting to examine to what extent it conforms to this idealistic expectation. Buddhism, which undoubtedly is the most rational of all the religions, does not have any evidence of having created over its near millennium long tenure in India such an order of the society which could claim liberty, equality and fraternity of Ambedkar's conception. Ambedkar's argument that the Bhikku Sangha in Buddhism was the prototype of this kind of society becomes invalid once we call into question the role of Sangha in the production process. Before that, the order that envisaged nostalgically to recreate the value of the vanishing *Gana Rajya* in microcosm against the evil of rising monarchies, cannot just sublimate to the era of capitalism without being an alley of exploiters unless it transforms itself in some way as a catalyst for the revolution. The moral tenets of Buddhism likewise cannot submerge the lure of surplus extraction, that is its dominating ethos. If at all, it may help it become more pronounced by weakening the resistance of the exploited masses. As we empirically see, the Buddhism of his conception could not produce even a trace of morality in its adherents. On the contrary, for the masses it presents the distorted, if not inverted, worldview; it orients them to look inwards for their misery and be blind to the reality that some one exploits him. He could certainly derive mental peace and pleasure but it is a state of an intoxicated mind. Keeping in mind the causal links in Ambedkar's adoption of these instruments, the redefinition project needs to address these issues afresh.

The strategy of the ruling class always stresses on diversion of peoples' attention from their real problems and their disarmament - both in physical and ideological terms. They invariably have a multi-layered strategy in place for this purpose. The vanguard parties of the ruling classes open up sentimental fronts and attempt to divert the attention of people as their real problems get aggravated. Secondly, their time-tested methods of adulterating radical ideas with the masses are always in operation. Towards this end, we see all the ruling parties vying with each other in co-opting Ambedkar. 'Ambedkar' represents a potentially dangerous ideological weapon in the hands of the Indian proletariat and so the ruling class will be hell bent on blunting its edge. They will do everything to eulogise him not only for wooing dalits for their immediate electoral gains but also to neutralise him as the radical ideological force by propagandising a distorted version of the latter. Dalits will have to exercise vigil over their ideological assets even after redefining Ambedkar.

5

Ambedkar's Views

Men are mortal. So are ideas. An idea needs propagation as much as a plant needs watering. Otherwise both will wither and die.

Ideal Society and State

The conception of secular state is derived from the liberal democratic tradition of west. No institution which is maintained wholly out of state funds shall be used for the purpose of religious instruction irrespective of the question whether the religious instruction is given by the state or any other body.

If you ask me, my ideal would be the society based on liberty, equality and fraternity. An ideal society should be mobile and full of channels of conveying a change taking place in one part to other parts.

To idealise the real which more often than not is full of inequities is a very selfish thing to do. It is only when a person finds a personal advantage in things, as they are that he tries to idealise the real. To proceed to make such an ideal real is nothing short of criminal. It means perpetuating inequity on the ground that whatever is settled is settled for all times. Such a view is opposed to all morality. No society with ideal conscience has ever accepted it. On the contrary whatever progress in improving the terms of associated life between individuals and classes has been made in the course of history, is due entirely to the recognition of the ethical doctrine that whatever is wrongly settled is never settled and must be resettled.

In every country the intellectual class is the most influential class. This is the class which can foresee, advise and lead. In no country does the mass of the people live the life for intelligent thought and action. It is largely imitative and follows the intellectual class. There is no exaggeration in saying that the entire destination of the country depends upon its intellectual class. If the intellectual class is honest and independent, it can be trusted to take the initiative and give a proper lead when a crisis arises. It is true that the intellect by itself is no virtue. It is only a means and the use of a means depends upon the ends which an intellectual person pursues. An intellectual man can be a good man but he may easily be a rogue. Similarly an intellectual class may be a band of high-souled persons, ready to help, ready to emancipate erring humanity or it may easily be a gang of crooks or a body of advocates of narrow clique from which it draws its support.

My final words of advice to you are educate, agitate and organise; have faith in yourself. With justice on our side I do not see how we can loose our battle. The battle to me is a matter of joy. The battle is in the fullest sense spiritual. There is nothing material or social in it. For ours is a battle not for wealth or for power. It is battle for freedom. It is the battle of reclamation of human personality.

You must abolish your slavery yourselves. Do not depend for its abolition upon god or a superman. Remember that it is not enough that a people are numerically in the majority. They must be always watchful, strong and self-respecting to attain and maintain success. We must shape our course ourselves and by ourselves. Untouchability shuts all doors of opportunities for betterment in life for Untouchables. It does not offer an Untouchable any opportunity to move freely in society; it compels him to live in dungeons and seclusion; it prevents him from educating himself and following a profession of his choice.

Untouchability has ruined the Untouchables, the Hindus and ultimately the nation as well. If the depressed classes gained their self-respect and freedom, they would contribute not only to their own progress and prosperity but by their industry intellect and courage would contribute also to the strength and prosperity of the nation. If the tremendous energy Untouchables are at present required to fritter away in combating the stigma of Untouchability had been saved them, it would have been applied by them to the promotion of education and development of resources of their nation as a whole.

There have been many Mahatmas in India whose sole object was to remove Untouchability and to elevate and absorb the depressed classes, but everyone has failed in their mission. Mahatmas have come, Mahatmas have gone but the Untouchables have remained as Untouchables.

A historian ought to be exact, sincere and impartial; free from passion, unbiased by interest, fear, resentment or affection; and faithful to the truth, which is the mother of history the preserver of great actions, the enemy of oblivion, the witness of the past, the director of the future.

From the point of view of annihilation of caste, the struggle of the saints did not have any effects on society. The value of a man is axiomatic and self-evident; it does not come to him from the gilding of Bhakti. The saints did not struggle to establish this point. On the contrary their struggle had very unhealthy effect on the depressed classes. It provided the Brahmins with an excuse to silence them by telling them that they would be respected if they attained the status of Chokhamela.

It is mischievously propagated by Hindu scriptures that by serving the upper classes the Shudras achieve salvation. Untouchability is another appellation of slavery. No race can be raised by destroying its self-respect. So if you really want to uplift the Untouchables, you must treat them in the social order as free citizens, free to carve out their destiny.

What you have lost others have gained. Your humiliations are a matter of pride with others. You are made to suffer wants, privations and humiliations not because it was pre-ordained by the sins committed in your previous birth, but because of the overpowering tyranny and treachery of those who are above you. You have no lands because others have usurped them; you have no posts because others have monopolised them. Do not believe in fate; believe in your strength.

Learn to live in this world with self-respect. You should always cherish some ambition of doing something in this world. But remember that the age of selflessness has ended. A new epoch is set in. All things are now possible because of your being able to participate in the politics and legislature of your country.

Some people think that religion is not essential to the society. I do not hold this view. I consider the foundations of religion are essential to the society. At the roots of Hindu social system lies a Dharma as prescribed in the Manusmriti. Such being the case I do not think it is possible to abolish the inequality in the Hindu society unless foundations of the Smriti-religion is removed and a better one laid in its place. I however, despair of Hindu society, being able to reconstruct itself on such a better foundation.

My religious conversion is not inspired by any material motive. This is hardly anything I cannot achieve even while remaining an Untouchable. There is no other feeling than that of a spiritual feeling underlying my religious conversion. Hinduism does not appeal to my conscience. My self-respect cannot assimilate Hinduism. In your case change of religion is imperative for worldly as well as spiritual ends. Do not care for the opinion of those who foolishly ridicule the idea of conversion for material ends. Why should you live under the fold of that religion which has deprived you of honour, money, food and shelter?

I tell you, religion is for man and not man for religion. If you want to organise, consolidate and be successful in this world, change this religion. The religion that does not recognise you as a human being, or give you water to drink, or allow you to enter in temples is not worthy to be called a religion. The religion that forbids you to receive education and comes in the way of your material advancement is not worthy of the appellation 'religion'. The religion that does not teach its followers to show humanity in dealing with its co-religionists is nothing but a display of a force. The religion that teaches its followers to suffer the touch of animals but not the touch of human beings is not a religion but a mockery. The religion that compels the ignorant to be ignorant and the poor to be poor is not a religion but a visitation!

The basic idea underlying religion is to create an atmosphere for the spiritual development of the individual. This being the situation, it is clear that you cannot develop your personality at all in Hinduism.

In Hinduism, conscience, reason and independent thinking have no scope for development.

It is your claim to equality which hurts them. They want to maintain the *status quo*. If you continue to accept your lowly status ungrudgingly, continue to remain dirty, filthy, backward, ignorant, poor and disunited, they will allow you to live in peace. The moment you start to raise your level, the conflict starts. Untouchability is not transitory or temporary feature; it is eternal, it is lasting. Frankly it can be said that the struggle between the Hindus and the Untouchables is a never-ending conflict. It is eternal because the religion which assigns you the lowest status in society is itself divine and eternal according to the belief of the so-called high caste Hindus. No change warranted by change of time and circumstances is possible.

I have never claimed to be a universal leader of suffering humanity. The problem of the untouchables is quite enough for my slender strength. I do not say that other causes are not equally noble. But knowing that life is short, one can only serve one cause and I have never aspired to do more than serve the Untouchables.

Every man must have a philosophy of life, for everyone must have a standard by which to measure his conduct. And philosophy is nothing but a standard by which to measure.

Negatively I reject the Hindu social philosophy propounded in Bhagvad Gita, based as it is on the Triguna of Sankhya Philosophy which in my judgement is a cruel perversion of the philosophy of Kapila, and which had made the caste system of graded inequality the law of Hindu social life.

Positively, my social philosophy may be said to be enshrined in three words: liberty, equality and fraternity. Let no one however say that I have borrowed my philosophy from the French Revolution. I have not. My philosophy has its roots in religion and not in political science. I have derived them from the teachings of my master, the Buddha.

Indians today are governed by two different ideologies. Their political ideal set in the preamble of the Constitution affirms a life of liberty, equality and fraternity. Their social ideal embodied in their religion denies them.

Unlike a drop of water which loses its identity when it joins the ocean, man does not lose his being in the society in which he lives. Man's life is independent. He is born not for the development of the society alone, but for the development of his self.

Freedom of mind is the real freedom. A person whose mind is not free though he may not be in chains, is a slave, not a free man. One whose mind is not free, though he may not be in prison, is a prisoner and not a free man. One whose mind is not free though alive, is no better than dead. Freedom of mind is the proof of one's existence.

What is the proof to judge that the flame of mental freedom is not extinguished in the mind of person? To whom can we say that his mind is free. I call him free who with his conscience awake realises his rights, responsibilities and duties. He who is not a slave of circumstances and is always ready and striving to change them in his flavour, I call him free.

One who is not a slave of usage, customs, of meaningless rituals and ceremonies, of superstitions and traditions; whose flame of reason has not been extinguished, I call him a free man. He who has not surrendered his free will and abdicated his intelligence and independent thinking, who does not blindly act on the teachings of others, who does not blindly accept anything without critically analysing and examining its veracity and usefulness, who is always prepared to protect his rights, who is not afraid of ridicule and unjust public criticism, who has a sound conscience and self-respect so as not become a tool in the hands of others, I call him a free man. He who does not lead his life under the direction of others, who sets his own goal of life according to his own reasoning and decides for himself as to how and in what way life should be lead, is a free man. In short, who is a master of his own free will, him alone I call a free man.

Caste cannot be abolished by inter caste dinners or stray instances of inter caste marriages. Caste is a state of mind. It is a disease of mind. The teachings of the Hindu religion are the root cause of this disease. We practice casteism and we observe Untouchability because we are enjoined to do so by the Hindu religion. A bitter thing cannot be made sweet. The taste of anything can be changed. But poison cannot be changed into nectar.

What struck me most was that my community still continues to accept a position of humiliation only because caste Hindus persist in dominating over them. You must rely on your own strength, shake off the notion that you are in any way inferior to any community.

Constitutional morality is not a natural sentiment. It has to be cultivated. We must realise that our people have yet to learn it. Democracy in India is only a top dressing on an Indian soil which is essentially undemocratic.

Majorities are of two sorts: (1) communal majority, and (2) political majority. A political majority is changeable in its class composition. A political majority grows. A communal majority is born. The admission to a political majority is open. The door to a communal majority is closed. The politics of political majority are free to all to make and unmake. The politics of communal majority are made by its own members born in it.

The minorities in India have loyally accepted the rule of the majority which is basically a communal majority and not a political majority. It is for the majority to realise its duty not to discriminate against minorities. Whether the minorities will continue or will vanish must depend upon this habit of majority. The moment the majority looses the habit of discriminating against the minority, the minorities can have no ground to exist. They will vanish.

We want our own people, people who will fight tooth and nail for our interest and secure privilege for the under-privileged; people who will undo the wrongs done to our people; people who will voice our grievances fearlessly; people who can think, lead and act; people with principles and character. Such people should be sent to the legislatures. We must send such people to Legislatures who will be slaves to none but remain free to their conscience and get our grievances redressed.

Why does a human body become deceased? The reason is that as long as the human body is not free from suffering, mind cannot be happy. If a man lacks enthusiasm, either his body or mind is in a deceased condition.... Now what saps the enthusiasm in man? If there is no enthusiasm, life becomes drudgery — a mere burden to be dragged. Nothing can be achieved if there is no enthusiasm. The main reason for this lack of enthusiasm on the part of a man is that an individual looses the hope of getting an opportunity to elevate himself. Hopelessness leads to lack of enthusiasm. The mind in such cases becomes deceased.... When is enthusiasm created? When one breaths an atmosphere where one is sure of getting the legitimate reward for one's labour, only then one feels enriched by enthusiasm and inspiration.

Equality

The fundamental principle of Buddhism is equality... Buddhism was called the religion of Shudras. There was only one man who raised his voice against separatism and Untouchability and that was Lord Buddha.

The teachings of Buddha are eternal, but even then Buddha did not proclaim them to be infallible. The religion of Buddha has the capacity to change according to times, a quality which no other religion can claim to have...Now what is the basis of Buddhism? If you study carefully, you will see that Buddhism is based on reason. There is an element of flexibility inherent in it, which is not found in any other religion.

I am myself a believer in Ahimsa (non-violence). But I make a distinction between Ahimsa and meekness. Meekness is weakness and weakness is voluntarily imposed upon oneself is not a virtue. I am believer in Ahimsa but in the sense defined by the saint Takuma. Takuma has quite rightly said that Ahimsa consisted of two things: (1) love and kindness towards all creatures, and (2) destruction of evil doers. The second part of this definition is often lost sight of that the doctrine of Ahimsa becomes so ridiculous.

Religion must mainly be a matter of principles only. It cannot be a matter of rules. The moment it degenerates into rules, it ceases to be a religion, as it kills responsibility which is an essence of the true religious act.

We must begin by acknowledging that there is a complete absence of two things in Indian Society. One of these is equality. On the social plane we have an India based on the principles of graded inequality, which means elevation for some and degradation for others. On the economic plane we have a society in which there are some who have immense wealth as against many who live in abject poverty.

The second thing we are wanting in is the recognition of the principle of fraternity. What does fraternity mean? Fraternity means a sense of common brotherhood of all Indians, all Indians being one people. It is a principle that gives solidarity to social life. It is difficult thing to achieve. It seems to me that there lies a heavy duty to see that democracy does not vanish from the earth as a governing principle of human relationship. If we believe in it, we must both be true and loyal to it. We must not only be staunch in our faith in democracy but we must resolve to see that whatever we do, we do not help the enemies of democracy to uproot the principles of liberty, equality and fraternity.

It follows that we must strive along with other democratic countries to maintain the basis of democratic civilization. If democracy lives we are sure to reap the benefit of it. If democracy dies it will be our doom. On that there can be no doubt.

The basis of my politics lies in the proposition that the Untouchables are not a subdivision or subsection of Hindus, and that they are a separate and distinct element in the national life of India.

The true function of law consists in repairing the faults in society. Unfortunately ancient societies never dared to assume the function of repairing their own defects; consequently they decayed. This country has seen the conflict between ecclesiastical law and secular law long before Europeans sought to challenge the authority of the Pope. Kautilya's Arthshastra lays down the foundation of secular law. In India unfortunately ecclesiastical law triumphed over secular law. In my opinion this was the one of the greatest disasters in the country. The unprogressive nature of the Hindu society was due to the notion that the law cannot be changed.

Civilization has never been a continuous process. There were states and societies which at one time had been civilised. In the course of time something happened which made these societies stagnant and decayed. This could be illustrated by India's history itself. There could be no doubt that one of the countries which could boast of ancient civilization is India. When the inhabitants of Europe were living under the barbaric conditions, this country had reached the highest peak of civilization, it had parliamentary institutions when the people of Europe were mere nomads.

I measure the progress of a community by the degree of progress which women have achieved.

Justice has always evoked ideas of equality, of proportion of compensation. Equity signifies equality. Rules and regulations, right and righteousness are concerned with equality in value. If all men are equal, then all men are of the same essence, and the common essence entitles them of the same fundamental rights and equal liberty... In short justice is another name of liberty, equality and fraternity.

Anyone who studies working of the system of social economy based on private enterprise and pursuit of personal gain will realise how it undermines, if it does not actually violate the individual rights on which democracy rests. How many have to relinquish their rights in order to gain their living? How many have to subject themselves to be governed by private employers?

I hate injustice, tyranny, pompousness and humbug, and my hatred embraces all those who are guilty of them. I want to tell my critics that I regard my feelings of hatred as a real force. They are only the reflexes of love I bear for the causes I believe in and I am in no wise ashamed of it.

Indifferentism is the worst kind of disease that can affect people. Political tyranny is nothing compared to the social tyranny and a reformer who defies society is a more courageous man than a politician who defies Government.

Every man who repeats the dogma of Mill that one country is no fit to rule another country must admit that one class is not fit to rule another class.

One cannot have any respect or regard for men who take the position of the reformer and then refuse to see the logical consequences of that position, let alone following them out in action. History shows that where ethics and economics come in conflict, victory is always with economics. Vested interests have never been known to have willingly divested themselves unless there was sufficient force to compel them.

This condition obtains even where there is no slavery in the legal sense. It is found where as in caste system, some persons are forced to carry on the prescribed callings which are not their choice.

India is a peculiar country and her nationalists and patriots are a peculiar people. A patriot and a nationalist in India is one who sees with open eyes his fellow men treated as being less than man. But his humanity does not rise in protest. He knows that men and women for no cause are denied their rights. But it does not prick his civil sense of helpful action. He finds a whole class of people shut out from public employment. But it does not rouse his sense of justice and fair play.

Hundreds of evil practices that injure man and society are perceived by him. But they do not sicken him with disgust. The patriot's one cry is power for him and his class. I am glad I do not belong to that class of patriots. I belong to that class which takes its stand on democracy and which seeks to destroy monopoly in every form. Our aim is to realise in practice our ideal of one man one value in all walks of life — political, economical and social.

There is no nation of Indians in the real sense of the world, it is yet to be created. In believing we are a nation, we are cherishing a great delusion. How can people divided into thousand of castes be a nation? The sooner we realise that we are not yet a nation, in a social and psychological sense of the world, the better for us.

It is not enough to be electors only. It is necessary to be law-makers; otherwise those who can be law-makers ill be the masters of those who can only be electors.

Democracy

Walter Bagehot defined democracy as ' Government by discussion'. Abraham Lincoln defined democracy as ' A Government of the people, by the people and for the people'.

My definition of democracy is — a form and a method of Government whereby revolutionary changes in the social life are brought about without bloodshed. That is the real test. It is perhaps the severest test. But when you are judging the quality of the material you must put it to the severest test.

Democracy is not merely a form of Government. It is primarily a mode of associated living, of conjoint communicated experience. It is essentially an attitude of respect and reverence towards our fellow men.

A democratic form of Government presupposes a democratic form of a society, The formal framework of democracy is of no value and would indeed be a misfit if there was no social democracy. It may not be necessary for a democratic society to be marked by unity, by community of purpose, by loyalty to public ends and by mutuality of sympathy. But it does unmistakably involve two things. The first is an attitude of mind, and attitude of respect and equality towards their fellows. The second is a social organisation free from rigid social barriers. Democracy is incompatible and inconsistent with isolation and exclusiveness resulting in the distinction between the privileged and the unprivileged.

Democracy is not a Form of Government, but a form of social organisation.

What we must do is not to content ourselves with mere political democracy. We must make our political democracy a social democracy as well. Political democracy cannot last unless there is at the base of it, a social democracy. What does social democracy mean? It means a way of life which recognises liberty, equality and fraternity as the principles of life. These principles of liberty, equality and fraternity are not to be treated as separate items. They form a union in the sense that, to divorce one from the other is to defeat the very purpose of democracy. Liberty cannot be divorced from equality, nor can liberty and equality be divorced from fraternity.

Without social union, political unity is difficult to be achieved. If achieved, it would be as precarious as a summer sapling, liable to be uprooted by the gust of wind. With mere political unity, India may be a state. But to be a state is not to be a nation and a state which is not a nation has small prospects of survival in the struggle of existence. This is especially true where nationalism — the most dynamic force of modern times, is seeking everywhere to free itself by the destruction and disruption of all mixed states. The danger to a mixed and composite state, therefore lies not so much in external aggression as in the internal resurgence of nationalities which are fragmented, entrapped, suppressed and held against their will.

The idea of fundamental rights has become a familiar one since their enactment in the American Constitution and in the

Constitution framed by the Revolutionary France. The idea of making a gift of fundamental rights to every individual is no doubt very laudable. The question is how to make them effective? The prevalent view is that once the rights are enacted in law then they are safeguarded.

This again is an unwarranted assumption. As experience proves, rights are protected not by law but by social and moral conscience of the society. If social conscience is such that it is prepared to recognise the rights which law proposes to enact, rights will be safe and secure. But if the fundamental rights are opposed by the community, no Law, no Parliament, no Judiciary can guarantee them in the real sense of the world. What is the use of Fundamental rights to the Untouchables in India? As Burke said, there is no method found for punishing the multitude. Law can punish a single solitary recalcitrant criminal. It can never operate against the whole body of people who choose to defy it. Social conscience is the only safeguard of all rights, fundamental or non-fundamental.

Rights are real only if they are accompanied by remedies. It is no use giving rights if the aggrieved person has no legal remedy to which he can resort when his rights are invaded.

Lost rights are never regained by appeals to the conscience of the usurpers, but by relentless struggle.... Goats are used for sacrificial offerings and not lions.

For a successful revolution it is not enough that there is discontent. What is required is a profound and thorough conviction of the justice, necessity and importance of political and social rights. I feel that the Constitution is workable, it is flexible and it is strong enough to hold the country together both in peacetime and in wartime. Indeed, if I may say so, if things go wrong under the new Constitution, the reason will not be that we had a bad Constitution. What we will have to say is that Man was vile.

Equality may be a fiction but nonetheless one must accept it as a governing principle.

What are we having this liberty for? We are having this liberty in order to reform our social system, which is full of inequality, discrimination and other things, which conflict with our fundamental rights.

Our object in framing the Constitution is rally two-fold: (1) To lay down the form of political democracy, and (2) To lay down that our ideal is economic democracy and also to prescribe that every Government whatever is in power shall strive to bring about economic democracy. The directive principles have a great value, for they lay down that our ideal is economic democracy.

If I find the Constitution being misused, I shall be the first to burn it.

On the 26th January 1950, we are going to enter into a life of contradictions. In politics we will have equality and in social and economic life we will have inequality. In politics we will be recognising the principle of one man one vote and one vote one value. In our social and economic life, we shall by reason of our social and economic structure, continue to deny the principle of one man one value. How long shall we continue to live this life of contradictions? How long shall we continue to deny equality in our social and economic life? If we continue to deny it for long, we will do so only by putting our political democracy in peril. We must remove this contradiction at the earliest possible moment else those who suffer from inequality will blow up the structure of democracy which this Constituent Assembly has so laboriously built up.

There can be no gain saying that political power in this country has too long been the monopoly of the few, and the many are not beasts of burden but also beasts of prey.

The monopoly has not merely deprived them of their chance of betterment, it has sapped them of what may be called the significance of life. Those downtrodden classes are tired of being governed. They are impatient to govern themselves. This urge of self-realisation in the downtrodden must not be allowed to devolve into class struggle or class war.

It would lead to the division of the House. That would indeed be a day of disaster. For, as has been well-said by Abraham Lincoln: "A house divided against cannot stand very long". Therefore, the sooner room is made for realisation of their aspiration, the better for the few, the better for the country, the better for the independence and the better for the continuance of its democratic structure. This can only be done by the establishment of equality and fraternity in all walks of life.

It is disgraceful to live at the cost of one's self-respect. Self-respect is the most vital factor in life. Without it, man is a cipher. To live worthily with self-respect, one has to overcome difficulties. It is out of hard and ceaseless struggle alone that one derives strength, confidence and recognition.

Cultivation of mind should be the ultimate aim of human existence.

Sincerity is the sum of all moral qualities.

Man is mortal. Everyone has to die some day or the other. But one must resolve to lay down one's life in enriching the noble ideals of self-respect and in bettering one's human life. We are not slaves. Nothing is more disgraceful for a brave man than to live life devoid of self-respect.

My social philosophy may be said to be enshrined in three words: liberty, equality and fraternity. My philosophy has roots in religion and not in political science. I have derived them from the teachings of my master, the Buddha.

Emerson has said that consistency is a virtue of an ass. No thinking human being can be tied down to a view once expressed in the name of consistency. More important than consistency is responsibility. A responsible person must learn to unlearn what he has learned. A responsible person must have the courage to rethink and change his thoughts. Of course there must be good and sufficient reason for unlearning what he has learned and for recasting his thoughts. There can be no finality in rethinking.

John Dewey said: "Every society gets encumbered with what is trivial, with what is dead wood from the past and what is positively perverse. As a society becomes more enlightened, it realises that it is responsible not to conserve and transmit the whole of its achievement, but only such as makes a better future society".

There is nothing fixed, nothing eternal, nothing sanatan; everything is changing, change is the law of life for individuals as well as for society. In a changing society there must be constant revolution of old values.

No civilised society of today presents more survivals of primitive times than does the Indian society. Its religion is essentially primitive and its tribal code, in spite of the advance of time and civilization, operates in all its pristine vigour even today. Indian society still savours of the clan system, even though there are no clans.

An ideal society should be mobile, should be full of channels for conveying a change taking place in one part to other parts. In an ideal society there should be many interests consciously communicated and shared.

The strength of a society depends upon the presence of points of contacts, possibilities of interaction between different groups that exist in it. These are what Carlyle calls "Organic filaments", i.e. the elastic threads which helps to bring the disintegrating elements together and to reunite them.

Hero-worship

Heroes and hero-worship is a hard fact in India's political life. I agree that hero-worship is demoralising for the devotee and dangerous to the country. I welcome the criticism so far as it conveys the caution that you must know your man is really great before you start worshipping him. This unfortunately is not an easy task. For in these days with the Press in hand it is easy to manufacture Great Men. Carlyle used a happy phrase when he described the Great Men of history as so many bank notes. Like bank notes they represent gold. What we have to see that they are not forged notes. I admit that we ought to be more cautious in our worship of Great Men. For in this country we have arrived at such a stage when alongside the notice boards saying "Beware of pickpockets", we need to have notice boards saying "Beware of Great Men". Even Carlyle who defended the worship of Great Men warned his readers how: "Multitudes of Great Men have figured in history who were false and selfish."

Hero-worship in the sense of expressing our unbound admiration is one thing. To obey the hero is a totally different kind of worship. There is nothing wrong in the former while the latter is no doubt a most pernicious thing. The former is man's respect for which is noble and of which the great men are only an embodiment. The latter is the serf's fealty to his lord. The former is consistent with respect, but the latter is a sign of debasement. The former does not take away one's intelligence to think and independence to act. The latter makes one perfect fool. The former involves no disaster to the state. The latter is a source of positive danger to it.

In India, 'Bhakti' or what may be called the path of devotion or hero-worship plays a part in politics unequalled in magnitude by the part it plays in the politics of any other of the world. 'Bhakti' in religion may be a road to salvation of the soul. But in politics, 'Bhakti' or hero-worship is a sure road to degradation and to eventual dictatorship.

The questions which President Roosevelt propounded for the American public to consider will arise here, if they have not already arisen: Who shall rule — wealth or man? Which shall lead — money or intellect? Who shall fill the public stations — educated and patriotic free men or the feudal serf's of the corporate capital? For the president, Indian politics, at any rate the Hindu part of it, instead of being spiritualised has become grossly commercialised, so much so that it has become a byword for corruption. Many men of culture are refusing to concern themselves in this cesspool. Politics has become a kind of sewage system intolerably unsavoury and insanitary. To become a politician is like going to work in the drain.

History bears out the proposition that political revolutions have always been preceded by social and religious revolutions. Social reform in India has few friends and many critics. Law and order are the medicine of the body politic and when the body politic gets sick, medicine must be administered.

The world owes much to rebels who would dare to argue in the face of the pontiff (high priest) and insist that he is not infallible. A people and their religion must be judged by social standards based on social ethics. No other standard would have any meaning if religion is held to be necessary good for the well-being of the people.

Ethnologists are of the opinion that men of pure race exist nowhere and that there has been admixture of all races in all parts of the world — especially is this the case with the people if India. Mr. D. R. Bhandarkar has stated: "There is hardly a class or caste in India which has not a foreign strain in it. There is as an admixture of alien blood not only among the warrior classes — the Rajputs and Marathas — but among the Brahmins who are under the happy delusion that they are free from all foreign elements.

The question is not whether a community lives or dies, the question is on what plane does it live. There are different modes of survival. But all are not equally honourable. For an individual as well as a society, there is a gulf between merely living and living worthily. To fight in a battle and live in a glory is one mode. To beat a retreat to surrender and to live the life of a captive is also a mode of survival.

The sovereignty of scriptures of all religions must come to an end if we want to have a united integrated modern India.

Law and religion are two forces which govern the conduct of men. At times they act as handmaids to each other. At other times they act as check and counter-check. Of the two forces, Law is personal while religion is impersonal. Law being personal it is capable of being unjust and iniquitous. But religion being impersonal, it can be impartial, it is capable of defeating the inequity committed by law. Religion is believed to ennoble man and not degrade him. Hinduism is an exception.

I like the religion that teaches liberty, equality and fraternity. The relationship between husband and wife should be one of closest friends.

To open or not to open the temples is a question for you to consider and not for me to agitate. If you think it is bad manners not to believe in the sanctity of human beings, then throw open the doors and be a gentleman, but if you wish to remain a orthodox Hindu then shut the doors and damn yourself, for I don't care to come. We are Indians, firstly and lastly

Given the time and circumstances, nothing under the sun shall stop this country from becoming a super power.

Being grateful has limitations, no man can be grateful at the cost of his dignity, no woman at the cost of her chastity and no country at the cost of its freedom.

A great man is different from an eminent one in that he is ready to be the servant of the society.

So long as you do not achieve social liberty, whatever freedom is provided by the law is of no avail to you.

On 26th Jan. 1950, India will be an independent country. What would happen to her independence? Will she maintain or will she lose it again? This is the first thought that comes to my mind. It is not that India was never an independent country. The point is that she once lost the independence she had. Will she lose it a second time? It is this thought which makes me most anxious for the future. What perturbs me greatly is the fact that not only India has once beforelost her independence, but she lost it by treachery of some of her own people...

Will history repeat itself ?It is this thought which fills me with anxiety. This anxiety is deepened by the realisation of the fact that in addition to our old enemies in the form of castes and creeds, we are going to have many political parties with diverse and opposing political creeds. Will Indians place the country above their creed or creed above their country? I do not know, But this much is certain that if the parties place creed above country, our independence will be put in jeopardy a second time and probably be lost forever. This eventuality we all must resolutely guard against. We must be determined to defend our independence with the last drop of our blood!

Bahujan Philosophy

Indian History

This is in response to letter from Dr. Choudhrie in DV of Sept. 1-15. I am glad to know that he is trying to study Ancient Indian History. Not only it is illuminating, but it throws ample light on the happenings of today. One finds that from times immemorial, the struggle between the so-called upper caste savarnas on one side and the rest of population on other side is going on. It had assumed different names, shapes and forms during the course of different periods of history, and the history of India is nothing but the history of conflict between these two ideologies, as is well demonstrated by Dr. Ambedkar.

The present name for this is bahujan-vad and bahujan-virodh-vad. The present day protagonists of these are Phuley, Shahu and Ambedkar on one side and Tilak, Gandhi and Golwalkar on the other. All the leaders of Christians and Muslims need to understand this point and explain it to the gullible ignorant and illiterate Christian and Muslim masses, instead of thinking in lines of proletising Dalits. These are the only two ideologies in present day India, and sooner the people understand this, earlier they will be freed from their slavery.

Unchristian Side of the Indian Church

In his rejoinder to Dr. Chaudhrie's letter, VTR has very aptly described the situation. If I remember it correctly, in his article of above name published in DV some two years ago, he had commented that the missionaries are educating the children of oppressors, who tomorrow will come to power and see that these very schools be closed.

It is like feeding milk to the serpents' offsprings. He had also suggested that at least 50 per cent of seats in all Christian convents must be given only to SCs and STs at no charge, and the deficit be made good by charging double fees from the children of oppressors. I think that article was a master piece.

Ambedkar's Advice to Christians

I like to make all conversant with one of the speeches of Dr. Ambedkar, during the period of active consideration of choice of religion to adopt. May be, this might clear doubts, if any. The speech delivered to Indian Christians of Sholapur. Published in 'Janata' of 5.2.1938, reproduced from 'Dnyanodaya'

"From the available religions and personalities in the world, I consider only two — Buddha and Christ for conversion. We want a religion for me and my followers which will teach equality freedom among men, and how man must behave with men and God, how child should behave with father, etc.

"Missionaries feel they have done their duty when they convert an untouchable to Christianity. They do not look after their political rights. I find this is a big fault in Christians. Because they have not entered into politics up till now. It is difficult for any institution to survive without political support. We, Untouchables, though are ignorant and illiterate, we are in movement. That is why we have 15 seats in the Legislative Assembly. Students are getting scholarships, there are government hostels. Such is not the case of Christian students. If an untouchable student getting scholarship get converted, his scholarship is stopped though his financial status remains same. If you were in politics, things would have been opposed.

"Your society is educated. Hundreds of boys and girls are metric. These people have not agitated against this injustice unlike the uneducated untouchables. If any girl becomes a nurse or any boy becomes a teacher they are involved in their own affairs, they do not get involved in public affairs. Even clerks and officers are busy in their work, he ignores the social injustice. Your society is so much educated, how many are District judges or magistrates? I tell you, this is because of your neglect towards politics, because there in nobody to talk of and fight for your rights. ..."

Hindu Muslim Riots and Dalits

A letter by Dr. Ambedkar sent from England at the time of Third Round Table Conference published in "Janata" of 24.12.1932.

"When Hindus and Muslims fight among themselves, the Untouchables tend to incline towards Muslims. They feel, they would be benefited if they develop friendship with Muslims. But Untouchables should keep in mind that it is not all that true as it appears and so they should be very careful. What I experienced at the time of Sarada Act about the Muslim policy, can not called satisfactory. I got first severe jolt when I found that almost all the Muslims got ready to oppose the essential Act like Sarada Act along with the obsolete and puranic, fundamentalists and revivalist orthodox Hindus. And at the time of Round Table Conference, I got second experience now that their attitude can be how narrow and retrograde, like that of sanatani orthodox Hindus. A special telegram from the Brahmin President of Varnashram Brahman Sangha was received recently by a Muslim delegate, Mr. Gazanavi. It was a message that Muslims should cooperate with orthodox Hindus in opposing the Untouchables temple entry movement. It was also suggested that, if India gets freedom, it would be dangerous to the religion of both Hindus as well as Muslims, and so the religious Muslims should be careful about the swaraj like religious Hindus. The sanatani Brahmins also requested Mr. Gaznavi to put forward the side of sanatani Hindus by the Muslim delegates in the RTC! Thus, it could be said that these orthodox Brahmins have materialised the proverb that 'we are orthodox Brahmins and our relatives are Muslims'. Mr. Gaznavi has published this telegram in 'Times' here. The fact, that the orthodox Bengali Muslim like Mr. Gaznavi should be entrusted the job of preserving the religion of Hindus, by the orthodox Hindus, and that he should accept it, should be borne in mind by all the reformists in India. It is an excellent example of how an orthodox sanatani Hindu is ready to pray even an 'yavan' or a 'mlenchha' when he finds the life of his 'dharma' is in danger (from untouchables). And the 'dharma' of Hindus is such a provokative (vigna-santoshi) one, that whenever any thing new happens, or due to time any change takes place in traditional customs, they shout that, dharm' is in danger. Just like a sanatani Hindu, the Indian Muslim also is a strange object. He is averse to all social reforms. His corelegionists outside India have turned to be social revolutionaries. A Muslim patriot like Kemal Pasha has quashed all customs and traditions which are hurdles against the progress of nation and human life. I have great respect and affinity for Kemal Pasha. But the Indian Muslims, even the patriots and nationalists like Shaukat Ali, do not like Kemal Pasha and Amanullah. Because they are reformists, and in the eyes of a Indian Muslim, reform is a sacrilege."

6

Post-Ambedkar Dalit Movements

The Legacy of the Messiah

Babasaheb Ambedkar has undoubtedly been the central figure in the epistemology of the dalit universe. It is difficult to imagine anything serious or important in their collective life that is totally untouched by Ambedkar. For the dalit masses he is everything together; a scholar par excellence in the realm of scholarship, a Moses or messiah who led his people out of bondage and ignominy on to the path of pride, and a Bodhisatva in the pantheon of Buddhism. He is always bedecked with superlatives, quite like God, whatever may be the context in dalit circles.

It is not difficult to see the reason behind the obeisance and reverence that dalits have for Ambedkar. They see him as one who devoted every moment of his life thinking about and struggling for their emancipation, who took the might of the establishment head on in defence of their cause; who sacrificed all the comforts and conveniences of life that were quite within his reach to be on their side; who conclusively disproved the theory of caste based superiority by rising to be the tallest amongst the tall despite enormous odds, and finally as one who held forth the torch to illuminate the path of their future. Few in the history of millenniums of their suffering had so much as looked at them as humans and empathised with them as fellow beings. He was their own among these few. It was he, who forsook his high pedestal, climbed down to their level, gave them a helping hand and raised them to human stature. It is a commonplace occurrence to see dalits right from the humble landless labourer in villages to the highly placed bureaucrat in corridors of power, emotionally attributing their all to him. They all believe that but for him, they would still be living like their forefathers, with spittoons around their necks and broom sticks to their behind.

It is thus natural for dalits to place him at the centre as their beacon and conduct their collective affairs as directed by its beam. This beam however is not monochromatic like a laser beam, to use an analougy from physics, but is composed of many light frequencies, the filters for which are controlled not by the masses but by some others. They manipulate this beam as per their desire, sometimes letting some frequencies pass and some times some other. They could selectively amplify some part and de-amplify the other and present an entirely different spectrum. What reaches the masses, thus, is not the holistic and true picture of 'Ambedkar' but its part, sometimes a distorted part, carefully filtered out and amplified by the 'technicians'. This fragmented and false Ambedkar is what reaches the masses. For them, Ambedkar is no more a historical personality named Bhimrao Ramji Ambedkar. He is already metamorphosed into a symbol - a symbol for their collective aspiration, an icon for the thesis of their emancipation. Because for the masses icons come handy. They are sans complexity of the main body, practical useable artefacts. Iconisation of the great heroes and their ideas at the hands of masses is thus inevitable. Human history is replete with such icons; rather it is largely made of them. The dalit politicians who never let the masses see the material aspects of their problems and kept them entangled in the cobweb of emotional issues have moreover promoted iconisation of Babasaheb Ambedkar.

This analysis is premised on a hypothesis that the history of post-Ambedkar dalit movement is largely influenced by the icons of Ambedkar that were produced by the socio-political dynamics of post-independence India. The process of iconisation, whatever be the motivations, has to have the basis, howsoever tenuous, in the material reality, in the facts about the subject. Being essentially a simplification of a complex reality, it involves the playing up of facts as per one's proclivities and propensities. The text therefore attempts to trace out the bases for various Ambedkar icons in Ambedkar himself and simultaneously highlights the motive force behind the underlying distortions that they embody. While it largely holds these icons responsible for the current sorry State of the dalit movement based on the near-monotheistic devotion of dalits towards Babasaheb Ambedkar, it still considers that the conceptual framework that he reflects could be used, not only to further the emancipatory struggles of dalits to its logical end but also to promote a true democratic revolution in India, provided it is seen in a radical light.

The analysis is divided into four parts. The first reviews the post-Ambedkar dalit movement, essentially in relation to certain significant milestones or trends and attempts to trace the specific icon of Ambedkar that underscores each. The second part discusses the general limitations of transpositioning the ideologies, characterising specific episodes in the history across the historical periods and in specific reviews the predominant profiles of the Ambedkar-icons. It outlines the need to redefine Ambedkar, if he is to be the ideological icon to guide the dalit movement to its logical end.

A review of the significant events and episodes in the dalit movement after the demise of Babasaheb Ambedkar is attempted here in order to identify the icons behind them and assess their characteristics.

Gaikwad and Others

After the death of Babasaheb Ambedkar, the mantle of leadership fell upon the shoulders of Dadasaheb Gaikwad. He appeared to be the natural choice, by virtue of his stature in the movement as well as his age. He had grown up to be Ambedkar's trusted lieutenant through frontline participation in all the battles, right from the days of Mahad. He represented a typical activist of the Ambedkarian movement and had a mass identity. He seemed to know the exact pulse of dalit masses. It is interesting to note that the question of land that by and large constitutes the crux of the dalit problem (as recognised by innumerable scholars even today) was and could only be taken up by Gaikwad. It was the biggest and by far the most glorious event in the post-Ambedkar dalit movement. Even during the days of Babasaheb Ambedkar, the mass struggle for land had never materialised in direct terms and at such a scale. At the most, it could be said to have materialised symbolically in the form of a struggle for abolition of 'Khoti' — a kind of landlordism that prevailed in the Konkan region of Maharashtra. At any rate, as a mass struggle for land at the national level, it did not have any parallel in Indian history. It was the first time that the economic dimension of the dalit problem was effectively integrated with their social oppression. It had gained an overwhelming support from the masses all over the country. Scores of dalit families went to jail and many dalit hamlets remained deserted for days.

However, although it had caught the fancy of dalit masses, the rest of the dalit leadership thought otherwise. They disproved Gaikwad's struggle as being communist and declared that it had no place in Ambedkarian agenda. They highlighted Ambedkar's statement that mass struggles were the grammar of anarchy in the constitutional regime and should not have any place in a parliamentary democracy. They argued that if the land question was at all important, it could have been taken up judicially in the Supreme Court of India. Fortunately, none suggested parliamentary solution. It was perhaps considered infeasible as none could muster requisite majority to effect the people oriented fundamental changes after the Poona Pact. In tacit terms, the other leaders were accusing Gaikwad of being intellectually incapable of comprehending the subtleties of Ambedkar's ideology and hence unsuitable to step into his shoes.

Gaikwad, a rustic in the common man's Dhoti-Kurta attire, and not embellished with university degrees, could not be accepted by these people. They considered themselves the true heirs to the leadership after Ambedkar on the sole criterion that they fitted the Ambedkarian mould (as they conceived it) better than Gaikwad. This mould was based on the contemporary middle class cultural norms that Ambedkar displayed in his attire and general demeanour. They would conveniently forget that his western attire was basically a counter to Gandhi's belaboured austerity and a representation of modernity as against Gandhi's anti-modern views. Instead, they aped him in all appearances. They wore trousers and shirts, were suited and booted, had university degrees and could command better sophistry than Gaikwad. They would exhibit their law books as the key to the treasure left behind by Ambedkar. They could thus project themselves as better clones of Ambedkar to the gullible dalit masses. Gaikwad and the people of his ilk could be activists but not the leaders!

The first attempt to iconise Babasaheb Ambedkar and considerably successfully so, as the later times proved, is apparent in this early post-Ambedkar episode. That was the icon of a *'saheb'* — the epitaph used for an Englishman but later used as an honorific for natives, who were educated, westernised and placed in bureaucratic authority. It denoted someone far above the masses, one who was endowed with authority and power. It was the icon of a saviour. It projected leader as the saviour incarnate who would liberate them from their bondage and lead them to prosperity. All that masses had to do was to stand solidly behind him. They did not have any specific role in the project of their own emancipation other than being meek followers of the leader. This particular icon distanced the dalit leadership from the masses in every way in terms of physical attributes like appearance, clothes, language and lifestyle. It promoted blind following and servile notions. The leaders were to be treated as their quasi-monarch (a la *Bhim Raja*). They could not be questioned on equal terms. They bestowed favours by their very existence. Without leaders the masses could not exist. It obfuscated, mystified and externalised the problems of dalits, if not their very existence. The saheb syndrome that curiously settled among dalits as the general honorific, almost devoid of any attribute association, got significant reinforcement by this icon. Moreover, in so far as this syndrome reflected middle class aspirations and value associations, this icon helped petty-bourgeoisise the entire dalit movement.

Although, later the Dalit Panthers brought in a change in this leadership model, certainly in its physical attributes and so made it more people friendly, it approximately recoiled back to the old RPI (Republican Party of India) model with the demise of the spirit behind Panthers. This leadership model was certainly regressive as it reproduced the decadent feudal structure that dalits were so familiar with in real life; perhaps it was both, its cause as well as its effect. Paradoxically, its protagonists and promoters were the very people who seemed to claim a larger share of modernity. Gaikwad's equation with the masses and his charisma would not be easily swept away by their attempts but it is a fact that he could not take up mass based struggles thereafter and rather chose to fall prey to the enticements of power and pelf form Congress circle. Thus, this early icon of Ambedkar certainly blocked the emerging mass orientation of the dalit movement.

Tailist Pursuit of Power

The importance of dalits in the scheme of post-1947 politics was duly recognised by the ruling classes, then predominantly represented by the Congress party. It was vital for them to tie dalits to the parliamentary alternative. Hypothetically speaking, if the latent alienation and the proletarian consciousness of dalits were allowed to grow in an unhindered manner, revolutionary prospects for India would have been closer than in any other conceivable place in the world.

However, no ruling class would allow this to happen, much less the Indian one, which had impeccable credentials in its adeptness at keeping its victims within the institutional bondage for millenniums with mere soft strategies. Whatever the other motivations, there was certainly this element of strategy at work in making Ambedkar the chairman of the drafting committee for the Indian Constitution. It is said that it was done at the instance of none other than Mahatma Gandhi. For Gandhi — the super-strategist of the Congress, the Poona Pact with which he effectively blocked the political voice of dalits within the parliamentary framework, it was necessary to commit them to the latter for a long period. Could there be a better method to achieve this than getting Ambedkar- the undisputed leader of dalits, who had come to regard him as their Messiah, to author the Constitution!

It is a tribute to Gandhi's farsightedness and cunning that he prompted Nehru to make it happen. Gandhi and Nehru knew that the composition of the Constituent Assembly, surfeit with representation of the propertied classes by design, provided enough fortification not to let Ambedkar's ideology penetrate the Constitutional draft. But, at the same time, Ambedkar could be eulogised as its maker. The strategy killed several birds with one stone. It won the dalit commitment to the Constitution; it projected a progressive facet of the Indian ruling class to the world and planted false consciousness among dalits. Thus, although the content of the Constitution was decided by the ruling classes, the ruled ones were made to own it up. It was a feat of strategy certainly comparable in its import to that behind the caste institution. Behind its generosity and progressive veneer was hidden the trap which would effectively incapacitate the dalits for a long time to come. Once trapped they would stay in perpetual fragmentation in the turbulence of electoral game played by various sections of the ruling classes. Dalits constituting over 15 per cent of the total population are a significant factor in the number game of electoral politics. Their spread prevented them from winning any election on their own steam but at the same time none other could possibly win it without their support. Every ruling class political party would vie with each other to get them as a vote block on its side and still collectively prevent their coalescence into a class.

The mass struggle that materialised under the leadership of Gaikwad certainly shook the ruling classes. They had to devise special strategies to contain the threat of the emerging dalit challenge. It was a challenge indeed, although inadequately articulated, that had exactly touched the most sensitive nerve of the feudal structure, which still lay at the base of everything that mattered to dalits. The implementation of this strategy was soon seen in Gaikwad being befriended by Yashavantrao Chawhan, the then chief minister of Maharashtra and later the Deputy Prime Minister of the country. It culminated in the first alliance between the RPI and the Congress, which helped Gaikwad, and a few others reach the Parliament and Legislative Assemblies. The inauguration of the era of unprincipled alliances could be discerned right here. The Congress was undisputedly a representative party of the Indian ruling classes comprising the high caste capitalists and landlords. The alliance between this party and the party of the most exploited in the land, to say the least, could only be termed unholy.

In the face of it, it appears difficult to associate this phenomenon with Ambedkar who for the best part of his life had fought the Congress tooth and nail, criticised it ruthlessly and ultimately warned his followers to be away from it as it was the 'burning house'. It is interesting to note him standing out among his contemporaries, including the communists and socialists of all hues, in unambiguously characterising the Congress party as the representative of the capitalists and landlords and unmask its fake anti-imperialist facade.

However, as it always happened, in this case too his life-saga left enough strands to be picked up by the vested interests in support of the seemingly contrary act. Whatever the situational contexts and strategic compulsions, but it could be cited that the same Ambedkar had joined the Congress government at the centre under Nehru's Prime Ministership, had accepted the chairmanship of the drafting committee for the Indian Constitution on the basis of support from the Congress majority, and had accepted the Congress support for getting re-elected to the Constituent Assembly after the partition of the country. Whatever might have been his strategy in relenting his stand in accepting the Congress offers, it cannot be ignored that it eventually got subsumed in the universal strategy of the ruling classes to neutralise resistance struggles of the oppressed people.

Whenever the oppressed masses organised their resistance against the oppression, repression and co-option have been the age-old twin strategic tools in the repertoire of the ruling classes. Contrary to the general feeling that the latter is the recent phenomenon, associated with the spread of liberalism, these strategies have been iteratively used by the rulers from time immemorial, depending upon their perception of the intensity of peoples' struggles. One of the native examples of co-option could be had in the form of Buddha who symbolised a rebellion against the *Brahmin Dharma*, being projected as the ninth incarnation of the God Vishnu. More often than not, co-option being the low cost option is preferred by the ruling classes. What Congress had done in allying with RPI was precisely implementation of this strategy. On the side of RPI, the motivation to ally with any party flowed from, as it seems, the clarion call given by Ambedkar to dalits to become 'the ruling race'. It was supposed to mean the rule of the dalits, the have-nots — the rule of the working classes. It was however conveniently taken to mean being part of the ruling team, the ruling class, by the dalit leaders. Any pursuit of power, regardless of means, thus became a quasi-sacred obsession for the dalit leaders.

In absence of any explanation of the strategic contexts in which Ambedkar had accepted support from the Congress, it provided good enough grounds to sustain the de-shaped icon of Ambedkar in the minds of gullible masses. This icon froze the alternative of parliamentary structure as the only alternative for dalits and consequently impelled them to rely on electoral methods to gain power. The Poona Pact had already eliminated the possibility of shaping up their truly representative leadership through the electoral means and in corollary laid foundation for the proliferation of irresponsible leaders. It had permanently ordained the necessity for dalits to be in alliance with some or the other ruling class party for their political survival. This icon thus fortified the emasculation of dalits in the political sphere. It approved the in-camera parleys of the leaders for their tailist pursuit of power shorn of the mass line and established the bourgeois model of politicking. Dalit movement thus became permanently an adjunct of the ruling class.

Splits and Schism: Imperative of Electoral Commerce

Then came the era of disintegration. The RPI split and further split till people lost count of its factions. Three predominant reasons could be discerned for this disintegration: (i) The ruling class strategy of 'divide and rule', (ii) the lack of ideological coherence in the dalit movement, and (iii) the petty-bourgeoisie aspirations of its leadership. Apparently, these reasons reinforced each other and in that sense were not exclusive.

'Divide and Rule' is the well-known strategy of the ruling classes world over to basically weaken the ruled people. Indians generally attributed it to the colonial British policy but the fact is that more than any one else, it is ingrained in the blood of their own ruling class. It underlay their caste system in the form of a continuum of hierarchies that kept the people perpetually divided. This caste continuum has certainly played its obnoxious role even in avowedly 'caste annihilating' dalit movement in terms of providing potential fissures to crack along. As explained above, the post-independence reality, comprising mainly the 'Poona Pact' and enslavement of dalits within the framework of parliamentary democracy exposed dalits to ruling class enticements and resultantly led to their perpetual division. The strong dalit movement even if co-opted for the time being, posed the threat of re-emergence and challenge. It had to be simultaneously weakened to perpetuate their political subordination. The petty-bourgeoisie aspirations of dalit leaders made operationalisation of this strategy easy. Its feasibility was further enhanced by the ambivalence reflected in Ambedkar's sayings and doings from time to time, which provided scope for any one to interpret him the way one liked. It was his icon as the demigod of dalits that was used up by the competing commanders of his army to do whatever they liked.

This deification that he himself severally warned against and abhorred but which paradoxically had started well during his life time (celebration of his *Jayantis*) and grew after his death with an accelerated pace particularly because he himself became an essential icon in the neo-Buddhist rituals after his embracement of Buddhism less than two months ago. The mass *Dharmantar* — (change in religion), unprecedented in modern times and considered by many as the culmination of his life mission, released the flood of dalit religiosity that overwhelmed every other thing. It imparted him a quasi-spiritual aura as *Bodhisatva*. Many enthusiastically added a *sarana* in his name (*Bhimam saranam gachhami*) to the original *trisarana* of Buddhism. Thereafter the display of devotion towards Ambedkar became a surrogate for one's ideological allegiance to him.

Everyone vied with another to display his kind of devotion and in turn to emphasise superiority of his ideological ware for justifying his separate shop. The process of establishing the shop invariably relied upon the collection of clientele from one's own sub-caste and building up subordinate political nexus with some section of the ruling class. The ideological pretensions through the display of devotion to Ambedkar continued thereafter with the aim of expanding the clientele.

The ruling classes of course played their cards well in catalysing this divide in their pursuit of buying the dalit support. This electoral commerce paid off handsomely and created its own rationale and motivation for the permanent division of dalit leaders. Through this process, some of the leaders of the wretched, while serving their cause, amassed wealth worth crores of rupees, became industrialists, maintained fleets of cars, roamed around by air and taxis, without any evidence of the basic source of their prosperity.

It is a tribute to the political consciousness of dalits that while they starved and bled themselves over the issue of unity of these leaders, it never occurred to them to ask, even in a whisper, a question about the source of their material well being! Many blatantly indulged in the acts contrary to their profession for amassing wealth — some set up liquor factories and still remained the front rank leaders of the Buddhists, some allied with the rank castiest and communalist and still claimed to be ardent Ambedkarites. What counted was money and power. Paradoxically, the more affluent ones seemed to fit the bill better as they looked bigger 'sahebs', adding an additional aura to their leadership. Apart from the naked might of money in the electoral politics that tended to situate the moneyed men at the pedestal of power, the leadership model outlined above certainly contributed to their sustenance. With the money power they could invest into cultivation of their cronies and in turn command a better return in the wake of electoral parleys.

The splits were in a way a corollary of the leadership model and the over-reliance on the electoral politics sanctioned by the above-indicated icons. The leaders were always seen endowed with an uncommon wisdom that was really beyond the reach of masses. Leaders thus could do whatever they wanted without any scruples and they did it even breaking away from the party. As a result, the so-called giants who claimed the legacy of Ambedkar became contented with the identity of the parenthesised alphabets of their names after the RPI. They did not even worry about the fact that the formations represented by these parenthesised identities were basically a mere coagulation of their own sub-castes, in their respective geographical areas. It was a qualitative leap backwards for the ones who had proudly launched upon the annihilation of castes as their mission. Every one claimed to be a better follower of Ambedkar than the other is, and in the process, proliferated his icons by projecting one's proprietary models.

Dalit Panthers

The degeneration that set in continued unabated till the birth of Dalit Panthers in early-1970s. There could be varied explanations for the paradigm shift in dalit politics (movement) marked by Dalit Panthers. Remarkably, they spoke the language of defiance and militancy, which created waves. These waves had shaken the foundations of the established order in the country and in essence demonstrated what the wrath of the wretched could be! It provided a valuable insight that was pathetically missing in the dalit politics. Going by their manifesto, dalit panthers had broken many new grounds in terms of radicalising the political space for the dalit movement. They imparted the proletarian — radical class identity to dalits and linked their struggles to the struggles of all oppressed people over the globe. The clear cut leftist stand reflected by this document undoubtedly ran counter to the accepted legacy of Ambedkar as projected by the various icons, although it was sold in his name as an awkward tactic.

It reflected a historical dilemma characteristic of the Indian situation. The pathos of casteism integral with the dalit experience essentially brought in Ambedkar, as his was the only articulate framework that took cognisance of it. But, for the other contemporary problems of depravations Marxism provided a scientific framework to bring about a revolutionary change. Although, have-nots from both dalits and non-dalits craved for a fundamental change, the former adhered to what appeared to be Ambedkarian methods of socio-political change and the latter to what came to be the Marxian method which tended to see every social process as the reflection of the material reality. Both caused erroneous interpretations.

It is to the credit of Panthers that the assimilation of these two ideologies was attempted for the first time in the country but unfortunately it proved abortive in absence of the efforts to rid each of them of its obfuscating influence and stress their non-contradictory essence. Neither, there was theoretical effort to integrate these two ideologies, nor was there any practice combining social aspects of caste with say, the land question in the village setting. Essentially, it remained an emotional and a poetic negation of the *status quo*, craving for the broad revolutionary change and on ideological plane inevitably reflected an amalgam of Ambedkar and Marx. This ideological amalgam could not be acceptable to those under the spell of the prevailing Ambedkar-icons and therefore this revolutionary seedling in the dalit movement died a still death.

The possibility of the radical shift in the paradigm of dalit politics indicated by the manifesto was totally submerged by the reactionary upsurge of the new version of orthodox Ambedkarism. The reactionaries objected to the radical content of the programme alleging that the manifesto was doctored by the radicals — the Naxalites. There is no denying the fact that the Naxalite movement which had erupted quite like the Dalit Panther, as a disenchantment with and negation of the established politics, saw a potential ally in the Panthers and tried to forge a bond right at the level of formulation of policies and programme of the latter. But even if the Panthers had chosen to pattern their programme on the ten-point programme of the Black Panther Party (BPP) in the USA, which had been the basic inspiration for their formation, it would not have been any less radical.

The amount of emphasis on the material aspects of life that one finds in the party programme of the BPP could still have been inimical to the established icon of Ambedkar. Radicalism was the premise for the very existence of the Dalit Panther and hence the quarrel over its programme basically reflected the clash between the established icon of Ambedkar and his radical version proposed in the programme. The fact that for the first time the Dalit Panther exposed dalits to a radical Ambedkar and brought a section of dalit youth nearer to accepting it certainly marks its positive contribution to the dalit movement.

There were material reasons for the emergence of Dalit Panthers, as there are for any episode or event. Children of the Ambedkarian movement had started coming out of universities in large numbers in the later part of 1960s, just to face the blank future staring at them. The much-publicised Constitutional provisions for them turned out to be a mirage. Their political vehicle was getting deeper and deeper into the marsh of parliamentarism. It ceased to see the real problems of people.

The air of militant insurgency that had blown all over the world during those days also provided them the source material to articulate their anger. Unfortunately, quite like the BPP, they lacked the suitable ideology to channel this anger for achieving their goal. Interestingly, as they reflected the positive aspects of the BPP's contributions in terms of self-defence, mass organising techniques, propaganda techniques and radical orientation, they did so in the case of BPP's negative aspects too. Like Black Panthers they also reflected 'TV mentality' (to think of a revolutionary struggle like a quick-paced TV programme), dogmatism, neglect of economic foundation needed for the organisation, lumpen tendencies, rhetoric outstripping capabilities, lack of clarity about the form of struggle and eventually corruptibility of the leadership. The Panthers' militancy by and large remained confined to their speeches and writings. One of the reasons for its stagnation was certainly its incapability to escape the petit bourgeois ideological trap built up with the icons of Ambedkar. It would not get over the ideological ambivalence represented by them. Eventually, the petit-bourgeoise 'icon' of Ambedkar prevailed and extinguished the sparklet of new revolutionary challenge. It was completely sapped of its rebellious image and its vitality and soon got corrupted with a ridiculous prefix 'Bharatiya' to it. It survived as another living monument to the ideological bankruptcy and the degeneration of the dalit leadership. It went the RPI way and what remained of it were the numerous fractions engaged in internecine squabbles under the sly hands of the ruling classes.

The Dalit Panther phase represented the clash of two icons: one, that of a radical 'Ambedkar', as a committed rationalist, perpetually striving for the deliverance of the most oppressed people in the world. He granted all the freedom to his followers to search out the truth using the rationalist methodology as he did. He abhorred all kinds of humbug and hated to be bound by any dogma. He desired his followers to do the same. Like his mentor, the Buddha, he would exhort his followers not to take any thing for granted until their own experience corroborated it or their intellect supported it. The other is of the 'Ambedkar' who has forbidden the violent methods and advocated the constitutional ways for his followers, who was a staunch anti-Communist, ardent Buddhist, nay, Bodhisatva, who has given a permanent doctrine that was infallible. As it turned out, the radical icon of Ambedkar was projected without adequate conviction. It was implanted in an alien soil. There was no one committed to propagating such an image of Ambedkar, neither communists nor dalits. Eventually it remained as a veritable hodgepodge compared to the familiar set of icons coming from the other camp.

Kanshiram's Movement

The movement of Kanshiram markedly reflected a different strategy, which coined the 'Bahujan' identity encompassing all the SCs, STs, BCs, OBCs and religious minorities than 'dalit', which practically represented only the scheduled castes. Kanshiram started off with an avowedly apolitical organisation of government employees belonging to Bahujana, identifying them to be the main resource of these communities. It later catalysed the formation of an agitating political group creatively coined as DS4 — the Dalit Shoshit Samaj Sangharsh Samiti, which eventually became a full-fledged political party — the Bahujan Samaj Party (BSP).

Purely, in terms of electoral politics, which has some how become a major obsession with all the dalit parties, Kanshiram's strategy has proved quite effective, though in only certain parts of the country. He has given a qualitative impetus to the moribund dalit politics, locating itself into a wider space peopled by all the downtrodden of India. But he identified these people only in terms of their castes and communities. It may be said to his credit that he reflected the culmination of what common place icon of Ambedkar stood for. Kanshiram shrewdly grasped the political efficacy of this icon that sanctioned the pursuit of power in the name of downtrodden castes.

The religious minorities which potentially rears the sense of suffering marginalisation from the majority community could be easily added to it to make a formidable constituency in parliamentary parlance. Every one knew it but none did how to implement. Kanshiram has seemingly succeeded in this task at least in certain pockets. The careful analysis will show that the combination of certain historical developments and situational factors has been behind this success. As Kanshiram has amply experienced, it is not replicable elsewhere. It is bound to be short-lived and illusory unless this success is utilised to implement a revolutionary programme to forge a class identity among its constituents. If not, one will have to constantly exert to recreate the compulsions for their togetherness and allegiance.

In absence of any class-agenda, which is certainly the case of BSP, these compulsions could only be created through manipulative politics for which political power is an essential resource. BSP's unprincipled pursuit of power is basically driven by this exigency. It is futile to see in this game a process of empowerment of the subject people as could be seen (although not conclusively) from the statistical evidence of the cases of atrocities, and of overall situation of the poor people under its rule. There should be no lament over this as essentially it is where any kind of political acrobatics is destined to end in the prevailing system. The imperatives of this kind of strategy necessarily catapult the movement into the camp of the ruling classes as has exactly happened with BSP. BSP's electoral parleys with Congress, BJP, Akali Dal (Mann) that reached the stage of directly sharing State power in UP recently, essentially reflect this process of degeneration and expose its class characteristics today.

It seems to have sustaining support from the icon that BSP itself created, where Ambedkar was painted as the intelligent strategist who could turn any situation to his advantage, who used every opportunity to grab political power to achieve his objective. He is the person who saw in political power, a key to the woes of dalits and therefore exhorted them to grab it at any cost. He did not think highly of mass struggles except for tactical reasons to demonstrate the might of the leaders. For him, there existed only means not the values for securing one's goals. He did not see any permanent friend or foe in politics and joined even the Congress whom he had once declared as the enemy. He is seen as the person endowed with State authority (as a member of the Viceroy's Executive Council, Law Minister, and Chairman of the Drafting Committee for the Indian Constitution) — the sole source of his power to benefit his people. He was the sole arbiter of the interests of his people. Of course, he had disdain for all shades of communism.

Kanshiram's reading of Ambedkar ignores the fact that Ambedkar had to carve out space for his movement in the crevices left by the contradictions between various Indian political parties and groups on one side and the colonial power on the other. For most of his time, he sought maximisation of this space from the contending Muslim League and Congress, to name the predominant players, and eventually brought dalit issue to the national political agenda. Kanshiram stuffs his Ambedkar icon entirely with such kind of superfluity that it would look credible to the gullible dalit masses. This icon approves of his sole ideology that political power to his party (read him) could solve all dalit problems. His strategy till then has been to be in vantage position to decide who would be the King and thereby leverage his bargaining power. He did not care for democracy. To some extent this non-democratic stance spells his compulsions to have unitary command over his party structure as without it, his adversaries would gobble it up. He did not have any utility for any programme or manifesto, no concern for any issue howsoever burning, no qualms about policy or principles because, his sole obsession is to maximise his power by whatever means. In the rhetoric of empowering Bahujans, he does not even feel it necessary to demonstrate what exactly this empowering means and what benefits it would entail them. He never even spelt out what precisely ails his Bahujans except for highlighting their prejudiced social identities in worn-out casteist phraseology. That explains his entries into and exits from political alliances with any one with the same alacrity. The obsession with capturing power robbed him of certain fundamental values that Ambedkar never compromised.

The underlying value of the movement of Ambedkar was represented by liberty, equality and fraternity. Kanshiram does not seem to respect any value than the political and money power. In Ambedkar, one cannot miss an overflowing concern for the oppressed and wrath against the perpetrators of oppression. Kanshiram's concern scarcely transcended his speeches in his electoral rallies. It was with this concern and commitment that Ambedkar kept on referring to Marx and Marxism till his end, something as a touchstone to test his alternatives. Kanshiram simply abhorred it. Ambedkar struggled to formulate the dalit problem. Kanshiram either took it for granted or did not care for it at all. He never tried to articulate the nature of his Bahujanas' ailment except for the rhetorical reference to their subordination by the minority upper caste Hindus. For Ambedkar certain values, moral code, etc. were paramount, Kanshiram never seemed to be bothered by these issues. Ambedkar always foresaw plans and programmes; visualised appropriate structures for the downtrodden. Kanshiram expressed clear disdain for such things. For Ambedkar political power was a means, to Kanshiram it appears to be the end. Notwithstanding these broad differences, he has succeeded in luring the dalit masses in certain pockets of the country by projecting an Ambedkar icon that sanctioned his unscrupulous pursuits of power.

The crux of Kanshiram can be traced to his superfluous attempt to replicate Ambedkar's movement of 1920s as if the times had stood still for the bygone five decades. Ambedkar's mobilisation of dalit masses through struggles is vulgarised by him as the 'agit-prop' tool to collect people behind him. When Ambedkar realised the potency of political power, he launched his Indian Labour Party that reflected his urge to bring together the working class, transcending the caste lines. It is only when the political polarisation took communal turn that he abandoned his ILP project and launched the Scheduled Caste Federation. For Kanshiram, the talk sans caste and communities is perhaps an anathema. His casteist platform as such appears preordained by his ambition for power.

Ambedkar joined hands with a few political parties — one the communists (while joining the strike of mill workers) and the other is the Praja Samajwadi Party of Ashok Mehta in the 1952 elections. Although, he accepted the Congress support and offered to work in their government, he never tied up his political outfit to the Congress. It always appeared a politically expedient step for him as an individual without any organisational implication. Kanshiram's record so far clearly shows that he is ready to join hands with any one promising him the share of political power. Declaredly he would avoid the leftists of all hues and accept the friendship of the rank reactionaries of every kind. Ambedkar pointed at the capitalism and Brahminism as the twin enemy for his movement but Kanshiram enthusiastically embraced them without any pinch to his conscience. Ambedkar, in his own way, has been in search of suitable ideological carrier for the dalit movement. Kanshiram has no utility for such a thing.

Multiplicity of Brands, Little Differentiation

Apart from these broad political trends, there are many regional outfits like Dalit Mahasabha in Andhra Pradesh, Mass Movement in Maharashtra, Dalit Sena in Bihar and elsewhere, etc. some of which dabble directly into electoral politics and some of them do not. So far, none of them have a radically different icon of Ambedkar from the ones described above. They offer some proprietary ware claiming to be a shade better than that of others.

Hinduised Buddhism: Turning the Wheel Backwards

Another trend in the dalit movement emphasises the spread of Buddhism as its goal. As in politics, there are numerous organisations devoted to this task. According to them, Buddhism was the culmination of Ambedkar's mission and hence, the true

Ambedkarite not only had to be a Buddhist but also had to work for the spread of Buddhism. Ambedkar's declared vision of making India a Buddhist country spells a mission statement to them. Their activities revolve around building Buddhist viharas, becoming *Shramners and Bhikkus*; imbibing religious mode of living and engaging in quasi-studious pursuits like learning Pali, reading Buddhist scriptures, rewriting the episodes in history. At the renaissance some amount of excavation of skeletons is inevitable but it had become an obsession with the dalit intellectuals, who squandered considerable energies in dissecting the Hindu mythology to expose its cunning and rediscovering the Buddhist glories as their own legacy. One of the underlying motives in this enterprise was to project superiority of Buddhism and in turn their own as they believed that they were the original Buddhists. Paradoxically, all of them quibble over the distinction between 'Dharma' and 'Dhamma', claiming that Buddhism is Dhamma whereas others are the Dharmas. Unlike other religions, Buddhism does not have any place for rituals, gods or any permanent entity like soul, and is just a practicable moral code for living.

However, in practice, all kinds of mumbo jumbo that some times appears to be exceeding the familiar but on-the-wane rituals of Hinduism, are followed, so much so that not only Buddha but even Ambedkar is not spared from the godhood (*Bhim Bhagawan*). Of late, the relatively upwardly mobile (middle class) among dalits are increasingly getting attracted towards 'Vipasyana' — a kind of meditation that is said to have been practised by Buddha himself to get his enlightenment and so is 'prescribed' in Buddhism to be a good Buddhist. Many of them lately claim that it is the essence of Buddhism. It is amusing to see this mind-centric trend growing among dalits. In all this, Ambedkar's attempts at rationalisation and redefinition of Buddhism are completely forgotten. What rather is remembered is that he himself had given them the *'vidhi'* for marriage and for such other occasions; that he himself had devotedly said the three precepts and five oaths and stood through the long winding *Gathas* in the language of antiquity, that how he got into spiritual trance in front of the Buddha's statue when he visited Sarnath.

The icon they follow is that of a man incarnate of Buddha who analysed the problem of humanity and ultimately prescribed *nirvana* — a indescribable State marked by the extinction of all kind of craving. One who after Ashoka made greatest contributions to the revival and spread of Buddhism. It shows Ambedkar as a spiritual person who ultimately finds the roots of all the problems in the world within oneself and therefore preaches the virtue of moral rearmament and inner purity. The essence of being was to attain *nirvana,* the State of total contentment. It implied the futility of struggling against the material exploitation of dalits as their real salvation. It lay rather in extinguishing their own craving. It tended to internalise all their problems to themselves and stressed the need to cleanse their minds. Inevitably, it envisaged typical religious conduct from the followers with the highly pitched religious benchmarks available anywhere.

The sphere of religions abounds in such paradoxes. Its idiom basically promotes them. Buddhism could very well be conceived as the rebellion against the predominant creed of the establishment that prevailed more than 25 centuries ago, quite like Marxism in our times. Buddha was the first philosopher who forsook the futility of sterile philosophising and stressed the need to change the world. It is interesting to see in him as the first dialectician, some one in the same lineage as Hegel and Marx.

It is a historical to expect Buddha to give a solution to the problems of our times but it is important to appreciate the underscoring rational approach followed by him in his search. His conclusions are not important, as they are essentially constrained by the State of knowledge and overall development of the physical sciences during his times. What is important is to see the expanse of positive things that he could postulate at that time. Significantly, Buddha discarded the concept of God and soul and spoke against all kinds of rituals; he asked people to accept things only if it corresponded with their own experience or passed the test of their own intellect. He gave complete freedom to people to make amends to the *Dhamma* as per the needs of time. But, it could not escape the pressures of institutionalisation, which transformed it into a religion. They made him a God, wove stories that well competed with any mythology, built elaborate rituals to be followed and sapped it of its essential zeal of changing the world.

The paradox would be better illustrated by the responses of ardent Ambedkarites to the recent news about one Islamic Taliban commander threatening to dynamite two fourth-century monuments — 1,500-years-old statues of Buddha in central Afghanistan. The response came from highly educated non-resident Indian Ambedkarites. It was interesting in as much as they reveal what havoc the religious mindset that owes allegiance to Buddhism can play with even its human-centric tenets. They said that the dalits in India should immediately take out a massive procession to the consulate of Afghanistan and threaten them that no Afghan would be spared in India if they carried out destruction of the Buddha statues in Afghanistan.

It was a burst of anger at the first hearing of the news and was not to be meant but nonetheless it revealed the consciousness, the consciousness of Khomini or of any Hindu fundamentalist at work. It is one thing to speak against the fundamentalist vandalism and condemn it or even punish the responsible people in whatever way but it is quite another to don reverse fundamentalism to kill innocents to save dead stone statues in some distant land. It is important to realise the fact that even the Buddha's *Dhamma* whose roots are firmly in the soil of rationality and whose sole *raison d'etre* is the human suffering, could be mutilated to be its exact opposite by the very followers of Ambedkar who consciously cleansed it of the dust of irrationality and mysticism gathered over millennia.

SC/ST Associations: Facing a Dead End Ahead

One more significant trend in the dalit movement has its source in the policy of reservations in services of the State. Apart from the central and State governments, the large number of public sector undertakings that were floated by them, and other institutions established and promoted with public money, also came to be the State, attracting the constitutional provisions regarding reservations for the SCs and STs in services. The dalits in these sectors represented the collective investment and achievements of the dalit community, as reservations were the only hope for them to secure material well being. Although, they found themselves catapulted to modern sectors of economy, they found there were newer traps already in place, which clearly communicated the caste code for the modern organisations. The dalits had to conform their behaviour to this code for their survival. It reflected all the familiar prejudices against them. Their experience of the blatant violations of these provisions generally manifested in terms of backlogs in filling reservation posts, denial of promotions and general discriminatory treatment meted out in postings, transfers and other aspects of organisational life. The trade unions and management associations would not address their woes because they involved a contradiction between the interests of dalits and non-dalits. Thus, were born the SC/ST associations. Even after their countrywide proliferation, these associations do not have any locus standi with managements except for the ritualistic interviews during the annual visits of parliamentary committees on the welfare of SCs and STs.

It is a sad commentary on the functioning of the Constitution that over the last four decades it has driven these collectives to a State of hopelessness. The constitutional provisions regarding the reservations flow in the form of various circulars issued by the Government of India that are supposed to be implemented by its executive machinery. Over the years there has been a plethora of these circulars each written in such a convoluted language that even the highest court of law also felt it an arduous task to interpret them. One of the deliberate lacunae that exist in this scheme is that there is no effective onus on any one for the implementation of these provisions.

The executive can blatantly refuse to implement them under the plea of variant interpretation and drive the SC/ST employee or his association to the courts of law. Even if the poor employee or the SC/ST association could last the long winding court process over the years and succeed in getting the favourable verdict (a remote possibility though) the employer can still persist with his negative attitude. There are scores of cases of this kind where the petitioner employee or his association had to launch contempt proceeding against the employers and end up being bankrupt in the process. The helplessness of dalit employees in the services, in a way is the reflection of the sorry State of dalit politics. Since, there was no way these associations could effectively struggle, they landed up seeking petty favours from managements and in return being a black sheep during anti-management struggles.

The typical activities of these associations comprise celebration of the birth anniversaries of Ambedkar, representing dalit employees to the management or administration, and doing certain philanthropic and community service, depending upon the degree of their own organisation and resources. The icon that they seem to be following is that of a saviour, emancipator, to whom they need to pay their obeisance, to obey his commandments. Their community service for instance could be easily traced to Ambedkar's call to dalits to contribute 20 per cent of their earnings to the cause of the community. Although, rarely any dalit (save the poorest ones) goes so far as to sacrifice one fifth of his income over the cause of the community, none seem to refuse some symbolic contribution. Some better organised associations distribute notebooks, text books among slum children, run coaching and career counselling classes, organise relief works in the wake of calamities, open eateries in the dalit congregations like the ones at the Dikshyabhumi in Nagpur and Chaityabhumi in Mumbai. These are the gestures of repayment of the social debt.

They see in Ambedkar as the one who struggled to get them so many facilities and it is their bounden duty to take fullest advantage of the same. It was their sacred duty to occupy positions of power in bureaucracy. It is assumed, as Ambedkar appears to have assumed himself, that the educated dalits with bureaucratic authorities will serve the cause of their community in direct proportion to their relative position.

The myth is still sustained in spite of heaps of evidence to the contrary. Ambedkar's exhortation to 'agitate' is reduced down to making appeals to various authorities, having meetings with managements submitting memoranda and at the maximum, to filing the writ petitions in the courts — in short all that in the feasible range of the public service — rules. However, the constraints soon constitute the conscience. Ambedkar is reduced to a deity that imparts an identity. It is therefore that one curiously finds dalits celebrating the joint birth anniversaries of Babasaheb Ambedkar and Shivaji along with the Shiv Sena in the so-called den of Ambedkarism — the State of Maharashtra.

Kanshiram's Work

The rosy picture painted by the editor about dalits of UP is, I am afraid, not all that true. Whatever is achieved politically is not because of strengthening of chamar jati, but due to cooperation of all the various small castes. You only have to see the caste structure of seats of MPs contested by Kanshiram during last

Loksabha elections, or for that matter even in recent Vidhansabha elections. Kanshiram and Mayavati have not tried to strengthen only chamar caste, as is presumed by our editor. They have asked to strengthen all bahujans to come together and work for common good of all bahujans including dalits. They never worked for "separate but equal" castes. Neither Dr. Ambedkar, nor Shahu, nor Phuley worked on the lines mentioned by our editor. They always worked to bring all together, demolishing walls among the castes, never ever, they advocated salvation of any individual caste or that of an individual person within a caste. A letter by Dr. Ambedkar to a mang youth is proof thereof.

Kanshiram's 'Jati Todo Samaj Jodo'

Dr. Ambedkar confirmed in 'Annihilation of Castes', that the sanction behind the shastras must end. He had given special emphasis on the 'Manu' a smriti said to be written by a Brahmin pundit Sumati Bhargava at the time of counter-revolution started by Pushyamitra Shunga about 185 BC. This is the main book, Dr. Ambedkar attacked. It must be understood that though it is said to be religious scripture, Dr. Ambedkar considered it to be a political book, rather a law book, or you may call it the Constitution of Ancient and Medieval slave India. Only in Ambedkar's India a new Constitution is provided to this country, and that too not entirely to the satisfaction of its maker.

So the fundamental way is to make the bahujan samaj understand that they are not Hindus and hence they must stop considering themselves as Hindus. They shall not follow the tenets of Manu smriti. This is happening gradually, You find that the Adivasis, though they are being coerced by the manuvadis into believing that they must follow Hindu gods and Hindu religious worship, etc. are talking freely of Ambedkarism and are turning gradually away from BSO. This process is the process of 'Samaj jodo'. This can be attributed to the work of Kanshiram in post Ambedkar era. Again I have to make it clear that at this stage, without jeopardising stand for religious and social unity, we can only strive for political unity; the religious and social unity will have to wait. I feel, our editor, also means to achieve only political unity at this time, when he says, "What we need is not the 'unity' that destroys any identity, but an understanding and harmony which would help maintain and foster such identities to fight the oppressor."

Dalit Unity, not Enough

Without in any way denigrating the efforts of those who are striving for Dalit Unity, we feel, even if all the Dalits of India, of all castes, shades and colours, unite, they cannot achieve any power without the help of other oppressed castes, as they are only about 16 per cent or so. And if there is no power, caravan of Ambedkar will be on retrograde journey. Many non-dalit castes are realising the mischief done by Caste system, they are having dialogue with Dalits and uniting with them, as is seen in North Indian states. To think that those who talk of 'Unity' belong to a 'dominant caste' and so have an unfair vested interest in 'unity', will rather be an injustice to their efforts. The dominance they achieved is not the cause of their 'Unity talks', but it is the result of it. Before Phuley, Shahu and Ambedkar thought of Unity, the condition of all dalit castes was more or less same, none was dominant and all were subservient to BSO.

Should we not Destroy our Identity?

Are various leaders ready to give up their identity on argument that Dalit liberation must get priority over all other demands? One does not have to give up ones identity, if we are talking at this stage of only political unity. But if we unite only politically at this stage, a time will come, when we have to unite religiously and socially also. At that time, I would like to ask these leaders, "Can they afford not to dissolve their identities?" If they did, their castes would be wiped out by the BSO. One has only to see the way these sub-castes are fighting among themselves just for crumbs, they have forgotten that their real enemy, BSO, is safe and secure in its own citadel.

Even at this stage, infighting among the sub-castes is counter productive and injurious to the interest of their own caste. It is the leaders of BSO, who make them fight by showing a carrot to the stooges. It is a post Poona pact situation of proliferating chamachas, big and small. The members of Ambedkarite public have by now acquired enough knowledge and experience to identify these stooges and keep away from them. If some one likes to remind the people of this situation, let him not be labelled as selfish and his warnings condemned as being of "educated-meaning brain washed", person of a 'dominant' caste.

7

Golden Words of Ambedkar

His Comments on Different Concerns

Ethics and Economics

History shows that where ethics and economics come in conflict, victory is always with economics. Vested interests have never been known to have willingly divested themselves unless there was sufficient force to compel them.

Equality

Equality may be a fiction but nonetheless one must accept it as e governing principle.

Fate

Do not believe in fate. Believe in your strength.

Force

Force, it cannot be denied, is the medicine of the body politic and must be administered when the body politic becomes sick. But just because force is the medicine of the body politic, it cannot be allowed to become its daily bread.

Fraternity

Fraternity is the name for the disposition of an individual to treat men as the object of reverence and love and the desire to be in unity with his fellow beings.

Freedom

Freedom of the nation, if it is to be a reality, must vouchsafe the freedom of the different classes comprised in it, particularly of those who are treated as the servile classes.

Society

Making of the individual a sharer or partner in the associated activity so that he feels its success as his success and its failure as his failure is the real thing that binds men and makes a society of them. The society must have either the sanction of law or the sanction of morality to hold it together. Without either, society is sure to go to pieces.

More than political or religious, man is a social animal. He may not have, need not have religion; he may not have needed not have politics. He must have society; he cannot do without society.

Slave

Tell the slave he is a slave and he will revolt.

To a slave, his master may be better or worse. But there cannot be a good master. A good man cannot be a master and a master cannot be a good man.

Slavery

Slavery does not merely mean a legalised form of subjection. It means a state of society in which some men are forced to accept from others the purposes, which control their conduct.

Strike

Strike is a civil wrong and not a crime, and making a man serve against his will is nothing less than making him a slave.

Survival

It is not survival but the quality, the plane of survival that is important.

There is no honour in mere survival. What matters is the plane of survival. One can survive by unconditional surrender. One can survive by beating a cowardly retreat and one can survive by fighting.

State Socialism

State socialism should be prescribed by the law of the Constitution so that it will be beyond the reach of a Parliamentary majority to suspend, and amend or abrogate it. It is only this that one can achieve the triple object. Namely, to establish Socialism, retain Parliamentary Democracy and avoid Dictatorship.

Unconstitutional Methods

When there was no way left for constitutional methods for achieving economic and social objectives, there was some justification for unconstitutional methods for achieving economic and social objectives. But where constitutional methods are open there can be no justification for these unconstitutional methods. These methods are nothing but the Grammar of Anarchy.

Unity

If unity is to be an abiding factor, it must be founded on a sense of kinship, in the feeling of being kindred. In short, it must be spiritual.

Law

Law is the abode of all worldly happiness.

Law and Fraternity

Law is secular which anybody may break while fraternity or religion is sacred which everybody must respect.

Leisure

Leisure means the lessening of the toil and effort necessary for satisfying the physical wants of life.

Liberty

Liberty falls under two classes. There is civil liberty and there is political liberty. Civil liberty refers to: (i) liberty of movement, which is another name for freedom from arrest without due process of law; (ii) liberty of speech (which of course includes liberty of thought, liberty of reading writing and discussion); and (iii) liberty of action.

The first kind of liberty is of course fundamental. Not only fundamental, it is also most essential. About its value, there can be no manner of doubt. The second kind of liberty, which may be called freedom of opinion, is important for many reasons.

It is a necessary condition of all progress: intellectual, moral, political and social. Where it does not exist the *status quo* becomes stereotyped and all originality even the most necessary is discouraged. Liberty of action means doing what one likes to do. It is not enough that liberty of action should be formal.

It must be real. So understood, liberty of action means effective power to do specific things. There is no freedom where they're also no means of taking advantage of it. Real liberty of action exists only where exploitation has been annihilated, where no suppression of one class by another exists, where there is no unemployment, no poverty and where a person is free from the fear of losing his job, his home, and his food as a consequence of his action.

Political liberty consists in the right of the individual to share in the framing of laws and in the making and unmaking of governments.

Liberty, Equality, Fraternity

Liberty cannot be divorced from equality, equality cannot be divorced from liberty. Nor can liberty and equality be divorced from fraternity. Without equality, liberty would produce the supremacy of the few over the many. Equality without liberty would kill individual initiative. Without fraternity, liberty and equality could not become a natural course of things.

Linguistic State

A linguistic State with its regional language as its official language may easily develop into an independent nationality. The road between an independent nationality and an independent State is very narrow. If this happens, India will cease to be modern India we have and will become the medieval India consisting of a variety of States indulging in rivalry and warfare.

Lost Rights

Lost rights are never regained by begging and by appeals to the conscience of the usurpers, but by relentless struggle.

Love and Hatred

No one can hope to make any effective mark upon his time and bring the aid that is worth bringing to great principles and struggling causes if he is not strong in his love and his hatred.

Machinery

Machinery and modern civilization are indispensable for emancipating man from leading the life of a brute, and for providing him with leisure and making a life of culture possible.

The slogan of a democratic society must be machinery and more machinery, civilization and more civilization.

Man's Power

A man's power is dependent upon: (1) physical heredity, (2) social inheritance or endowment in the form of parental care, education, accumulation of scientific knowledge, everything that enables him to be more efficient than the savage and finally, (3) on his own efforts.

Mind

Man is what mind makes of him.

For inspiration and enthusiasm one must have a healthy and sound mind. Man derives inspiration if his mind is free to develop.

The world cannot be reformed except by the reformation of the mind of the man, and the mind of the world.

Misery

Man's misery is the result of man's inequity to man. Only righteousness can remove this inequity and the resultant misery.

Glory

Glory to those who devote their time, talents and their all to the annihilation of slavery.

Glory to those who would keep on their struggle for the liberation of the enslaved in spite of heavy odds, carping humiliations, storms and dangers till the down-trodden secure their human rights.

Great Men

A great man must be motivated by the dynamics of a social purpose and must act as the scourge and the scavenger of the society.

Happiness

Poverty gives rise to sorrow. But removal of poverty does not necessarily give rise to happiness. Not high standard of living but a standard of culture is what gives happiness.

Hero-worship

Bhakti (hero-worship) in religion may be a road to salvation of the self. But in politics, bhakti or hero-worship is a sure road to degradation and to eventual dictatorship.

Hero-worship in the sense of expressing our unbounded admiration is one thing. To obey the hero is a totally different kind of hero-worship. There is nothing wrong in the former while the latter is no doubt a most pernicious thing. The former is only man's respect for everything which is noble and of which the Great Man is only an embodiment. The former is consistent with respect, but the latter is a sign of debasement.

Hinduism and Buddhism

There is a great difference between Buddhism and Hinduism. Buddhism means casteless society based on equal rights. Hinduism on the other hand is primarily based on caste system; a system which encourages aloofness, inequality and exploitation.

Unlike Hinduism, Buddhism lays no emphasis on the attainment of heaven. Nor it is necessary. To be happy in the present life, one should practice the ethics of morality, non-violence (ahimsa), equality and universal brotherhood. This is an eternal truth taught by the Buddha.

Hinduism

Inequality is the soul of Hinduism.

To the Untouchables, Hinduism is a veritable chamber of horrors. The iron law of caste, the heartless law of karma and the senseless law of status by birth are veritable instruments of torture, which Hinduism has forged against the Untouchables.

History

They cannot make history who forget history.

It is quite wrong to hold that man is not a factor in the making of history. Man is necessary to rub two pieces of flint to make fire.

Man is a factor in the making of history and the environmental forces, whether impersonal or social, if they are, they are the first and not the last things.

History of India: The history of India is said to begin with the Aryans who invaded India, made it their home and established their culture. Whatever may be the virtues of the Aryans, their culture, their religion and their social system, we know very littler about their political history. Indeed notwithstanding the superiority that is claimed for the Aryans as against the non-Aryans, the Aryans have left very little their political achievements for history to speak of. The political history of India begins with the rise of a non-Aryan people called Nagas, who were a powerful people, whom the Aryans were unable to conquer, with whom the Aryans had to make peace, and whom the Aryans were compelled to recognise as their equals. Whatever fame and glory India achieved in ancient times in the political field, the credit for it goes entirely to the Non-Aryan Nagas. It is they who made India great and glorious in the annals of the world.

There is only one period in Indian history, which is a period of freedom, greatness and glory. This is the period of Maurya Empire. At all other times, the country suffered from defeat and darkness.

It must be recognised that there has never been such as a common Indian culture, that historically there have been three Indias, Brahminic India, Buddhist India and Hindu India, each with its own culture. Secondly, it must be recognised that the history of India before the Muslim invasions is the history of a mortal conflict between Brahmanism and Buddhism. Any one who does not recognise these two facts will never to able to write a true history of India, a history which will disclose the meaning and purposes running through it.

Ideas

Men are mortal. So are ideas. An idea needs propagation as much as a plant needs watering. Both will otherwise wither and die.

Ideal Society

My (Dr. B. R. Ambedkar) ideal would be a society based on Liberty, Equality and Fraternity. An ideal society should be mobile, should be full of channels for conveying a change taking place in one part to other parts. In an ideal society there should be many interests consciously communicated and shared. There should be varied and free points of contact with other modes of association. In other words, there must be social endosmosis.

Indians First and Last

I do not want that our loyalty as Indians should be in the slightest way affected by any competitive loyalty whether that loyalty arises out of our religion, out of our culture or out of our language. I want all people to be Indians first, Indian last and nothing else but Indians.

Indifferentism

Indifferentism is the worst kind of disease that can infect a people.

Instructions

What instructs me, amuses me.

Intellectuals

There is a world of difference between one who is learned and who is an intellectual. The former is class-conscious and is alive to the interests of his class. The latter is emancipated being who is free to act without being swayed by class considerations.

Language

One language can unite people. Two languages are sure to divide people. This is an inexorable law.

Culture is conserved by language.

Rights

Rights are protected not by law but by the social and moral conscience of society. If social conscience is such that it is prepared to recognise the laws which law chooses to enact, rights will be safe and secure. But if fundamental rights are opposed by the community, no law, no Parliament, no judiciary can guarantee them in real sense of the word.

Secularism

The conception of a secular state is derived from the liberal democratic tradition of the west. No institution, which is maintained wholly out of state funds, shall be used for the purpose of religious instruction irrespective of the question whether the religious instruction is given by the state or by any other body.

It (secular state) does not mean that we shall not take into consideration the religious sentiments of the people. All that a secular state means is that this Parliament shall not be competent to impose any particular religion upon the rest of the people. That is the only limitation that the Constitution recognises.

Self-help

You must stand on your own feet and fight as best you can for your rights. Power and, prestige will come to you through struggle. It is not enough that a people are numerically in majority. They must be always watchful, strong, well-educated and self-replicating to attain and maintain success.

Whatever might be one's ideal, either of national progress or of self-development, one should patiently exert oneself to reach it. One should concentrate one's mind and might on one's goal.

Self-respect

Self-respect is the most vital factor in life. Without it, man is a mere cipher.

Nothing is more disgraceful for a brave man than to live a life devoid of self-respect and without love for the country.

Learn to live in this world with self-respect.

No race can be raised by destroying its self-respect.

Social Conscience

Social conscience is the only safeguard of all rights, fundamental or non-fundamental.

Social Democracy

Social democracy means a way of life, which recognises liberty, equality and fraternity as the principle of life.

A democratic form of Government presupposes a democratic form of society. The formal framework of democracy is of no value and would indeed be misfit if there were no social democracy. The politicians never realised that democracy was not a form of government; it was essentially a form of society. It may not be necessary for a democratic society to be marked by unity, by community of purpose, by loyalty to public ends and by mutuality of sympathy. But it does unmistakably involve two things. The first is an attitude of mind, an attitude of respect and equality towards their fellows. The second is a social organisation free from rigid social barriers.

Social Evils

Wherever there are social evils, the health of the body politic requires that they shall be removed before they become the symbols of suffering and injustice. For it is the social and economic of revolution or decay.

Social Tyranny

Political tyranny is nothing compared to social tyranny and a reformer, who defies society, is a much more courageous man than a politician, who defies Government.

National Feeling

The national feeling is a feeling of a corporate sentiment of oneness which makes those who are charged with it feel that they are kith and kin.

National Language

Since Indians wish to unite and develop a common culture it is the duty of the all Indians to own up Hindi as their language.

Philosophy of Life

Every one should have a philosophy of life, for every one must have a standard by which to measure his conduct. And philosophy is nothing but a standard by which to measure. My social philosophy may be said to be enshrined in three words: Liberty, equality and fraternity. Let no one, however, say that I have borrowed my philosophy from the French Revolution. I have not. My philosophy has roots in religion and not in political science. I have derived them from the teachings of my master, the Buddha.

Philosophy and Religion

The difference between philosophy and religion may be put in two ways. Philosophy is concerned with knowing truth. Religion is concerned with the love of truth. Philosophy is static. Religion is dynamic.

Political Power

Political power is the key to all social progress.

Political power is the most precious thing in the life of a community especially if its position is constantly being challenged and the community is required to maintain it by meeting challenge. Political power is the only means by which it can sustain its position.

Political Revolutions

Puritanism founded the new world. It was Puritanism, which won the war of American Independence, and Puritanism was a religious movement. The same is true of the Muslim Empire. Before the Arabs became a political power, they had undergone a thorough religious revolution started by Prophet Muhammad. Even Indian History supports the same conclusion. The political revolution led by Chandragupta was preceded by the religious and social revolution of Buddha. The political revolution led by Shivaji was preceded by the religious and social reform brought about by the saints of Maharashtra. The political revolution of the Sikhs was preceded by the religious and social revolution led by Guru Nanak.

Politics

Politics is nothing if not realistic. There is very little in it that is academic.

Poverty

Renunciation of riches by those who have it may be a blessed state. But poverty can never be. To declare poverty to be a blessed state is to pervert religion, to perpetuate vice and crime, to consent to make earth a living hell.

The poor are made to suffer wants, privations and humiliations not because it was pre-ordained by the sins committed in their previous births, but because of the overpowering tyranny and treachery of those who are above them.

The sooner the poor remove the foolish belief that their miseries were pre-ordained, the better.

The thought that poverty is an inevitability and is inborn and inseparable is entirely erroneous.

Power and Wisdom

Power is one thing, and wisdom and prudence quite a different thing.

Progress

The good things of this earth do not fall from heaven. Every progress has its bill of costs and only those who pay for it will have that progress.

Rebels

The world owes much to rebels who would dare to argue in the face of pontiff and insist that he is not infallible.

Nationality

Nationality means "Consciousness of kind, awareness of the existence of that tie of kinship".

Nationalism

Nationalism means "The desire for separate national existence for those who are bound by their tie of kinship".

Noble Life

Man is mortal. Every one is to die some day or other. But one must resolve to lay down one's life in enriching the noble ideals of self-respect and in bettering human life.

Man must eat to live and he should live and work for the well being of the society.

Dragging on life somehow or to live like a crow for a thousand years is not the only way and worthy way in this world. Life can be ennobled by sacrificing it for a lasting good such as the cause of truth, a vow, honour or country.

Better to die in the prime of youth for a great cause than to live like an oak and do nothing.

Norms

Ideals or norms are good and necessary. Neither a society nor an individual can do without a norm. But a norm must change with change in time and circumstances. No norm can be permanently fixed. There must always be room for revaluation of the values of our norm.

Parents

There will be no difference between parents and animals if they will not desire to see their children in a better position than their own.

Religion

Religion is not an opium as it is held by some. What good things I have in me or whatever have been the benefits of my education to society, I owe them to the religious feelings in me. I want religion but I do not want hypocrisy in the name of religion.

Man cannot live by bread alone. He has a mind which needs food for thought. Religion instils hope in man and drives him to activity.

Religion is for man and not man for religion.

Religion and slavery are incompatible.

Religion in the sense of morality must remain the governing principle in every society.

Religion if it is to function must be in accord with reason which is merely another name for science.

Religion must recognise the fundamental tenets of liberty, equality and fraternity. Unless a religion recognises these three fundamental principles of social life, religion will be doomed.

Religion must not sanctify or ennoble poverty.

Religion and Morality

As a matter of truth, morality has no place in religion.

The content of religion consists of God, soul, prayers, worship, rituals, ceremonies and sacrifices.

Morality comes in only wherein man comes in relation to man. Morality comes in into religion as a side wind to maintain peace and order.

Be good to your neighbour because you are both children of god. That is the argument of religion.

Every religion preaches morality but morality is not the root of religion. It is a wagon attached to it. It is attached and detached, as the occasion requires. The action of morality in the functioning of religion is therefore, casual and occasional.

Virtue in Danger

Where virtue is in danger, do not avoid fighting, do not be mealy mouthed.

Achievements

Nothing valuable in this world is achieved except by great efforts.

All great things in the world were achieved by patient industry and by undergoing toil and tribulations.

Ahimsa

Ahimsa Permo Dharma is an extreme Doctrine. It is a Jaina Doctrine. It is not Buddhist Doctrine. Buddha meant to make a distinction between 'will to kill' and 'need to kill'. What he banned was killing where there was nothing but the will to kill. Buddha made a distinction between principle and Rule. He did not make Ahimsa a matter of Rule. He enunciated it as a matter of Principle or way of life. A Principle leaves you freedom to act. A rule does not. Rule either breaks you or you break the rule.

Ambition

One should always cherish some ambition to do something in the world. They alone rise who strive.

Anarchy

In anarchy and dictatorship, liberty is lost.

Appeasement

Appeasement means buying off the aggressor by conniving at his acts of murder, arson and loot against innocent victims of his displeasure.

Appeasement sets no limits to the demands and aspirations of the aggressor.

Army

The ultimate guarantee of the independence of a country is a safe army - an army on which you can rely to fight for the country at all times and in any eventuality.

A safe army is better than a safe border.

Back to Nature

The call of back to nature means back to nakedness, back to squalor, back to poverty and back to ignorance for the vast mass of people.

Buddhism

I prefer Buddhism because it gives three principles in combination, which no other religion does. Buddhism teaches Prajna (understanding as against superstition and supernaturalism), *Karuna* (love), and *Samata* (equality). This is what man wants for a good and happy life.

Buddhist Culture

Even though Buddhism is almost extinct in India, yet it has given birth to a culture, which is far better and richer than the Brahminic culture. When the question of the National Flag and the National Emblem was being considered by the Constituent Assembly we could not find any suitable symbol from the Brahminic culture.

Ultimately, the Buddhist culture came to our rescue and we accepted the Wheel of Law (Dhamma Chakra) as the National Symbol.

Caste and Class

Caste System is not merely a division of labour. It is also a division of labourers. It is an hierarchy in which the divisions of labourers are graded one above the other.

Caste has killed public spirit. Caste has destroyed the sense of public charity. Caste has made public opinion impossible. Virtue has become caste-ridden and morality has become caste-bound. There is no sympathy to the deserving. There is no appreciation of the meritorious.

There cannot be a more degrading system of social organisation than the Chaturvarna. It is the system which deadens, paralyses and cripples the people from helpful activity.

Caste in the hands of the orthodox has been a powerful weapon for persecuting the reforms and for killing all reform.

These castes are anti-national. In the first place because they bring about separation in social life. They are anti-national also because they generate jealousy and antipathy between caste and caste. The Caste system is a system which is infested with the spirit of isolation and in fact it makes isolation of one Caste from another a virtue. There is isolation in the class system.

But it does not make isolation virtue nor does it prohibit social intercourse. The class system, it is true produces groups, but they are not akin to Caste groups. The groups in the class system are only non-social while the Castes in the Castes system are in their mutual relations definitively and positively anti-social.

Practically speaking, in a class structure, there is on the one hand, tyranny, vanity, pride, arrogance, greed selfishness and on the other insecurity, poverty, degradation, loss of liberty, self-reliance, independence dignity and self-respect.

The group set-up prevents an individual from acquiring consistency of mind, which is possible only when society has common ideals, common models.

The group set-up leads to stratification of classes. Those who are masters remain masters and those who are born in slavery remain slaves. Owners remain owners and workers remain workers. The privileged remain privileged and the serfs remain serfs.

Constitution

I feel that the Constitution is workable; it is flexible and it is strong enough to hold the country together both in peacetime and in wartime. Indeed, if I may say so, if things go wrong under the new Constitution the reason will not be that we had a bad Constitution. What we will have to say is that Man was vile.

Courage

The secret of freedom is courage and courage is born in combination of individuals into a party.

Culture

It is true that man shares the Constitution and functions of animals, nutritive, reproductive, etc. But these are not distinctively human functions. The distinctively human function is reason, the purpose of which is to enable man to observe, meditate, cogitate, study and discover the beauties of the universe and enrich his life and control the animal elements in his life.

What divides the brute from man is culture. Culture is not possible for the brute but it is essential for man.

The aim of human society must be to enable every person to lead a life of culture which means the cultivation of the mind as distinguished from the satisfaction of mere physical wants.

While the ultimate goal of a brute's life is reached once his physical appetites are satisfied, the ultimate goal of a man's existence is not reached unless and until he has fully cultivated his mind.

Democracy

Political Democracy rests on four premises, which may be set out in the following terms: (i) The individual is an end in himself, (ii) That the individual has certain inalienable rights, which must be guaranteed to him by the Constitution, (iii) That the individual shall not be required to relinquish any of his constitutional rights as a precondition precedent to the receipt of a privilege, (iv) That the State shall not delegate powers to private persons to govern others.

The soul of democracy is the doctrine of one man, one value.

Democracy is a form and method of government whereby revolutionary changes in the economic and social life of the people are brought about without bloodshed. Democracy is not merely a form of Government. It is primarily a mode of associated living of conjoined communicated experience. It is essentially an attitude of respect and reverence towards fellowmen.

Democracy is incompatible and inconsistent with isolation and exclusiveness, resulting in the distinction between the privileged and the unprivileged. Democracy cannot work without friction unless there is fellow-feeling among those who constitute the State.

The first thing required for the successful working of democracy is that there must be no glaring inequalities and there must be neither an oppressed class nor a suppressed class. The second thing required is the existence of opposition to show whether the Govt. is going wrong. The third thing is equality before law and in administration. The fourth is the observance of constitutional morality. The fifth point is the functioning of moral order in society, for moral is taken for granted in the democracy. The sixth thing is the requirement of public conscience.

A democratic Government can remain democratic only if it is worked by two parties ?a party in power and a party in opposition.

Despotism

To have popular government run by a single party is to let democracy become a mere form for despotism to play its part from behind it.

Despotism does not cease to be despotism because it is elective. Nor does despotism become agreeable because despots belong to our own kindred.

Dhamma

According to the Buddha, Dhamma consists of Prajna and Karuna. Prajna is understanding. The Buddha made Prajna one of the two corner-stones of His Dhamma because he did not wish to leave any room for superstition. Karuna is love. Because, without it society can neither live nor grow, that is why the Buddha made it the second corner-stone of his Dhamma. A unique amalgam of Prajna and Karuna is the Dhamma of the Buddha.

In Dhamma there is no place for prayers, pilgrimages, rituals, ceremonies or sacrifices.

Dhamma is righteousness, which means right relations between man and man in all spheres of life.

Duty

Blessed are those who are awakened to their duty to those among whom they are born.

The duty must be performed; let the efforts be successful or not; let the work be appreciated or not. When a man's sincerity of purpose and capacity are proved even his enemies come to respect him.

Education

Give up the idea that parents give 'Janma' to the child and not destiny (karma). They can mould the destiny of their children by giving them education.

Knowledge is the foundation of a man's life.

Education is as necessary for females as it is for males.

If ones education is detrimental to the welfare of the poor, the educated man is a curse to the society.

Character is more important than education.

8

Ambedkar's Speeches

Accomplishments of the Constituent Assembly of India

[Speech of Bharat Ratna Dr. Bhim Rao Ambedkar Detailing the Accomplishments of the Constiuent Assembly of India]

Sir, looking back on the work of the Constituent Assembly it will now be two years, eleven months and seventeen days since it first met on the 9th of December 1946. During this period the Constituent Assembly has altogether held eleven sessions. Out of these eleven sessions the first six were spent in passing the Objectives Resolution and the consideration of the Reports of Committees on Fundamental Rights, on Union Constitution, on Union Powers, on Provincial Constitution, on Minorities and on the Scheduled Areas and Scheduled Tribes. The seventh, eighth, ninth, tenth and the eleventh sessions were devoted to the consideration of the Draft Constitution. These eleven sessions of the Constituent Assembly have consumed 165 days. Out of these, the Assembly spent 114 days for the consideration of the Draft Constitution.

Coming to the Drafting Committee, it was elected by the Constituent Assembly on 29th August 1947. It held its first meeting on 30th August. Since August 30th it sat for 141 days during which it was engaged in the preparation of the Draft Constitution.

The Draft Constitution as prepared by the Constitutional Adviser as a text for the Draft Committee to work upon, consisted of 243 articles and 13 Schedules. The first Draft Constitution as presented by the Drafting Committee to the Constituent Assembly contained 315 articles and 8 Schedules. At the end of the consideration stage, the number of articles in the Draft Constitution increased to 386. In its final form, the Draft Constitution contains 395 articles and 8 Schedules. The total number of amendments to the Draft Constitution tabled was approximately 7,635. Of them, the total number of amendments actually moved in the House were 2,473.

I mention these facts because at one stage it was being said that the Assembly had taken too long a time to finish its work, that it was going on leisurely and wasting public money. It was said to be a case of Nero fiddling while Rome was burning. Is there any justification for this complaint? Let us note the time consumed by Constituent Assemblies in other countries appointed for framing their Constitutions. To take a few illustrations, the American Convention met on May 25th, 1787 and completed its work on September 17, 1787, i.e. within four months. The Constitutional Convention of Canada met on the 10th October 1864 and the Constitution was passed into law in March 1867 involving a period of two years and five months.

The Australian Constitutional Convention assembled in March 1891 and the Constitution became law on the 9th July 1900, consuming a period of nine years. The South African Convention met in October, 1908 and the Constitution became law on the 20th September 1909 involving one year's labour. It is true that we have taken more time than what the American or South African Conventions did. But we have not taken more time than the Canadian Convention and much less than the Australian Convention. In making comparisons on the basis of time consumed, two things must be remembered.

One is that the Constitutions of America, Canada, South Africa and Australia are much smaller than ours. Our Constitution as I said contains 395 articles while the American has just seven articles, the first four of which are divided into sections which total up to 21, the Canadian has 147, Australian 128 and South African 153 sections. The second thing to be remembered is that the makers of the Constitutions of America, Canada, Australia and South Africa did not have to face the problem of amendments. They were passed as moved. On the other hand, this Constituent Assembly had to deal with as many as 2,473 amendments. Having regard to these facts the charge of dilatoriness seems to me quite unfounded and this Assembly may well congratulate itself for having accomplished so formidable a task in so short a time.

Turning to the quality of the work done by the Drafting Committee, Mr. Naziruddin Ahmed felt it his duty to condemn it outright. In his opinion, the work done by the Drafting Committee is not only not worthy of commendation, but is positively below par. Everybody has a right to have his opinion about the work done by the Drafting Committee and Mr. Naziruddin is welcome to have his own. Mr. Naziruddin Ahmed thinks he is a man of greater talents than any member of the Drafting Committee. The Drafting Committee would have welcomed him in their midst if the Assembly had thought him worthy of being appointed to it. If he had no place in the making of the Constitution it is certainly not the fault of the Drafting Committee.

Mr. Naziruddin Ahmed has coined a new name for the Drafting Committee evidently to show his contempt for it. He calls it a Drafting committee. Mr. Naziruddin must no doubt be pleased with his hit. But he evidently does not know that there is a difference between drift without mastery and drift with mastery. If the Drafting Committee was drifting, it was never without mastery over the situation.

It was not merely angling with the off chance of catching a fish. It was searching in known waters to find the fish it was after. To be in search of something better is not the same as drifting. Although Mr. Naziruddin Ahmed did not mean it as a compliment to the Drafting committee. I take it as a compliment to the Drafting Committee. The Drafting Committee would have been guilty of gross dereliction of duty and of a false sense of dignity if it had not shown the honesty and the courage to withdraw the amendments which it thought faulty and substitute what it thought was better. If it is a mistake, I am glad the Drafting Committee did not fight shy of admitting such mistakes and coming forward to correct them.

I am glad to find that with the exception of a solitary member, there is a general consensus of appreciation from the members of the Constituent Assembly of the work done by the Drafting Committee. I am sure the Drafting Committee feels happy to find this spontaneous recognition of its labours expressed in such generous terms. As to the compliments that have been showered upon me both by the members of the Assembly as well as by my colleagues of the Drafting Committee I feel so overwhelmed that I cannot find adequate words to express fully my gratitude to them. I came into the Constituent Assembly with no greater aspiration than to safeguard the interests of he Scheduled Castes. I had not the remotest idea that I would be called upon to undertake more responsible functions. I was therefore greatly surprised when the Assembly elected me to the Drafting Committee. I was more than surprised when the Drafting Committee elected me to be its Chairman. There were in the Drafting Committee men bigger, better and more competent than myself such as my friend Sir Alladi Krishnaswami Ayyar. I am grateful to the Constituent Assembly and the Drafting Committee for reposing in me so much trust and confidence and to have chosen me as their instrument and given me this opportunity of serving the country.

The credit that is given to me does not really belong to me. It belongs partly to Sir B. N. Rau, the Constitutional Adviser to the Constituent Assembly who prepared a rough draft of the Constitution for the consideration of the Drafting Committee. A part of the credit must go to the members of the Drafting Committee who, as I have said, have sat for 141 days and without whose ingenuity of devise new formulae and capacity to tolerate and to accommodate different points of view, the task of framing the Constitution could not have come to so successful a conclusion. Much greater, share of the credit must go to Mr. S.N. Mukherjee, the Chief Draftsman of the Constitution. His ability to put the most intricate proposals in the simplest and clearest legal form can rarely be equalled, nor his capacity for hard work. He has been as acquisition tot he Assembly. Without his help, this Assembly would have taken many more years to finalise the Constitution. I must not omit to mention the members of the staff working under Mr. Mukherjee. For, I know how hard they have worked and how long they have toiled sometimes even beyond midnight. I want to thank them all for their effort and their cooperation (Cheers).

The task of the Drafting Committee would have been a very difficult one if this Constituent Assembly has been merely a motley crowd, a tasseleted pavement without cement, a black stone here and a white stone there is which each member or each group was a law unto itself. There would have been nothing but chaos. This possibility of chaos was reduced to nil by the existence of the Congress Party inside the Assembly which brought into its proceedings a sense of order and discipline. It is because of the discipline of the Congress Party that the Drafting Committee was able to pilot the Constitution in the Assembly with the sure knowledge as to the fate of each article and each amendment. The Congress Party is, therefore, entitled to all the credit for the smooth sailing of the Draft Constitution in the Assembly.

The proceedings of this Constituent Assembly would have been very dull if all members had yielded to the rule of party discipline. Party discipline, in all its rigidity, would have converted this Assembly into a gathering of yes' men. Fortunately, there were rebels. They were Mr. Kamath, Dr. P. S. Deshmukh, Mr. Sidhva, Prof. K. T. Shah and Pandit Hirday Nath Kunzru. The points they raised were mostly ideological. That I was not prepared to accept their suggestions, does not diminish the value of their suggestions nor lessen the service they have rendered to the Assembly in enlivening its proceedings. I am grateful to them. But for them, I would not have had the opportunity which I got for expounding the principles underlying the Constitution which was more important than the mere mechanical work of passing the Constitution.

Finally, I must thank you Mr. President for the way in which you have conducted the proceedings of this Assembly. The courtesy and the consideration which you have shown to the Members of the Assembly can never be forgotten by those who have taken part in the proceedings of this Assembly. There were occasions when the amendments of the Drafting Committee were sought to be barred on grounds purely technical in their nature. Those were very anxious moments for me. I am, therefore, specially grateful to you for not permitting legalism to defeat the work of Constitution-making.

As much defence as could be offered to the Constitution has been offered by my friends Sir Alladi Krishnaswami Ayyar and

Mr. T. T. Krishnamachari. I shall not therefore enter into the merits of the Constitution. Because I feel, however good a Constitution may be, it is sure to turn out bad because those who are called to work it, happen to be a bad lot. However had a Constitution may be, it may turn out to be good if those who are called to work it, happen to be a good lot.

The working of a Constitution does not depend wholly upon the nature of the Constitution. The Constitution can provide only the organs of State such as the Legislature, the Executive and the Judiciary. The factors on which the working of those organs of the State depend are the people and the political parties they will set up as their instruments to carry out their wishes and their politics. Who can say how the people of India and their purposes or will they prefer revolutionary methods of achieving them? If they adopt the revolutionary methods, however good the Constitution may be, it requires no prophet to say that it will fail. It is, therefore, futile to pass any judgement upon the Constitution without reference to the part which the people and their parties are likely to play.

The condemnation of the Constitution largely comes from two quarters, the Communist Party and the Socialist Party. Why do they condemn the Constitution? Is it because it is really a bad Constitution? I venture to say no'. The Communist Party want a Constitution based upon the principle of the Dictatorship of the Proletariat. They condemn the Constitution because it is based upon parliamentary democracy. The Socialists want two things. The first thing they want is that if they come in power, the Constitution must give them the freedom to nationalise or socialise all private property without payment of compensation. The second thing that the Socialists want is that the Fundamental Rights mentioned in the Constitution must be absolute and without any limitations so that if their Party fails to come into power, they would have the unfettered freedom not merely to criticise, but also to overthrow the State.

These are the main grounds on which the Constitution is being condemned. I do not say that the principle of parliamentary democracy is the only ideal form of political democracy. I do not say that the principle of no acquisition of private property without compensation is so sacrosanct that there can be no departure from it. I do not say that Fundamental Rights can never be absolute and the limitations set upon them can never be lifted. What I do say is that the principles embodied in the Constitution are the views of the present generation or if you think this to be an overstatement, I say they are the views of the members of the Constituent Assembly. Why blame the Drafting Committee for embodying them in the Constitution? I say why blame even the Members of the Constituent Assembly? Jefferson, the great American statesman who played so great a part in the making of the American Constitution, has expressed some very weighty views which makers of Constitution, can never afford to ignore. In one place he has said:

> "We may consider each generation as a distinct nation, with a right, by the will of the majority, to bind themselves, but none to bind the succeeding generation, more than the inhabitants of another country."

In another place, he has said:

> "The idea that institutions established for the use of the national cannot be touched or modified, even to make them answer their end, because of rights gratuitously supposed in those employed to manage them in the trust for the public, may perhaps be a salutary provision against the abuses of a monarch, but is most absurd against the nation itself. Yet our lawyers and priests generally inculcate this doctrine, and suppose that preceding generations held the earth more freely than we do; had a right to impose laws on us, unalterable by ourselves, and that we, in the like manner, can make laws and impose burdens on future generations, which they will have no right to alter; in fine, that the earth belongs to the dead and not the living;"

I admit that what Jefferson has said is not merely true, but is absolutely true. There can be no question about it. Had the Constituent Assembly departed from this principle laid down by Jefferson it would certainly be liable to blame, even to condemnation. But I ask, has it? Quite the contrary. One has only to examine the provision relating to the amendment of the

Constitution. The Assembly has not only refrained from putting a seal of finality and infallibility upon this Constitution as in Canada or by making the amendment of the Constitution subject tot he fulfilment of extraordinary terms and conditions as in America or Australia, but has provided a most facile procedure for amending the Constitution. I challenge any of the critics of the Constitution to prove that any Constituent Assembly anywhere in the world has, in the circumstances in which this country finds itself, provided such a facile procedure for the amendment of the Constitution.

If those who are dissatisfied with the Constitution have only to obtain a 2/3 majority and if they cannot obtain even a two-thirds majority in the Parliament elected on adult franchise in their favour, their dissatisfaction with the Constitution cannot be deemed to be shared by the general public.

There is only one point of constitutional import to which I propose to make a reference. A serious complaint is made on the ground that there is too much of centralisation and that the States have been reduced to Municipalities. It is clear that this view is not only an exaggeration, but is also founded on a misunderstanding of what exactly the Constitution contrives to do. As to the relation between the Centre and the States, it is necessary to bear in mind the fundamental principle on which it rests. The basic principle of Federalism is that the Legislative and Executive authority is partitioned between the Centre and the States not by any law to be made by the Centre but by the Constitution itself. This is what Constitution does.

The States under our Constitution are in no way dependent upon the Centre for their legislative or executive authority. The Centre and the States are coequal in this matter. It is difficult to see how such a Constitution can be called centralism. It may be that the Constitution assigns to the Centre too large a field for the operation of its legislative and executive authority than is to be found in any other federal Constitution. It may be that the residuary powers are given to the Centre and not to the States. But these features do not form the essence of federalism. The chief mark of federalism as I said lies in the partition of the legislative and executive authority between the Centre and the Units by the Constitution. This is the principle embodied in our Constitution.

There can be no mistake about it. It is, therefore, wrong to say that the States have been placed under the Centre. Centre cannot by its own will alter the boundary of that partition. Nor can the Judiciary. For as has been well said:

> "Courts may modify, they cannot replace. They can revise earlier interpretations as new arguments, new points of view are presented, they can shift the dividing line in marginal cases, but there are barriers they cannot pass, definite assignments of power they cannot reallocate. They can give a broadening construction of existing powers, but they cannot assign to one authority powers explicitly granted to another."

The first charge of centralisation defeating federalism must therefore fall.

The second charge is that the Centre has been given the power to override the States. This charge must be admitted. But before condemning the Constitution for containing such overriding powers, certain considerations must be borne in mind. The first is that these overriding powers do not form the normal feature of the Constitution. Their use and operation are expressly confined to emergencies only.

The second consideration is: Could we avoid giving overriding powers to the Centre when an emergency has arisen? Those who do not admit the justification for such overriding powers to the Centre even in an emergency, do not seem to have a clear idea of the problem which lies at the root of the matter. The problem is so clearly set out by a writer in that well-known magazine "The Round Table" in its issue of December 1935 that I offer no apology for quoting the following extract from it. Says the writer:

> "Political systems are a complex of rights and duties resting ultimately on the question, to whom, or to what authority, does the citizen owe allegiance. In normal affairs the question is not present, for the law works smoothly, and a man, goes about his business obeying one authority in this set of matters and another authority in that. But in a moment of crisis, a conflict of claims may arise, and it is then apparent that ultimate allegiance cannot be divided. The issue of

> allegiance cannot be determined in the last resort by a juristic interpretation of statutes. The law must conform to the facts or so much the worse for the law. When all formalism is stripped away, the bare question is, what authority commands the residual loyalty of the citizen. Is it the Centre or the Constituent State?"

The solution of this problem depends upon one's answer to this question which is the crux of the problem. There can be no doubt that in the opinion of the vast majority of the people, the residual loyalty of the citizen in an emergency must be to the Centre and not to the Constituent States.

For it is only the Centre which can work for a common end and for the general interests of the country as a whole. Herein lies the justification for giving to all Centre certain overriding powers to be used in an emergency. And after all what is the obligation imposed upon the Constituent States by these emergency powers? No more than this - that in an emergency, they should take into consideration alongside their own local interests, the opinions and interests of the nation as a whole. Only those who have not understood the problem, can complain against it.

Here I could have ended. But my mind is so full of the future of our country that I feel I ought to take this occasion to give expression to some of my reflections thereon. On 26th January 1950, India will be an independent country (Cheers). What would happen to her independence? Will she maintain her independence or will she lose it again? This is the first thought that comes to my mind. It is not that India was never an independent country. The point is that she once lost the independence she had. Will she lost it a second time?

It is this thought which makes me most anxious for the future. What perturbs me greatly is the fact that not only India has once before lost her independence, but she lost it by the infidelity and treachery of some of her own people. In the invasion of Sind by Mahommed-Bin-Kasim, the military commanders of King Dahar accepted bribes from the agents of Mahommed-Bin-Kasim and refused to fight on the side of their King. It was Jaichand who invited Mahommed Gohri to invade India and fight against Prithvi Raj and promised him the help of himself and the Solanki Kings. When Shivaji was fighting for the liberation of Hindus, the other

Maratha noblemen and the Rajput Kings were fighting the battle on the side of Moghul Emperors. When the British were trying to destroy the Sikh Rulers, Gulab Singh, their principal commander sat silent and did not help to save the Sikh Kingdom. In 1857, when a large part of India had declared a war of independence against the British, the Sikhs stood and watched the event as silent spectators.

Will history repeat itself? It is this thought which fills me with anxiety. This anxiety is deepened by the realisation of the fact that in addition to our old enemies in the form of castes and creeds we are going to have many political parties with diverse and opposing political creeds. Will Indian place the country above their creed or will they place creed above country? I do not know. But this much is certain that if the parties place creed above country, our independence will be put in jeopardy a second time and probably be lost for ever. This eventuality we must all resolutely guard against. We must be determined to defend our independence with the last drop of our blood (Cheers).

On the 26th of January 1950, India would be a democratic country in the sense that India from that day would have a government of the people, by the people and for the people. The same thought comes to my mind. What would happen to her democratic Constitution? Will she be able to maintain it or will she lost it again. This is the second thought that comes to my mind and makes me as anxious as the first.

It is not that India did not know what is Democracy. There was a time when India was studded with republics, and even where there were monarchies, they were either elected or limited. They were never absolute. It is not that India did not know Parliaments or Parliamentary Procedure.

A study of the Buddhist Bhikshu Sanghas discloses that not only there were Parliaments-for the Sanghas were nothing but Parliaments - but the Sanghas knew and observed all the rules of Parliamentary Procedure known to modern times. They had rules regarding seating arrangements, rules regarding Motions, Resolutions, Quorum, Whip, Counting of Votes, Voting by Ballot, Censure Motion, Regularisation, Res Judicata, etc. Although these rules of Parliamentary Procedure were applied by the Buddha to the meetings of the Sanghas, he must have borrowed them from the rules of the Political Assemblies functioning in the country in his time.

This democratic system India lost. Will she lost it a second time? I do not know. But it is quite possible in a country like India — where democracy from its long disuse must be regarded as something quite new - there is danger of democracy giving place to dictatorship. It is quite possible for this new born democracy to retain its form but give place to dictatorship in fact. If there is a landslide, the danger of the second possibility becoming actuality is much greater.

If we wish to maintain democracy not merely in form, but also in fact, what must we do? The first thing in my judgement we must do is to hold fast to constitutional methods of achieving our social and economic objectives. It means we must abandon the bloody methods of revolution. It means that we must abandon the method of civil disobedience, non-cooperation and satyagraha. When there was no way left for constitutional methods for achieving economic and social objectives, there was a great deal of justification for unconstitutional methods. But where constitutional methods are open, there can be no justification for these unconstitutional methods. These methods are nothing but the Grammar of Anarchy and the sooner they are abandoned, the better for us.

The second thing we must do is to observe the caution which John Stuart Mill has given to all who are interested in the maintenance of democracy, namely, not "to lay their liberties at the feet of even a great man, or to trust him with power which enable him to subvert their institutions". There is nothing wrong in being grateful to great men who have rendered life-long services to the country. But there are limits to gratefulness. As has been well said by the Irish Patriot Daniel O'Connel, no man can be grateful at the cost of his honour, no woman can be grateful at the cost of her chastity and no nation can be grateful at the cost of its liberty.

This caution is far more necessary in the case of India than in the case of any other country. For in India, Bhakti or what may be called the path of devotion or hero-worship, plays a part in its politics unequalled in magnitude by the part it plays in the politics of any other country in the world. Bhakti in religion may be a road to the salvation of the soul. But in politics, Bhakti or hero-worship is a sure road to degradation and to eventual dictatorship.

The third thing we must do is not to be content with mere political democracy. We must make our political democracy a social democracy as well. Political democracy cannot last unless there lies at the base of it social democracy. What does social democracy mean? It means a way of life which recognises liberty, equality and fraternity as the principles of life. These principles of liberty, equality and fraternity as the principles of life. These principles of liberty, equality and fraternity are not to be treated as separate items in a trinity. They form a union of trinity in the sense that to divorce one from the other is to defeat the very purpose of democracy.

Liberty cannot be divorced from equality, equality cannot be divorced from liberty. Nor can liberty and equality be divorced from fraternity. Without equality, liberty would produce the supremacy of the few over the many. Equality without liberty would kill individual initiative. Without fraternity, liberty would produce the supremacy of the few over the many. Equality without liberty would kill individual initiative. Without fraternity, liberty and equality could not become a natural course of things.

It would require a constable to enforce them. We must begin by acknowledging the fact that there is complete absence of two things in Indian Society. One of these is equality. On the social plane, we have in India a society based on the principle of graded inequality which we have a society in which there are some who have immense wealth as against many who live in abject poverty. On the 26th of January 1950, we are going to enter into a life of contradictions. In politics we will have equality and in social and economic life we will have inequality.

In politics we will be recognising the principle of one man one vote and one vote one value. In our social and economic life, we shall, by reason of our social and economic structure, continue to deny the principle of one man one value. How long shall we continue to live this life of contradictions? How long shall we continue to deny equality in our social and economic life? If we continue to deny it for long, we will do so only by putting our political democracy in peril. We must remove this contradiction at the earliest possible moment or else those who suffer from inequality will blow up the structure of political democracy which is Assembly has to laboriously built up.

The second thing we are wanting in is recognition of the principle of fraternity. What does fraternity mean? Fraternity means a sense of common brotherhood of all Indians-if Indians being one people. It is the principle which gives unity and solidarity to social life. It is a difficult thing to achieve. How difficult it is, can be realised from the story related by James Bryce in his volume on American Commonwealth about the United States of America.

The story is- I propose to recount it in the words of Bryce himself- that-

> "Some years ago the American Protestant Episcopal Church was occupied at its triennial Convention in revising its liturgy. It was thought desirable to introduce among the short sentence prayers a prayer for the whole people, and an eminent New England divine proposed the words `O Lord, bless our nation'. Accepted one afternoon, on the spur of the moment, the sentence was brought up next day for reconsideration, when so many objections were raised by the laity to the word nation' as importing too definite a recognition of national unity, that it was dropped, and instead there were adopted the words `O Lord, bless these United States."

There was so little solidarity in the USA at the time when this incident occurred that the people of America did not think that they were a nation. If the people of the United States could not feel that they were a nation, how difficult it is for Indians to think that they are a nation. I remember the days when politically-minded Indians, resented the expression "the people of India". They preferred the expression "the Indian nation." I am of opinion that in believing that we are a nation, we are cherishing a great delusion. How can people divided into several thousands of castes be a nation? The sooner we realise that we are not as yet a nation in the social and psychological sense of the world, the better for us. For then only we shall realise the necessity of becoming a nation and seriously think of ways and means of realising the goal. The realisation of this goal is going to be very difficult - far more difficult than it has been in the United States. The United States has no caste problem. In India there are castes. The castes are anti-national. In the first place because they bring about separation in social life. They are anti-national also because they generate jealousy and antipathy between caste and caste. But we must overcome all these difficulties if we wish to become a nation in reality. For fraternity can be a fact only when there is a nation. Without fraternity equality and liberty will be no deeper than coats of paint.

These are my reflections about the tasks that lie ahead of us. They may not be very pleasant to some. But there can be no gainsaying that political power in this country has too long been the monopoly of a few and the many are only beasts of burden, but also beasts of prey. This monopoly has not merely deprived them of their chance of betterment, it has sapped them of what may be called the significance of life. These downtrodden classes are tired of being governed. They are impatient to govern themselves. This urge for self-realisation in the downtrodden classes must no be allowed to devolve into a class struggle or class war. It would lead to a division of the House. That would indeed be a day of disaster. For, as has been well said by Abraham Lincoln, a House divided against itself cannot stand very long. Therefore the sooner room is made for the realisation of their aspiration, the better for the few, the better for the country, the better for the maintenance for its independence and the better for the continuance of its democratic structure. This can only be done by the establishment of equality and fraternity in all spheres of life. That is why I have laid so much stresses on them.

I do not wish to weary the House any further. Independence is no doubt a matter of joy. But let us not forget that this independence has thrown on us great responsibilities. By independence, we have lost the excuse of blaming the British for anything going wrong. If hereafter things go wrong, we will have nobody to blame except ourselves. There is great danger of things going wrong. Times are fast changing. People including our own are being moved by new ideologies. They are getting tired of Government by the people. They are prepared to have Governments for the people and are indifferent whether it is

Government of the people and by the people. If we wish to preserve the Constitution in which we have sought to enshrine the principle of Government of the people, for the people and by the people, let us resolve not to be tardy in the recognition of the evils that lie across our path and which induce people to prefer Government for the people to Government by the people, nor to be weak in our initiative to remove them. That is the only way to serve the country. I know of no better.

Speech at Mahad

[*25 December 1927 is a watershed in the history of the Dalit movement. On this day, Dr. Ambedkar began an agitation by the Dalits to draw water from the Chavadar Lake at Mahad. The water of this lake was hitherto reserved for caste Hindus. The Manusmriti was burnt here as a mark of Dalit Proust against untouchability. The following is the historic speech made by Dr Ambedkar on this occasion*]

Gentlemen, you have gathered here today in response to the invitation of the Satyagraha Committee. As the Chairman of that Committee, I gratefully welcome you all.

Many of you will remember that on the 19th of last March all of us came to the Chavadar Lake here. The caste Hindus of Mahad had laid no prohibition on us; but they showed they had objections to our going there by the attack they made. The fight brought results that one might have expected. The aggressive caste Hindus were sentenced to four months' rigorous imprisonment, and are now in jail. If we had not been hindered on 19th March, it would have been proved that the caste Hindus acknowledge our right to draw water from the lake, and we should have had no need to begin our present undertaking.

Unfortunately we were thus hindered, and we have been obliged to call this meeting today. This lake at Mahad is public property. The caste Hindus of Mahad are so reasonable that they not only draw water from the lake themselves but freely permit people of any religion to draw water from it, and accordingly people of other religions such as the Islamic do make use of this permission. Nor do the caste Hindus prevent members of species considered lower than the human, such as birds and beasts, from drinking at the lake. Moreover, they freely permit beasts kept by untouchables to drink at the lake.

Caste Hindus are the very founts of compassion. They practise no *hinsa* and harass no one. They are not of the class of miserly and selfish folk who would grudge even a crow some grains of the food they are eating. The proliferation of sanyasis and mendicants is a living testimony to their charitable temperament. They regard altruism as religious merit and injury to another as a sin.

Even further, they have imbibed the principle that injury done by another must not be repaid but patiently endured, and so, they not only treat the harmless cow with kindness, but spare harmful creatures such as snakes. That one Atman or Spiritual Self dwells in all creatures has become a settled principle of their conduct. Such are the caste Hindus who forbid some human beings of their own religion to draw water from the same Chavadar Lake! One cannot help asking the question, why do they forbid us alone?

It is essential that all should understand thoroughly the answer to this question. Unless you do, I feel, you will not grasp completely the importance of today's meeting. The Hindus are divided, according to sacred tradition, into four castes; but according to custom, into five: Brahmins, Kshatriyas, Vaishyas, Shudras and Atishudras. The caste system is the first of the governing rules of the Hindu religion. The second is that the castes are of unequal rank. They are ordered in a descending series of each meaner than the one before.

Not only are their ranks permanently fixed by the rule, but each is assigned boundaries it must not transgress, so that each one may at once be recognised as belonging to its particular rank. There is a general belief that the prohibitions in the Hindu religion against intermarriage, interdining, interdrinking and social intercourse are bounds set to degrees of association with one another. But this is an incomplete idea. These prohibitions are indeed limits to degrees of association; but they have been set to show people of unequal rank what the rank of each is. That is, these bounds are symbols of inequality.

Just as the crown on a man's head shows he is a King, and the bow in his hand shows him to be a Kshatriya, the class to which none of the prohibitions applies is considered the highest of all and the one to which they all apply is reckoned the lowest in rank. The strenuous efforts made to maintain the prohibitions are for the reason that, if they are relaxed, me inequality settled by religion will break down and equality will take its place.

The caste Hindus of Mahad prevent the untouchables from drinking the water of the Chavadar Lake not because they suppose that the touch of the untouchables will pollute the water or that it will evaporate and vanish. Their reason for preventing the untouchables from drinking it is that they do not wish to acknowledge by such a permission that castes declared inferior by sacred tradition are in fact their equals.

Gentlemen! you will understand from this the significance of the struggle we have begun. Do not let yourselves suppose that the Satyagraha Committee has invited you to Mahad merely to drink the water of the Chavadar Lake of Mahad.

It is not as if drinking the water of the Chavadar Lake will make us immortal. We have survived well enough all these days without drinking it. We are not going to the Chavadar Lake merely to drink its water. We are going to the Lake to assert that we too are human beings like others. It must be clear that this meeting has been called to set up the norm of equality.

I am certain that no one who thinks of this meeting in this light will doubt that it is unprecedented. I feel that no parallel to it can be found in the history of India. If we seek for another meeting in the past to equal this, we shall have to go to the history of France on the continent of Europe. A hundred and thirty-eight years ago, on 24 January 1789, King Louis XVI had convened, by royal command, an assembly of deputies to represent the people of the kingdom. This French National Assembly has been much vilified by historians.

The Assembly sent the King and the Queen of France to the Guillotine; persecuted and massacred the aristocrats; and drove their survivors into exile. It confiscated the estates of the rich and plunged Europe into war for fifteen years. Such are the accusations levelled against the Assembly by the historians. In my view, the criticism is misplaced; further, the historians of this school have not understood the gist of the achievement of the French National Assembly. That achievement served the welfare not only of France but of the entire European continent. If European nations enjoy peace and prosperity today, it is for one reason: the revolutionary French National Assembly convened in 1789 set new principles for the organisation of society before the disorganised and decadent French nation of its time, and the same principles have been accepted and followed by Europe.

To appreciate the importance of the French National Assembly and the greatness of its principles, we must keep in mind die state of French society at the time. You are all aware that our Hindu society is based on the system of castes. A rather similar system of classes existed in the France of 1789: the difference was that it was a society of three castes. Like the Hindu society, the French had a class of Brahmins and another of Kshatriyas. But instead of three different castes of Vaishya, Shudra and Atishudra, there was one class that comprehended these.

This is a minor difference. The important thing is that the caste or class system was similar. The similarity to be noted is not only in the differentiation between classes: the inequality of our caste system was also to be found in the French social system. The nature of the inequality in the French society was different: it was economic in nature. It was, however, equally intense. The thing to bear in mind is there is a great similarity between the French National Assembly that met on 5 May 1789 at Versailles and our meeting today. The similarity is not only in the circumstances in which the two meetings took place but also in their ideals.

That Assembly of the French people was convened to reorganise French society. Our meeting today too has been convened to reorganise Hindu society. Hence, before discussing on what principles our society should be reorganised, we should all pay heed to the principles on which the French Assembly relied and the policy it adopted. The scope of the French Assembly was far wider than that of our present meeting.

It had to carry out the threefold organisation of the French political, social and religious systems. We must confine ourselves to how social and religious reorganisation can be brought about. Since we are not, for the present, concerned with political reorganisation, let us see what the French Assembly did in the matter of the religious and social reorganisation of their nation. The policy adopted by the French National Assembly in this area can be seen plainly by anyone from three important proclamations issued by that Assembly. The first was issued on 17 June 1789. This was a proclamation about the class systems in France. As said before, French society was divided into three classes.

The proclamation abolished die three classes and blended them into one. Further, it abolished the seats reserved separately for the three classes (or estates) in die political assembly. The second proclamation was about the priests. By ancient custom, to appoint or remove these priests was outside the power of die nation, that being die monopoly of a foreign religious potentate, the Pope. Anyone appointed by the Pope was a priest, whether or not he was fit to be one in the eyes of those to whom he was to preach.

The proclamation abolished the autonomy of die religious orders and assigned to the French nation the authority to decide who might follow this vocation, who was fit for it and who was not, whether he was to be paid for preaching or not, and so on. The third proclamation was not about the political, economic or religious systems.

It was of a general nature and laid down the principles on which all social arrangements ought to rest. From that point of view, the third proclamation is the most important of the three; it might be called the King of these proclamations. It is renowned the world over as the declaration of human birthrights.

It is not only unprecedented in the history of France; more than that, it is unique in the history of civilized nations. For every European nation has followed the French Assembly in giving it a place in its own Constitution. So one may say that it brought about a revolution not only in France but the whole world. This proclamation has seventeen clauses, of which the following are important:

- All human beings are equal by birth; and they shall remain equal till death. They may be distinguished in status only in the public interest. Otherwise, their equal status must be maintained.
- The ultimate object of politics is to maintain these human birthrights.
- The entire nation is the mother-source of sovereignty. The rights of any individual, group or special class, unless

they are given by the nation, cannot be acknowledged as valid on any other ground, be it political or religious.

- Any person is free to act according to his birthright. Any limit placed upon this freedom must be only to the extent necessary to permit other persons to enjoy their birthrights. Such limits must be laid down by law: they cannot be set on the grounds of the religion or on any other basis than the law of the land.
- The law will forbid only such actions as are injurious to society. All must be free to do what has not been forbidden by law. Nor can anyone be compelled to do what the law has not laid down as a duty.
- The law is not in the nature of bounds set by any particular class. The right to decide what the law shall be rests with the people or their representatives. Whether such a law is protective or punitive, it must be the same for all. Since justice requires that all social arrangements be based on the equality of all, all individuals are equally eligible for any kind of honour, power and profession. Any distinction in such matters must be owing to differences of individual merit; it must not be based on birth.

I feel our meeting today should keep the image of this French National Assembly before the mind. The road it marked out for the development of the French nation, the road that all progressed nations have followed, ought to be the road adopted for the development of Hindu society by this meeting. We need to pull away the nails which hold' the framework of caste-bound Hindu society together, such as those of the prohibition of intermarriage down to the prohibition of social intercourse so that Hindu society becomes all of one caste. Otherwise untouchability cannot be removed nor can equality be established.

Some of you may feel that since we are untouchables, it is enough if we are set free from the prohibitions of interdrinking and social intercourse. That we need not concern ourselves with the caste system; how does it matter if it remains? In my opinion this is a total error. If we leave the caste system alone and adopt only the removal of untouchability as our policy, people will say that we have chosen a low aim. To raise men, aspiration is needed as much as outward efforts. Indeed it is to be doubted whether efforts are possible without aspiration. Hence, if a great effort is to be made, a great aspiration must be nursed. In adopting an aspiration one need not be abashed or deterred by doubts about one's power to satisfy it.

One should be ashamed only of mean aspirations; not of failure that may result because one's aspiration is high. If untouchability alone is removed, we may change from Atishudras to Shurdas; but can we say that this radically removes untouchability? If such puny reforms as the removal of restrictions on social intercourse, etc. were enough for the eradication of untouchability, I would not have suggested that the caste system itself must go. Gentlemen! you all know that if a snake is to be killed it is not enough to strike at its tail - its head must be crushed. If any harm is to be removed, one must seek out its root and strike at it. An attack must be based on the knowledge of the enemy's vital weakness.

Duryodhana was killed because Bheema struck at his thigh with his mace. If the mace had hit Duryodhana's head he would not have died; for his thigh was his vulnerable spot. One finds many instances of a physician's efforts to remove a malady proving fruitless because he has not perceived fully what will get rid of the disease; similar instances of failure to root out a social disease because it is hot fully diagnosed are rarely recorded in history; and so one does not often become aware of them. But let me acquaint you with one such instance that I have come across in my reading. In the ancient European nation of Rome, the patricians were considered upper class, and die plebians, lower class.

All power was in the hands of the patricians, and they used it to ill-treat the plebians. To free themselves from this harassment, the plebians, on the strength of their unity, insisted that laws should be written down for the facilitation of justice and for the information of all. Their patrician opponents agreed to this; and a charter of twelve laws was written down. But this did not rid the oppressed plebians of their woes. For the officers who enforced the laws were all of the patrician class; moreover the chief officer, called the tribune, was also a patrician. Hence, though the laws were uniform, there was partiality in their enforcement. The plebians then demanded that instead of the administration being in the hands of one tribune there should be two tribunes, of whom one should be elected by the plebians and the other by the patricians. The patricians yielded to this too, and the plebians rejoiced, supposing they would now be free of their miseries. But their rejoicing was short-lived.

The Roman people had a tradition that nothing was to be done without the favourable verdict of the oracle at Delphi. Accordingly, even the election of a duly elected tribune - if the oracle did not approve of him - had to be treated as annulled, and another had to be elected, of whom the oracle approved. The priest who put the question to the oracle was required, by sacred religious custom, to be one born of parents married in the mode the Romans called conferatio; and this mode of marriage prevailed only among the patricians; so that die priest of Delphi was always a patrician.

The wily priest always saw to it that if the plebians elected a man really devoted to their cause, the oracle went against him. Only if the man elected by the plebians to the position of tribune was amenable to the patricians, would the oracle favour him and give him the opportunity of actually assuming office. What did the plebians gain by their right to elect a tribune? The answer must be, nothing in reality. Their efforts proved meaningless because they did not trace the malady to its source. If they had, they would, at the same time that they demanded a tribune of their election, have also settled the question of who should be the priest at Delphi. The disease could not be eradicated by demanding a tribune; it needed control of the priestly office; which the plebians failed to perceive. We too, while we seek a way to remove untouchability, must enquire closely into what will eradicate the disease; otherwise we too may miss our aim. Do not be foolish enough to believe that removal of the restrictions on social intercourse or interdrinking will remove untouchability.

Remember that if the prohibitions on social intercourse and interdrinking go, the roots of untouchability are not removed. Release from these two restrictions will, at the most, remove untouchability as it appears outside the home; but it will leave untouchability in die home untouched. If we want to remove untouchability in the home as well as outside, we must break down the prohibition against intermarriage. Nothing else will serve. From another point of view, we see that breaking down the bar against intermarriage is the way to establish real equality. Anyone must confess that when the root division is dissolved, incidental points of separateness will disappear by themselves. The interdictions on interdining, interdrinking and social intercourse have all sprung from the one interdiction against intermarriage.

Remove the last and no special efforts are needed to remove the rest. They will disappear of their own accord. In my view the removal of untouchability consists in breaking down the ban on intermarriage and doing so will establish real equality. If we wish to root out untouchability, we must recognise that the root of untouchability is in the ban on intermarriage. Even if our attack today is on the ban against interdrinking, we must press it home against the ban on intermarriage; otherwise untouchability cannot be removed by the roots. Who can accomplish this task? It is no secret that the Brahmin class cannot do it.

While the caste system lasts, the Brahmin caste has its supremacy. No one, of his own will, surrenders power which is in his hands. The Brahmins have exercised their sovereignty over all other castes for centuries. It is not likely that they will be willing to give it up and treat the rest as equals. The Brahmins do not have the patriotism of the Samurais of Japan. It is useless to hope that they will sacrifice their privileges as the Samurai class did, for the sake of national unity based on a new equality. Nor does it appear likely that the task will be carried out by other caste Hindus. These others, such as the class comprising the Marathas and other similar cartes, are a class between the privileged and those without any rights.

A privileged class, at the cost of a little self-sacrifice, can show some generosity. A class without any privileges has ideals and aspirations; ' for, at least as a matter of self-interest, it wishes to bring about a social reform. As a result it develops an attachment to principles rather than to self-interest. The class of caste Hindus other than Brahmins lies in between: it cannot practise the generosity possible to the class above and it does not develop the attachment to principles that develops in the class below. This is why this class is seen to be concerned not so much about attaining equality with the Brahmins as about maintaining its status above the untouchables.

For the purposes of the social reform required, the class of caste Hindus other than Brahmins is feeble. If we are to await its help, we should fall into the difficulties that the farmer faced, who depended on his neighbour's help for his harvesting, as in the story of the mother lark and her chicks found in many textbooks.

The task of removing untouchability and establishing equality that we have undertaken, we must carry out ourselves. Others will not do it. Our life will gain its true meaning if we consider that we are born to carry out this task and set to work in earnest. Let us receive this merit which is awaiting us.

This is a struggle in order to raise ourselves; hence we are bound to undertake it, so as to remove the obstacles to our progress. We all know how at every turn, untouchability muddies and soils our whole existence. We know that at one time our people were recruited in large numbers into the troops. It was a kind of occupation socially assigned to us and few of us needed to be anxious about earning our bread. Other classes of our level have found their way into the troops, the police, the courts and the offices, to earn their bread. But in the same areas of employment you will no longer find the untouchables.

It is not that the law debars us from these jobs. Everything is permissible as far the law is concerned. But the Government finds itself powerless because other Hindus consider us untouchables and look down upon us, and it acquiesces in our being kept out of Government jobs. Nor can we take up any decent trade. It is true, partly, that we lack money to start business, but the real difficulty is that people regard us as untouchables and no one will accept goods from our hands.

To sum up, untouchability is not simple matter; it is the mother of all our poverty and lowliness and it has brought us to the abject state we are in today. If we want to raise ourselves out of it, we must undertake this task. We cannot be saved in any other way. It is a task not for our benefit alone; it is also for the benefit of the nation.

Hindu society must sink unless the untouchability that has become a part of the four-castes system is eradicated. Among the resources that any society needs in the struggle for life, a great resource is the moral order of that society. And everyone must admit that a society in which the existing moral order upholds things that disrupt the society and condemns those that would unite the members of the society, must find itself defeated in any struggle for life with other societies. A society which has the opposite moral order, one in which things that unite are considered laudable and things that divide are condemned, is sure to succeed in any such struggle.

This principle must be applied to Hindu society. Is it any wonder that it meets defeat at every turn when it upholds a social order that fragments its members, though it is plain to anyone who sees it that the four-castes system is such a divisive force and that a single caste for all, would unite society? If we wish to escape these disastrous conditions, we must break down the framework of the four-castes system and replace it by a single caste system.

Even this will not be enough. The inequality inherent in the four-castes system must be rooted out. Many people mock at the principles of equality. Naturally, no man is another's equal. One has an impressive physique; another is slow-witted. The mockers think that, in view of these inequalities that men are born with, the egalitarians are absurd in telling us to regard them as equals. One is forced to say that these mockers have not understood fully the principle of equality.

If the principle of equality means that privilege should depend, not on birth, wealth, or anything else, but solely on the merits of each man, then how can it be demanded that a man without merit, and who is dirty and vicious, should be treated on a level with a man who his merit and is clean and virtuous? Such is a counter-question sometimes posed. It is essential to define equality as giving equal privileges to men of equal merit.

But before people have had an opportunity to develop their inherent qualities and to merit privileges, it is just to treat them all equally. In sociology, the social order is itself the most important factor in the full development of qualities that any person may possess at birth. If slaves are constantly treated unequally, they will develop no qualities other than those appropriate to slaves, and they will never become fit for any higher status. If the clean man always repulses the unclean man and refuses to have anything to do with him, the unclean man will never develop the aspiration to become clean. If the criminal or immoral castes are given no refuge by the virtuous castes, the criminal castes will never learn virtue. The examples given above show that, although an equal treatment may not create good qualities in one who does not have them at all, even such qualities where they exist need equal treatment for their development; also, developed good qualities are wasted and frustrated without equal treatment.

On the one hand, the inequality in Hindu society stunts the progress of individuals and in consequence stunts society. On the other hand, the same inequality prevents society from bringing into use powers stored in individuals. In both ways, this inequality is weakening Hindu society, which is in disarray because of the four-castes system.

Hence, if Hindu society is to be strengthened, we must uproot the four-castes system and untouchability, and set the society on the foundations of the two principles of one caste only and of equality. The way to abolish untouchability is not any other than the way to invigorate Hindu society. Therefore I say that our work is beyond doubt as much for the benefit of the nation as it is in our own interest. Our work has been begun to bring about a real social revolution. Let no one deceive himself by supposing that it is a diversion to quieten minds entranced with sweet words. The work is sustained by strong feeling, which is the power that drives the movement. No one can now arrest it. I pray to God that the social revolution which begins here today may fulfil itself by peaceful means.

None can doubt that the responsibility of letting the revolution take place peacefully rests more heavily on our opponents than on us. Whether this social revolution will work peacefully or violently will depend wholly on the conduct of the caste Hindus. People who blame the French National Assembly of 1789 for atrocities forget one thing. That is, if the rulers of France had not been treacherous to the Assembly, if the upper classes had not resisted it, had not committed the crime of trying to suppress it with foreign help, it would have had no need to use violence in the work of the revolution and the whole social transformation would have been accomplished peacefully.

We say to our opponents too: please do not oppose us. Put away the orthodox scriptures. Follow justice. And we assure you that we shall carry out our programme peacefully.

9

Ambedkar's Life at a Glance

1891, April 14: Bhimrao Ramji Ambedkar was born in the British-founded town of Mhow, an important military centre near Indore, Madhya Pradesh. He was the fourteenth and last child of Ramji Sankpal and Bhimabai Murbadkar Sankpal. The family's ancestral town was Ambavade (in the Ratnagiri District of Maharashtra).

1894-96: When Bhimrao's father retired from his career with the British Army in 1894, he settled for a time in Dapoli (in Ratnagiri District). The young Bhimrao had his earliest education there.

1896: The family moved to Satara, where Ramji Sakpal found a job with the Public Works Department in Goregaon; Bhimrao was enrolled in school in Satara.

1896: Bhimabai Sakpal died; of her fourteen children, only three sons (Balaram, Anandrao, Bhimrao) and two daughters (Manjula, Tulasa) survived her. The children were cared for by their paternal aunt Mira, who had a disabling hunchback but did her best to look after them.

1900: Bhimrao entered the Government Middle School at Satara.

1901: Ramji Sakpal, who had remarried in 1898, moved his family from Satara to Bombay, the capital city of Bombay Presidency. They found housing in the Dabak Chawl, Lower Parel. Bhimrao soon entered Elphinstone High School in Bombay.

1906: Bhimrao's marriage was arranged, with Ramabai, nine-year-old daughter of Bhiku Dhutre of Wanand, near Dapoli. Some accounts have it that she was related to Gopal Baba Walangkar.

1907: Bhimrao passed the Matriculation Examination that entitled him to enrol in a college affiliated with Bombay University; his marks were average, his best subject was Persian (which he studied in place of Sanskrit).

1908: Bhimrao entered Elphinstone College, a college affiliated with Bombay University.

1910: Shivram Janba Kamble, another early caste reformer, organised a second Mahar conference at Jejuri; this resulted in a memorandum sent to the British government. Young Bhimrao met the reform-minded Gaikwar of Baroda, Sayaji Rao III (r.1875-1939), who then approved a scholarship of Rs. 25 a month for his education.

1912: Bhimrao passed the B.A. Examination (special subjects: Economics and Politics) from Bombay University, and prepared to take a position in the administration of Baroda State. His oldest son, Yashwant, was born.

1913: He had barely begun at his new post when he learned by telegram that his father was gravely ill; he rushed home just in time for a last farewell. "It was February 2, 1913, the saddest day in Bhimrao Ambedkar's life."

1913: The Gaekwar of Baroda announced his decision to offer scholarships to send students for higher education at Columbia University. A scholarship of 11.50 British pounds a month, for three years, was awarded to the young Ambedkar.

1913: Arriving in New York during the third week in July, Bhimrao was housed in Hartley Hall. But he didn't care for the food, and only stayed for a week. In August, he moved from Hartley Hall to "Cosmopolitan Club" (554 West 114th Street), a housing club maintained by a group of Indian students. He finally settled in a dormitory, Livingston Hall (since renamed Wallach

Hall, with his friend Naval Bhathena, a Parsi; the two remained friends for life.

1915: The young graduate student passed his M.A. exam in June, majoring in Economics, with Sociology, History, Philosophy, and Anthropology as other subjects of study; he presented a thesis, "Ancient Indian Commerce". For his outstanding achievement, he was honored by students and professors of the Faculty of Arts at a special dinner. In 1916 he offered another M.A. thesis, "National Dividend of India — A Historic and Analytical Study"; it was this one that later became the nucleus of his Ph.D. dissertation.

1916: On May 9th, he read his paper "Castes in India: Their Mechanism, Genesis, and Development" before a seminar conducted by the anthropologist Prof. Alexander Goldenweiser (1880-1940). Dr. Ambedkar was very proud of this paper, and remained so. He promptly got it published in the *Indian Antiquary* (May 1917). As late as 1936 he wrote that only shortage of time prevented him from reworking *Annihilation of Caste* so as to include in it this early seminar paper. In June, he went to London, and in October he was admitted to Gray's Inn for Law, and to the London School of Economics and Political Science for Economics, where he was allowed to start work on a doctoral thesis. He often worked in the British library reading room.

1917: The term of his scholarship from Baroda ended, so that he was obliged to go back to India in June with his work unfinished; he was, however, given permission to return and finish within four years. He sent his precious and much-loved collection of books back on a steamer — but it was torpedoed and sunk by a German submarine. He was appointed Military Secretary to the Gaikwar of Baroda; he had agreed to join the Baroda service as a condition of his scholarship. But this experience was not a happy one. Even to reach Baroda, he had to pay his own expenses; he used the damages paid by Thomas Cook and Company for his torpedoed luggage. And when he arrived in Baroda, things went from bad to worse. Meeting in Calcutta with Annie Besant as its president, for the first time in its history the Indian National Congress adopted a resolution endorsing "the justice and righteousness of removing all disabilities imposed by custom upon the Depressed Classes."

1918: After the Baroda fiasco, he tried to find ways to make a living for his growing family. With the help of Parsi friends, he became a private tutor, and found some work as an accountant. He also started an investment consulting business, but it failed when his clients learned that he was an untouchable. Finally, he became Professor of Political Economy in the Sydenham College of Commerce and Economics in Bombay. (This position came about through the recommendation of his London acquaintance, Lord Sydenham, former Governor of Bombay). He was mostly successful with his students, but some of the other professors objected to his sharing the same drinking-water jug that they all used.

1919: He testified both orally and in writing before the Southborough Committee, which was investigating franchise matters in the light of the planned Montagu-Chelmsford reforms. He demanded separate electorates and reserved seats for the untouchables: "The real social divisions of India then are: (1) Touchable Hindus. (2) Untouchable Hindus. (3) Mohammedans. (4) Christians. (5) Parsees. (6) Jews."

1920: Dr. Ambedkar started a weekly paper, "Mooknayak" (Leader of the Voiceless), in Marathi, with the help of the reform-minded Shahu I (1884-1922), Maharaja of Kolhapur. In the first issue, he called India a "home of inequality," and described Hindu society as "a tower which had several storeys without a ladder or an entrance. One was to die in the story in which one was born." The depressed classes must be saved "from perpetual slavery, poverty, and ignorance"; herculean efforts must be made "to awaken them to their disabilities." In March, he spoke at a Depressed Classes Conference in Mangaon in Kolhapur State; it was attended by the Maharaja of Kolhapur, who publicly praised him as a future national leader. At the end of the conference, the Maharaja and his courtiers shocked the tradition-minded by actually dining with Ambedkar and his caste members. In May, the Maharajah of Kolhapur convened another such conference, in Nagpur, a town later to acquire a major symbolic significance in Dr. Ambedkar's life. Having resigned from his teaching position, in July he returned to London, relying on his own savings, supplemented by loans from the Maharaja of Kolhapur and his friend Naval Bhathena. He returned to the London School of

Economics, and to Gray's Inn to read for the Bar. He lived in poverty, and studied constantly in the British Museum.

1922: Through unremitting hard work, Ambedkar once again overfulfilled all expectations: he completed a thesis for a M.Sc. (Econonics) degree at London School of Economics, and was called to the Bar, and submitted a Ph.D. thesis in economics to the University of London. He planned to do further research in economics at the University of Bonn (and also toyed with the idea of studying Sanskrit there). He sent to the university a handwritten letter and CV in German, but the whole project didn't work out. He soon had to return to London to deal with challenges to his thesis.

1923: His Ph.D. thesis at the University of London, "The Problem of the Rupee", was challenged on political grounds (for its allegedly subversive, anti-British implications), but was resubmitted and finally accepted; it was at once published in London and was "dedicated to the memory of my father and mother, as a token of my abiding gratitude for the sacrifices they made and the enlightenment they showed in the matter of my education."

1924: Back in India, Dr. Ambedkar began to practice as a barrister in Bombay, and also began to lecture part-time at Batliboi's Accountancy Training Institute. He founded the "Bahishkrit Hitakarini Sabha" (Group for the Wellbeing of the Excluded), to help the depressed classes mobilise. Its motto was "Educate, Agitate, Organise."

1925: He published his London School of Economics M.A. thesis as "The Evolution of Provincial Finance in British India"; it was dedicated to the Gaikwar of Baroda (for his help in the matter of my education), and had an introduction by Prof. Seligman. He also gave testimony before the Royal Commission on Indian Currency and Finance.

1926: The Governor of Bombay nominated him as a member of the Bombay Legislative Council; he took his duties seriously, and often delivered speeches on economic matters. He led the satyagraha at Mahad to exercise the right of Untouchables to draw water from the Chavdar Tank. He ceremonially took a drink of water from the tank, after which local caste Hindus rioted, and Brahmins took elaborate measure for the ritual purification of the tank.

1927: On January 1st, he held a meeting at the Koregaon Victory Memorial, 17 miles from Poona, which commemorates the defeat of the Peshwa's forces and the inauguration of British rule. The names of Mahar soldiers who fought with the British are inscribed there on a marble tablet. Such meetings still take place annually there on that day. On June 8, he was formally awarded the Ph.D. degree from Columbia University. His Ph.D. thesis was "The Evolution of Provincial Finance in British India". On December 24th, he addressed a Second Depressed Classes Conference in Mahad; he attacked the Laws of Manu, and then a copy of this ancient text was publicly burned, to the shock and horror of many caste Hindus.

1928: Dr. Ambedkar was appointed professor at the Government Law College, Bombay; his term of appointment ended in 1929. Dr. Ambedkar was selected as a member of the Bombay Presidency Committee to work with the Simon Commission, drafting guidelines for political change in India. Congress decided to boycott the Simon Commission because it had no Indians on it. Dissenting from the views of many of his colleagues, Dr. Ambedkar prepared a detailed report setting out his own recommendations.

1929: Dr. Ambedkar closed his second journal, "Bahishkrit Bharat" (Excluded India), which he had started in 1927, and replaced it with the "Janata" (The People), which was published until 1956, when it took on the name "Prabuddha Bharata" (after his conversion). On Oct. 23, during a visit to Chalisgaon, he had a bad accident, and was confined to bed until the last week of December.

1930: On Aug. 8, Dr. Ambedkar presided over the Depressed Classes Congress at Nagpur, and made a major speech: he endorsed dominion status, and criticised Gandhi's Salt March and Civil Disobedience Movement as inopportune; but he also criticised British colonial misgovernment, with its famines and immiseration. He argued that the "safety of the depressed classes" hinged on their "being independent of the Government and the Congress" both: "We must shape our course ourselves and by ourselves."

His conclusion emphasised self-help: "Political power cannot be a panacea for the ills of the depressed classes. Their salvation lies in their social elevation. They must cleanse their evil habits. They must improve their bad ways of living.... They must be educated.... There is a great necessity to disturb their pathetic contentment and to instil into them that divine discontent which is the spring of all elevation." Dr. Ambedkar was invited by the Viceroy to be a delegate to the Round Table Conference, and left for London in October. He participated extensively in the work of the Round Table Conference, often submitting written statements of his views. His views at the time were described in an unpublished manuscript later found among his papers: "The Untouchables and the Pax Britannica".

1932: The All-Indian Depressed Classes Conference, held at Kamtee near Nagpur on May 6th, backed Dr. Ambedkar's demand for separate electorates, rejecting compromises proposed by others. Gandhi, in Yeravda jail, started a fast to the death against the separate electorates granted to the depressed classes by Ramsay MacDonald's Communal Award. By September 23, a very reluctant Dr. Ambedkar was obliged by the pressure of this moral blackmail to accept representation through joint electorates instead. The result was the Poona Pact. In 1933, Gandhi replaced his journal "Young India" with a new one called "Harijan," and undertook a 21-day "self-purification fast" against untouchability. Dr. Ambedkar participated in the work of the Joint Committee on Indian Legislative Reform, examining a number of significant witnesses.

1935: Dr. Ambedkar was appointed principal of the Government Law College, and became a professor there as well; he held these positions for two years. In May, Dr. Ambedkar's wife Ramabai died after a long illness. Her great wish had been to make a pilgrimage to Pandharpur, but since as an untouchable she would not have been allowed to enter the temple, her husband had never allowed her to go. On Oct. 13th, Dr. Ambedkar presided over the Yeola Conversion Conference, held in Yeola, in Nasikh District. He advised the depressed classes to abandon all agitation for temple-entry privileges; instead, they should leave Hinduism entirely and embrace another religion. He vowed, "I solemnly assure you that I will not die as a Hindu." The struggle for social justice began to receive increasing attention and support from progressive writers. Mulk Raj Anand's powerful novel "Untouchable" (1935) was followed by "Coolie" (1936), with a foreword by E. M. Forster; both works called international attention to caste and class injustices. In Hindi, there was the work of Premchand. In December, Dr. Ambedkar was invited by the Jat-Pat-Todak Mandal of Lahore, a caste-reform organisation, to preside over its annual conference in the spring of 1936.

1935/36: He composed (or began to compose?), but did not publish, a brief, moving, and largely autobiographical memoir called *Waiting for a Visa.*

1936: On April 13-14th, he addressed the Sikh Mission Conference in Amritsar, and reiterated his intention of renouncing Hinduism. In late-April, the Jat-Pat-Todak Mandal realised the radical nature of its guest's planned speech, and withdrew its earlier invitation. On May 15th, Dr. Ambedkar published the speech he would have given, with an introductory account of the whole controversy. The result, a slim little book called The Annihilation of Caste, became famous at once. On May 31st, Dr. Ambedkar addressed the Mumbai Elaka Mahar Parishad (Bombay Mahar Society), during a meeting at Naigaum (Dadar), in Bombay. He spoke in Marathi, to his own people, with vividness and poignancy: "What Path to Salvation?". This was the only time he addressed an audience expressly limited to Mahars. In August, he founded his first political party, the Independent Labour Party, which contested 17 seats in the 1937 General Elections, and won 15.

1937: Dr. Ambedkar published the second edition of "The Annihilation of Caste", adding a concluding appendix that featured a debate with Gandhi over the speech. This work remained a best-seller, going through many editions in the coming years — and exciting much controversy. "It was logic on fire, pinching and pungent, piercing and fiery, provocative and explosive."

1938: Over Dr. Ambedkar's vigorous protests in January, Congress adopted Gandhi's own term "Harijans" (Children of God) as the official name for the "Scheduled Castes." In protest against a term that he considered condescending and meaningless, Dr. Ambedkar and his party staged a walkout from the Bombay

Legislative Assembly. Dr. Ambedkar made a number of significant speeches to the Assembly, during 1938-39.

1939: In January, he delivered to the Gokhale Institute of Politics and Economics a lecture called "Federation versus Freedom". During the debate over Congress's plan to leave the government in protest at not having been consulted about the declaration of war on Germany, Dr. Ambedkar made his own loyalties very clear: "Wherever there is any conflict of interests between the country and the untouchables, so far as I am concerned, the untouchables' interests will take precedence over the interests of the country. I am not going to support a tyrannising majority simply because it happens to speak in the name of the country.... As between the country and myself, the country will have precedence; as between the country and the depressed classes, the depressed classes will have precedence." In November, Congress left the government. Jinnah arranged the celebration of a "Day of Deliverance," and Dr. Ambedkar enthusiastically joined him. Dr. Ambedkar was careful to emphasise, however, that this was an anti-Congress rather than an anti-Hindu move; if Congress interpreted it as anti-Hindu, the reason could only be, he said, that Congress was a Hindu body after all.

1940: In December, Dr. Ambedkar published the first edition of his "Thoughts on Pakistan". In this work, he argued that though partition would be an unfortunate thing, it wouldn't be the worst possible outcome, and if the Muslims wanted it they had a perfect right to claim it.

1942: He founded his second political party, the All-India Scheduled Castes Federation, which didn't do so well in the elections of 1946. Dr. Ambedkar was inducted into the Viceroy's Executive Council as Labour Member, a position which he held until his resignation in June 1946. His thoughtful comments in that forum cover various topics. Congress started the "Quit India" movement. Dr. Ambedkar severely criticised this move. He described it as "both irresponsible and insane, a bankruptcy of statesmanship and a measure to retrieve the Congress prestige that had gone down since the war started. It would be madness, he said, to weaken law and order art a time when the barbarians were at the gates."

1943: On January 19th, he delivered the Presidential Address on the occasion of the 101st birth anniversary of Justice Mahadev Govind Ranade. It was published in book form in April, under the title "Ranade, Gandhi, and Jinnah". In September, he also prepared and published the vigorous memorandum, "Mr. Gandhi and the Emancipation of the Untouchables".

1944: On January 29th, he presided over the second meeting of the Scheduled Caste Federation, in Kanpur.

1945: In February, he published a revised version of "Thoughts on Pakistan"; this second, expanded edition was called "Pakistan; or Partition of India". A third edition of this book was published in 1946. On May 6th, he addressed the Annual Conference of the All India Scheduled Caste Federation, held at Parel, Bombay. This speech was soon published as "The Communal Deadlock and a Way to Solve It". In June, he published a political manifesto detailing the problems of dealing with Congress, and accusing it of many acts of betrayal: "What Congress and Gandhi Have Done to the Untouchables". The next year, he published a second edition, with major revisions in one chapter.

1946: In June, he founded Siddharth College, in Bombay; it was a project of the People's Education Society, which he had founded in 1945. In October, he published "Who Were the Shudras? How They Came to Be the Fourth Varna in the Indo-Aryan Society". He dedicated the book to the great early reformer Jotiba Phule.

1947: In March, he published "States and Minorities: What Are their Rights and How to Secure them in the Constitution of Free India", a memorandum on fundamental rights, minority rights, safeguards for the Depressed Classes, and the problems of Indian states. Independence and Partition came in August; Dr. Ambedkar accepted Nehru's invitation to become Minister of Law in the first Cabinet of independent India. On August 29th, he was appointed Chairman of the Drafting Committee for the new Constitution.

1948: On April 15th, Dr. Ambedkar married Dr. Sharda Kabir (a Saraswat Brahmin) in Delhi; she adopted the name Savita. He was now diabetic and increasingly ill, and she took care of him for the rest of his life. In October, he prepared a memorandum on "Maharashtra as a Linguistic Province", expressing his views for submission to the Linguistic Provinces Commission. He published "The Untouchables: a Thesis on the Origin of Untouchability", as a sequel to his book on the Shudras. As always on this subject, he wrote with passion. In the Preface he said, "The Hindu Civilization.... is a diabolical contrivance to suppress and enslave humanity. Its proper name would be infamy. What else can be said of a civilization which has produced a mass of people... who are treated as an entity beyond human intercourse and whose mere touch is enough to cause pollution?" In November, the Draft Constitution with its 315 articles and 8 schedules was formally introduced to the Constituent Assembly. Dr. Ambedkar concluded his speech: "I feel that the Constitution is workable; it is flexible and it is strong enough to hold the country together both in peace time and in war time. Indeed, if I may say so, if things go wrong under the new Constitution the reason will not be that we had a bad Constitution. What we will have to say is that Man was vile."

1950: Dr. Ambedkar gave several addresses about Buddhism; in May, he flew to Colombo, in Sri Lanka, to pursue further Buddhist connections.

1951: In February, he introduced in Parliament the "Hindu Code Bill" that he had drafted, which included greatly expanded rights for women; it proved very controversial, and consideration of it was postponed: on the Hindu Code Bill. In September, Dr. Ambedkar resigned from the Cabinet, embittered over the failure of Nehru and the Congress to back the Hindu Code Bill as they had earlier pledged to do. He became the Leader of the Opposition.

1952: Dr. Ambedkar received an honorary L.L.D. degree from Columbia University as part of its Bicentennial Special Convocation. The President described him as "one of India's leading citizens — a great social reformer and a valiant upholder of human rights."

1953: His political thinking included analysis of the issue of linguistic states; he published "Need for Checks and Balances" on this question. In 1955, he was still working on the subject, as the preface (dated Dec. 23, 1955) to "Thoughts on Linguistic States" testified.

1954: In the midst of his round of (increasingly embittered) Parliamentary and other activity, his health gave way; he was confined to bed for two months. While dedicating a new Buddhist vihara near Poona, Dr. Ambedkar announced that he was writing a book on Buddhism, and that as soon as it was finished, he planned to make a formal conversion to Buddhism. He also claimed that the image of Vithoba at Pandharpur was in reality an image of the Buddha, and said that he would write a thesis to prove this claim.

1956: Dr. Ambedkar brought the manuscript of "The Buddha and His Dhamma" to completion. "In February 1956, two new chapters are added to it: 'There is no god'; 'There is no soul'.... On March 15, 1956, Ambedkar wrote the preface to his book in his own handwriting and dictated it to Rattu [his secretary]." Printing began in May, but was slowed by constant last-minute revisions of the proofs. From June to October, he was bedridden in his Delhi residence. His eyes were failing, he suffered from side effects of the drugs he was given for his diabetes, he felt deeply depressed. His formal conversion took place on Oct. 14th in Nagpur, a town selected for reasons he explained in his moving speech, "Why Was Nagpur Chosen?". Many thousands of Mahars and other Dalits accepted Buddhism along with him. In November, he flew to Kathmandu to attend the Fourth World Buddhist Conference. On Dec. 2, he completed the manuscript of "The Buddha or Karl Marx", his last finished work, and gave it for typing. On the night of Dec. 5 or the early morning of Dec. 6, he died quietly in his sleep; on Dec. 7 there was a huge Buddhist-style funeral procession in Bombay, and he was cremated on the seashore.

10

Appendices

(Important Documents)

Gandhi and Ambedkar

'Inside every thinking Indian there is a Gandhian and a Marxist struggling for supremacy,' says noted historian and biographer Ramachandra Guha in the opening sentence of this publication. A significant portion of the book expands on this salvo. In short, it examines and discusses all those who comprise the life of thinking Indians today. Exclusive extracts from the book.

Mahatma Gandhi was not so much the Father of the Nation as the mother of all debates regarding its future. All his life he fought in a friendly spirit with compatriots whose views on this or that topic diverged sharply from his. He disagreed with Communists and the bhadralok on the efficacy and morality of violence as a political strategy. He fought with radical Muslims on the one side and with radical Hindus on the other, both of whom sought to build a state on theological principles. He argued with Nehru and other scientists on whether economic development in a free India should centre on the village or the factory. And with that other giant, Rabindranath Tagore, he disputed the merits of such varied affiliations as the English language, nationalism, and the spinning wheel.

In some ways the most intense, interesting and long-running of these debates was between Gandhi and Ambedkar. Gandhi wished to save Hinduism by abolishing untouchability, whereas Ambedkar saw a solution for his people outside the fold of the dominant religion of the Indian people. Gandhi was a rural romantic, who wished to make the self-governing village the bedrock of free India; Ambedkar an admirer of city life and modern technology who dismissed the Indian village as a den of iniquity. Gandhi was a crypto-anarchist who favoured non-violent protest while being suspicious of the state; Ambedkar a steadfast constitutionalist, who worked within the state and sought solutions to social problems with the aid of the state.

Perhaps the most telling difference was in the choice of political instrument. For Gandhi, the Congress represented all of India, the Dalits too. Had he not made their cause their own from the time of his first ashram in South Africa? Ambedkar however made a clear distinction between freedom and power. The Congress wanted the British to transfer power to them, but to obtain freedom the Dalits had to organise themselves as a separate bloc, to form a separate party, so as to more effectively articulate their interests in the crucible of electoral politics. It was thus that in his lifetime, and for long afterwards, Ambedkar came to represent a dangerously subversive threat to the authoritative, and sometimes authoritarian, equation: Gandhi = Congress = Nation.

Here then is the stuff of epic drama, the argument between the Hindu who did most to reform caste and the ex-Hindu who did most to do away with caste altogether. Recent accounts represent it as a fight between a hero and a villain, the writer's caste position generally determining who gets cast as hero, who as villain. In truth both figures should be seen as heroes, albeit tragic ones.

The tragedy, from Gandhi's point of view, was that his colleagues in the national movement either did not understand his concern with untouchability or even actively deplored it. Priests and motley shankaracharyas thought he was going too fast in his challenge to caste — and why did he not first take their permission? Communists wondered why he wanted everyone to clean their own latrines when he could be speaking of class struggle. And Congressmen in general thought Harijan work came in the way of an all-out effort for national freedom. Thus Stanley Reid, a former editor of the Times of India quotes an Indian patriot who complained in the late-30s that "Gandhi is wrapped up in the Harijan movement. He does not care a jot whether we live or die; whether we are bond or free."

The opposition that he faced from his fellow Hindus meant that Gandhi had perforce to move slowly, and in stages. He started by accepting that untouchability was bad, but added a cautionary caveat — that inter-dining and inter-marriage were also bad. He moved on to accepting inter-mingling and inter-dining (hence the movement for temple entry), and to arguing that all men and all varnas were equal. The last and most far-reaching step, taken only in 1946, was to challenge caste directly by accepting and sanctioning inter-marriage itself.

The tragedy, from Ambedkar's point of view, was that to fight for his people he had to make common cause with the British. In his book, Worshipping False Gods, Arun Shourie has made much of this. Shourie takes all of 600 pages to make two points: (i) that Ambedkar was a political opponent of both Gandhi and the Congress, and generally preferred the British to either; (ii) that Ambedkar cannot be called the "Father of the Constitution" as that implies sole authorship, whereas several other people, such as K. M. Munshi and B. N. Rau, also contributed significantly to the wording of the document. Reading Worshipping False Gods, one might likewise conclude that it has been mistakenly advertised as being the work of one hand. Entire chapters are based entirely on one or other volume of the Transfer of Power, the collection of official papers put out some years ago by Her Majesty's Stationery Office. The editor of that series, Nicholas Mansergh, might with reason claim co-authorship of Shourie's book. In a just world he would be granted a share of the royalties too.

Practised in the arts of over-kill and over-quote, Shourie is a pamphleteer parading as a historian. He speaks on Gandhi only as "Gandhiji" and of the national movement only as the "National Movement", indicating that he has judged the case beforehand. For to use the suffix and the capitals is to simultaneously elevate and intimidate, to set up the man and his movement as the ideal, above and beyond criticism. But the Congress' claim to represent all of India was always under challenge. The Communists said it was the party of landlords and capitalists. The Muslim League said it was a party of the Hindus. Ambedkar then appended a devastating caveat, saying that the party did not even represent all Hindus, but only the upper castes.

Shourie would deny that these critics had any valid arguments whatsoever. He is in the business of awarding, and more often withholding, certificates of patriotism. The opponents of the Congress are thus all suspect to him, simply because they dared point out that the National Movement was not always as national as it set out to be, or that the Freedom Struggle promised unfreedom for some. But how did these men outside the Congress come to enjoy such a wide following? This is a question Shourie does not pause to answer, partly because he had made up his mind in advance, but also because he is woefully ill-informed. Consider now some key facts erased or ignored by him.

That Ambedkar preferred the British to the Congress is entirely defensible. Relevant here is a remark of the 18th-century English writer Samuel Johnson. When the American colonists asked for independence from Britain, Johnson said: "How is it that we hear the greatest yelps for liberty among the drivers of Negroes?" Untouchability was to the Indian freedom movement what slavery had been to the American struggle, the basic contradiction it sought to paper over. Before Ambedkar, another outstanding leader of the lower castes, Jotiba Phule, also distrusted the Congress, in his time a party dominated by Poona Brahmins. He too preferred the British, in whose armies and factories low castes could find opportunities denied to them in the past. The opening up of the economy and the growth of the colonial cities also helped many untouchables escape the tyranny of the village. The British might have been unwitting agents of change; nonetheless, under their rule life for the lower castes was less unpleasant by far than it had been under the Peshwas.

Shourie also seems unaware of work by worthy historians on low-caste movements in other parts of India. Mark Juergensmeyer has documented the struggles of untouchables in Punjab, which under its remarkable leader Mangu Ram, rejected the Congress and the Arya Samaj to form a new sect, Adi-Dharm, which was opposed to both. Sekhar Bandyopadhyay has written of the Namasudras in Bengal, who like Ambedkar and his Mahars, were not convinced that a future Congress government would be sympathetic to their interests. And countless scholars have documented the rise of the Dravidian movement in South India, that took as its point of departure Brahmin domination of the Congress in Madras: the movement's founder, E. V. Ramaswamy "Periyar", also fought bitterly with Gandhi.

The leaders of these movements, and the millions who followed them, worked outside the Congress and often in opposition to it. Enough reason perhaps for Shourie to dismiss them all as anti-national. Indeed, Shourie's attitude is comparable to that of White Americans who question the patriotism of those Blacks who dare speak out against racism. For asking Blacks to stand up for their rights, men of such stature as W. E. B. Du Bois and Paul Robeson were called all kind of names, of which "anti-American" was much the politest. Later, the great Martin Luther King was persecuted by the most powerful of American agencies, the Federal Bureau of Investigation, whose director, J. Edgar Hoover, equated patriotism with acquiescence to White domination.

Much of the time, Shourie writes as if there is a singular truth, with him as its repository and guarantor. Time and again he equates Ambedkar with Jinnah as an "accomplice of Imperial politics". He dismisses all that Ambedkar wrote about Hinduism "caricature" and "calumnies". Not once does he acknowledge that there was much truth to the criticisms. There is not one admission here of the horrendous and continuing sufferings of Dalit as the hands of caste Hindus that might explain and justify Ambedkar's rhetoric and political choices. For Shourie, the fact that Ambedkar disagreed long and often with Gandhi is proof enough that he was anti-national. He even insinuates that Ambedkar "pushed Gandhi to the edge of death" by not interfering with the Mahatma's decision to fast in captivity. Of the same fast other historians have written, in my view more plausibly, that by threatening to die Gandhi blackmailed Ambedkar into signing a pact with him.

Somewhere in the middle of Worshipping False Gods, the author complains that Ambedkar's "statues, dressed in garish blue, holding a copy of the Constitution — have been put up in city after city." However, this aesthetic distaste seems rather pointless. For the background to the statues and the reverence they command lies in the continuing social practices of the religion to which Shourie and I belong. If caste lives, so will the memory of the man who fought to annihilate it. The remarkable thing is that 50 years after independence, the only politician, dead or alive, who has a truly pan-Indian appeal is B. R. Ambedkar. Where Gandhi is forgotten in his native Gujarat and Nehru vilified in his native Kashmir, Ambedkar is worshipped in hamlets all across the land. For Dalits everywhere he is the symbol of their struggle, the scholar, theoretician and activist whose own life represented a stirring triumph over the barriers of caste.

Shourie's attacks on Dalits and their hero follow in quick succession the books he has published attacking Communists, Christians and Muslims. Truth be told, the only category of Indians he has not attacked — and going by his present political persuasion will not attack — are high-caste Hindus. Oddly enough, this bilious polemicist and baiter of the minorities was once an anti-religious leftist who excoriated Hinduism. To see Shourie's career in its totality is to recall these words of Issac Deutscher, on the communist turned anti-communist.

He brings to his job the lack of scruple, the narrow-mindedness, the disregard of truth, and the intense hatred with which Stalinism has imbued him. He remains sectarian. He is an inverted Stalinist. He continues to see the world in black and white, but now the colours are differently distributed ... The ex-communist ... is haunted by a vague sense that he has betrayed either his former ideals or the ideals of bourgeois society ... He then tries to suppress the guilt and uncertainty, or to camouflage it by a show of extraordinary certitude and frantic aggressiveness. He insists that the world should recognise his uneasy conscience as the clearest conscience of all. He may no longer be concerned with any cause except one — self-justification.

Ambedkar is a figure who commands great respect from one end of the social spectrum. But he is also, among some non-Dalits, an object of great resentment, chiefly for his decision to carve out a political career independent of and sometimes in opposition to Gandhi's Congress. That is of course the burden of Shourie's critique but curiously, the very week his book was published, at a political rally in Lucknow the Samajvadi Party's Beni Prasad Verma likewise dismissed Ambedkar as one who "did nothing else except create trouble for Gandhiji". This line, that Ambedkar had no business to criticise, challenge or argue with Gandhi, was of course made with much vigour and malice during the national movement as well.

I think, however, that for Ambedkar to stand up to the uncrowned King and anointed Mahatma of the Indian people required extraordinary courage and will-power. Gandhi thought so too. Speaking at a meeting in Oxford in October 1931, Gandhi said he had "the highest regard for Dr. Ambedkar. He has every right to be bitter. That he does not break our heads is an act of self-restraint on his part." Writing to an English friend two years later, he said he found "nothing unnatural" in Ambedkar's hostility to the Congress and its supporters. "He has not only witnessed the inhuman wrongs done to the social pariahs of Hinduism", reflected this Hindu, "but in spite of all his culture, all the honours that he has received, he has, when he is in India, still to suffer many insults to which untouchables are exposed." In June 1936 Gandhi pointed out once again that Dr. Ambedkar "has had to suffer humiliations and insults which should make any one of us bitter and resentful." "Had I been in his place," he remarked, "I would have been as angry."

Gandhi's latter-day admirers might question Ambedkar's patriotism and probity, but the Mahatma had no such suspicions himself. Addressing a bunch of Karachi students in June 1934, he told them that "the magnitude of (Dr. Ambedkar's) sacrifice is great. He is absorbed in his own work. He leads a simple life. He is capable of earning one to two thousand rupees a month. He is also in a position to settle down in Europe if he so desires. But he does not want to stay there. He is only concerned about the welfare of the Harijians."

To Gandhi, Ambedkar's protest held out a lesson to the upper castes. In March 1936 he said that if Ambedkar and his followers were to embrace another religion, "We deserve such treatment and our task (now) is to wake up to the situation and purify ourselves." Not many heeded the warning, for towards the end of his life Gandhi spoke with some bitterness about the indifference to Harijan work among his fellow Hindus: "The tragedy is that those who should have especially devoted themselves to the work of (caste) reform did not put their hearts into it. What wonder that Harijan brethren feel suspicious, and show opposition and bitterness."

The words quoted in the preceding paragraphs have been taken from that reliable and easily accessible source: the Collected Works of Mahatma Gandhi. The 100 volumes of that set rest lightly on my shelves as, going by other evidence, they rest on the shelves of the man who compiled Worshipping False Gods. Perhaps the most perverse aspect of an altogether perverse book is that Shourie does not once tell us what Gandhi said or wrote about his great adversary. A curious thing or, on reflection, a not-so-curious thing: for if that scholarly courtesy was restored to, the case that Ambedkar was an anti-national careerist would be blown sky-high.

One of the few Gandhians who understood the cogency of the Dalit critique of the Congress was C. Rajagopalachari. In the second half of 1932, Rajaji became involved in the campaign to allow the so-called untouchables to enter the Guruvayoor temple in Kerala. The campaign was led by that doughty fighter for the rights of the dispossessed, K. Kelappan Nair. In a speech at Guruvayoor on December 20, 1932, Rajaji told the high castes that it would certainly help us in the fight for Swaraj if we open the doors of the temple (to Harijans). One of the many causes that keeps Swaraj away from us is that we are divided among ourselves. Mahatmaji received many wounds in London (during the Second Round Table Conference of 1931). But Dr. Ambedkar's darts were the worst. Mahatmaji did not quake before the Churchills of England. But as repressing the nation he had to plead guilty to Dr. Ambedkar's charges.

As it was, the managers of temples across the land could count upon the support of many among their clientele, the suvarna Hindus who agreed with the Shankaracharyas that the Gandhians were dangerous revolutionaries who had to be kept out at the gate. Unhappily, while upper-caste Hindus thought that Gandhi moved too fast, Dalits today feel he was much too slow. The Dalit politician Mayawati has, more than once, spoken of the Mahatma as a shallow paternalist who sought only to smooth the path for more effective long-term domination by the suvarna. Likewise, in his book Why I am Not a Hindu Kancha Illiah writes of Gandhi as wanting to "build a modern consent system for the continued maintenance of brahminical hegemony" — a judgement as unfair as Shourie's on Ambedkar.

Whereas in their lifetime Gandhi and Ambedkar were political rivals, now, decades after their death, it should be possible to see their contributions as complementing one another's. The Kannada critic D. R. Nagaraj once noted that in the narratives of Indian nationalism the "heroic stature of the caste-Hindu reformer", Gandhi, "further dwarfed the Harijan personality" of Ambedkar. In the Ramayana there is only one hero but, as Nagaraj points out, Ambedkar was too proud, intelligent and self- respecting a man to settle for the role of Hanuman or Sugreeva. By the same token, Dalit hagiographers and pamphleteers generally seek to elevate Ambedkar by diminishing Gandhi. For the scriptwriter and the mythmaker there can only be one hero. But the historian is bound by no such constraint. The history of Dalit emancipation is unfinished, and for the most part unwritten. It should, and will, find space for many heroes. Ambedkar and Gandhi will do nicely for a start.

Liberty, Equality, Community

A Lecture on Dr. Babasaheb Ambedkar's Vision of a New Social Order

Dr. Bhimrao Ramji Ambedkar's vision and life truly stands at the junction of the old and the new; coming from the depths of the society marked by hierarchies of inequality and involuted complexities of fixed exploitation to a leading role in the formation of a new order, symbolised by his role in the drafting of India's Constitution, symbol of a new order, Ambedkar was indeed a man marking the beginning of an era, a man whose life and thought encompassed both analysis of, rage about and struggle against the old exploitation and the visions of the new society. Whether or not the Constitution and the India that emerged from the struggle for freedom and equality truly represents Ambedkar's vision is a separate question; today I would like to focus on exactly what that vision was.

These are days of both assessing the past millennium and laying out our hopes and visions for the new one. It would not be an exaggeration to say that Ambedkar is here India's most significant figure. While Indira Gandhi and Mahatma Gandhi's names have been taken around the world as important figures of the millennium, it is not they nor any other of the rather bewildering collection of Indians mentioned (including Godse and Bacchan) but Dr. Bhimrao Ramji Ambedkar who has to be considered India's man of the millennium. Already awareness of the significance of Dalit and the role of Dalits in Indian society is spreading, and in the future when people look back on the traumas and changes that Indian society has undergone, and at the contributions its people have been making to global society, they will agree that it is Babasaheb who best represents the global-Indian heritage. Nehru was a national figure at most; his daughter Indira was also a national figure.

Mahatma Gandhi was indeed a global figure, who is recognised throughout the world today as a forerunner of the ecological movement. But Babasaheb's harsh judgement in 1939- "this Gandhi age is the dark age of India" I think will stand: the values that Gandhi represented, the proclamation of Hinduism and the glorification of a village society, in whatever idealised form, were ultimately backward values, the values of a pre-modern society. It was Babasaheb who stood within the Indian tradition of modernism, justice, freedom and equality and who gave the ideals of the French revolution local form and shape. I am using strong words here because the debate over these values is raging sharp and fierce today in India, because Babasaheb Ambedkar himself used strong words and took sharp positions on the issues involved, issues of development, freedom and equality.

Ambedkar's vision of a new social order can be summed up in the way in which he so often did, with the great slogan of the French revolution, "liberty, equality, fraternity." I would change the final term to "community" because I think it captures for our gender-concerned times the real meaning of the final term. Liberty, equality and community are the three most important components of a human vision for the new millennium.

In using these, I am quite aware that these great values of the Enlightenment and the French revolution are today under attack. They are under attack not only in India from advocates of pseudo-swadeshi who would see them as merely "western" but also world-wide, from post-modernists and eco-romanticists who think "progress" is impossible and from Leftists who have taken "liberalism" and "liberty" as bad words. It is important to assess this attack and Ambedkar's response. Part of this response has to do with the Indian context of his efforts. For this context was not only a heritage of caste inequality and oppression. It was also, and even more importantly, a heritage of Buddhism and other Indian traditions which Ambedkar saw as the beginnings of modernity, equality, liberty and community for India. In this sense the values that the French Revolution helped to give a world-wide push to are not really "western" at all, but world values. It is perhaps not accidental that "Enlightenment" is also a Buddhist term, perhaps with some different meaning. Prabuddh Bharat was the name Ambedkar gave to his final weekly newspaper, after Janata, after Bahishkrut Bharat. It was not only an equalitaritarian, free and fraternal India that he sought to achieve, but also an enlightened one, an India of rationality and science — an India true to its own heritage in linking with the most developed ones of Europe and elsewhere.

I will focus on three main points to summarise Dr. Ambedkar's vision of a new social order.

First, in contrast to the Gandhian and eco-romanticist position, Ambedkar shared with Marx and with liberal Enlightenment thinkers a belief in progress, a conviction that the history brought with it an advance in human welfare. In Marxist terms we can interpret this as the advance if the forces of production which brings with it an advance in human capacities; in liberal terms we can speak of an advance in freedom. Ambedkar also believed that human history is a history of progress, a forward movement and not simply a phase in endless cycles or final degeneration. He differed with Marx in interpreting the motive force of human history, so that it is also necessary to examine Ambedkar's views regarding the great debates on the role of idealism and materialism in human life and social structure.

Second, in today's India, indeed in the world, when Nehruvian statism is yielding to liberalism as a method and philosophy of economic development, it is necessary again to characterise Ambedkar's economic and political philosophy. This I would describe as a form of social liberalism and I will briefly trace his writings on economics and socialism, conclude with a look at his thinking in the final years of his life, expressed mainly in his essay "Buddha and Karl Marx." Last but not least, I would to examine Ambedkar's religious contributions, which are both at the practical level and at the level of philosophy. Here we must deal with his version of Buddhism, a "liberation theology" of Buddhism or more accurately, a Navayana Buddhism.

Ambedkar's Conception of History

Materialism, Idealism and Human Progress Is there such a thing as "progress" or "historical development"? At one time, it would have been surprising to even ask such a question. The greatest heritage of revolutionary values has been the belief that humans are emerging out of slavery, out of poverty, into a world that offers an improvement in human existence. It is still perhaps the confidence of the majority of humanity: millions greeted the stroke of midnight last December 31 and the new dawn of January 1 in the hope and confidence that the new millennium would bring, not necessarily a utopia, but at least a better world than existed earlier.

Yet in recent years the confidence that progress is possible has come under attack. Eco-romanticism, taking its justification from Mahatma Gandhi, tend to see history as heading into a downspin. We hear everywhere rhetoric of greater and greater destruction. We hear it even from some western interpretations of Buddhism. For instance, Sangharakshata — in spite of his similarities with Ambedkar at other points — sees a radical distinction between social and spiritual evolution, arguing that "the line of biological development is not single but double.

Every step in the evolutionary process results from a coalescence between an upward movement of material progress and a downward movement of psychic or spiritual degeneration" (1957) The Evolving Mind, a more nuanced book by another English member of the same order, also makes a distinction between material and mental evolution, arguing that Buddhism carries on a process of spiritual evolution while biological evolution comes to an end.

In this belief, historical development or social evolution has little to offer; humans must seek to evolve at the spiritual and mental level only. Even many self-styled Marxists seem to be falling under the rhetoric of despair, supporting eco-romanticists, and attacking not simply capitalism but any form of market economy (note about "market socialism"), any form of industrial development. Thus, combining an apparent Marxism with eco-romanticism, Maria Mies argues that the French revolution is finished; its ideals cannot be extended to Dalits, women or other sections of the marginalised in the world, and we must turn away from this vain effort to achieve "growth" to acceptance of a society based on limited needs, subsistence production, and stasis. Such ideas have a very wide spread today, not simply in India but just a much if not more in the US and Europe.

Ambedkar himself gave a very early answer to the romanticisation of a pre-industrial life and to the morality of "simple needs" in a 1918 essay reviewing a book by Bertrand Russell.

"This time-honoured complaint of the moralists against `love of money' is only a part of their general complaint against the goods of the world and finds its justification in the economic circumstances which gave rise to this particular belief....At a time when the whole world was living in `pain economy' as did the ancient world and when the productivity of human labour was extremely low and when no efforts could augment its return, in short, when the whole world was living in poverty it is but natural that moralists should have preached the gospel of poverty and renunciation of worldly pleasures only because they were not to be had..." This marks Ambedkar's disagreement with any romanticisation of poverty and with attempts to idealise an "eastern" pacifism and harmony with nature as contrasted with "western" aggressiveness and commercialism. In opposition to an ethic of subsistence and limiting needs, he urges the development of human productivity and the accumulation of wealth; he also goes on to cautiously distance himself from the condemnation of property so common to radicals and romanticists: "The trouble therefore one might say is not with property but with the unequal distribution of it". This position he retained lifelong; for his final writings on Buddhism distinguished it clearly from what he considered to be the glorification of poverty in Christian tradition.

Ambedkar, like Marx, is against exploitation, but not against development and accumulation. At a social level, he believes in progress in history, and at an individual level he gives legitimation to the honest and energetic efforts of "householders" to work and earn. While he does not fit into a clear historical materialist position, his writings show an evolutionary and "stagist" view of history.

For instance, in his early essay on "Philosophy of Hinduism" he analyses religions as associated with particular types of societies which he categorises in a series: "savage societies" and "antique civilised societies" and "modern civilized societies.". This is a social evolutionary model, though different from the more economically based versions offered by Marx or more conventional sociologists. History, then, does show us progress. What is its the motive force? Or, put in another way, what plays the basic role in determining social structure and conditioning human actions? This, of course, is the great question of sociological and historical materialism versus idealism (or pluralism); and basic positions might be marked out as deriving from Marx, Durkheim or Weber. Was Ambedkar an idealist because he gave so much importance to the role of religion and ideas in human action?

In his essay on Russell, he says rather offhandedly, "The economic and philosophical outlook of a society are more intimately connected than is commonly supposed and chipped of its exaggeration, the Economic Interpretation of History holds true". At the other end of his life, he would seem to have moved towards idealism. When settling his accounts with Marx he lists all the basic theses of Marx, states that most of them have been disproved, and says flatly, "Nobody now accepts the economic interpretation of history as the only explanation of history". In The Buddha and His Dhamma he very apparently gives the clear priority to "mind" as determinant. Under "What He Accepted" in existing Indian philosophical themes, he includes "recognition of the mind as the centre of everything. Mind precedes things, dominates them, creates them. If mind is comprehended all things are comprehended. Mind is the leader of all its faculties. Mind is the chief of all its faculties. The very mind is made up of those faculties. The first thing to attend to is the culture of the mind". Does this mean that Ambedkar has moved from a form of economic materialism to idealism as the main force in history? Supporting this thesis is the fact that his life work concludes with his religious and spiritual concerns, and that much of his writing on Indian history emphasises in practice the ideal-ideological factors. For example, "Revolution and Counter-Revolution in Indian History," his most sweeping study of the Indian past, classifies its stages in religious terms: Brahmanism, Buddhism and Hinduism.

Similarly, his studies on caste emphasise the role of the ideological force of Brahmanism in the creation and maintenance of this most important structure of Indian society.

However, I would argue that we can best characterise Ambedkar's view as pluralistic. As I have noted (Omvedt, 1998), though he has an implicit and very significant sociological theory, he was not a trained sociologist or historian, and does not spend any time developing or explicitly stating his methodology. If he had done so, he would probably have said, as Max Weber did, that he was emphasising the role of ideas primarily as a corrective factor. Just as Weber spend much of his professional life in debate with Marxist methodology and socialist ideas, so Ambedkar did also.

Not only do all of his writings show a concern for logical, Ambedkar was seriously concerned to have a rigorous scientific method. Thus, his discussion of karma in The Buddha and His Dhamma links it to causality. Though he stresses "mind" as central, even in this, his final and important work, his orientation is very much towards the material world, as shall be seen.

Even in his rejection of Marx, Ambedkar — who was never one to use words sloppily — rejects the "economic interpretation" as the "only explanation"; he never denies the role of material factors and economic impulses as a necessary part of any overall historical and social explanation.

This would be Weber's position. Ambedkar's philosophy of history is consistent with a pluralistic explanation of history, though not of a purely materialistic one.

Ambedkar's Political Economy: Social Liberalism

Throughout his life, , liberty, equality and fraternity (community), summed up in "social justice," which defined Ambedkar's orientation. However, his specific economic thinking can be said to have gone through three major stages.

The first phase is represented by his writings of the 1920s, which include two major books — the Problem of the Rupee and The Evolution of Provincial Finance in British India — and a number of articles. Ambedkar was trained in classical economics (i.e. in the economics of the earlier twentieth century which was already moving into Keynesianism). These show him as a liberal economist, though with significant influence of Keynesian. He argued for a low rupee, though one that would, as he saw it, balance the interests of workers (wage-earners) with those of capitalists and other entrepreneurs.

His study of the effects of British policy in India cite some of the critiques of British rule, in particular condemning the ways in which the British government was running India in the interest of British manufacturers.

"While the land tax prevented the prosperity of agricultural industry the customs taxes hampered the manufactures of the country. There were internal customs and external customs, and both were equally injurious to trade and industry". His economic writings of the 1920s reflect this. His economic theory, it has been recently and convincingly argued, was a liberal one, with concerns for responsible government financing that would be welcomed by liberalisers today. He retained, of course, an important concern for the role of the state, but he certainly believed in the potential of the market and trade for increasing individual and national wealth. In a recent analysis of his economics, S. Ambirajan has argued, I think correctly, that this is the main period for characterising Ambedkar's writings, since after this he did not usually write as an economist, and that the "Buddhist economics" of his last period was very different from the "small is beautiful" form usually associated with that.

However, the 1930s did usher in a second phase of Ambedkar's economic thinking. By then he had become heavily involved in social movements not only of Dalits but also of workers and peasants generally, and with this he came into contact with Indian communists and in many ways came under the influence of Marxism. This never really left him. It was during this period that his weekly Janata was filled with articles urging the unity of "peasants and workers" against "capitalists and landlords"; that he made his famous Mahad statement characterising the enemies of Dalits as "capitalism and Brahmanism."

In many ways, his economic and political thinking of this phase can be characterised as a form of what feminists used to describe as "dual systems" theory. Just as early socialist feminists in the US talked of "capitalism and patriarchy" or Black radicals of "capitalism and racism," so Ambedkar began to focus on "capitalism and Brahmanism." These, in a famous speech at Mahad in 1938, he said, "There are in my view two enemies which the workers of this country have to deal with. The two enemies are Brahmanism and Capitalism...By Brahmanism I do not mean the power, privileges and interests of the Brahmans as a community.

By Brahmanism I mean the negation of the spirit of Liberty, Equality and Fraternity. In that sense it is rampant in all classes and is not confined to the Brahmans alone, though they have been the originators of it" (reported in Times of India, February 14, 1938) In taking these Brahmanism and capitalism as the focus of struggle, Ambedkar was inclined to accept a Marxist explanation of social-economic exploitation with only the necessity of adding an appreciation for the role of caste as an autonomous, exploitative and oppressive social structure. This meant, in effect, taking Marxism as the theory with which to analyse capitalism and supplementing it with an analysis of caste focusing on religion and ideology. This period climaxed with the proclamation of the need for "state socialism" in States and Minorities. It is the Ambedkar of States and Minorities who is usually cited today by various types of socialists and Marxists as justification for their own position.

However, a "dual systems" approach to a theory of society and history is ultimately inadequate, and Ambedkar moved away from it. In fact by the late-1950s it would seem that he was already coming to a rejection of a Marxist approach to economic issues — leave alone criticising its inadequacy on social issues. The tumultuous political events of the time, mirrored in Ambedkar's continuing lead in Dalit struggles for equality and liberation, led to his this third and final period, which I would describe in terms of a search for a "Buddhist economics." As Ambirajan has rightly pointed out, this is not the "Buddhist economics" of "small is beautiful"; rather, in his final essay on "Buddha or Karl Marx," Ambedkar returns to an appreciation of the role of the private accumulation of wealth (i.e. of the "market" in conventional economic terms) and gives us a reinterpretation of state, market, community through a Buddhist parable. The householder, striving to increase his wealth honestly and forthrightly, provides the foundation of the economy. The King, symbolising the state, has the necessary role of ensuring against the poverty of the most oppressed — poverty which would result in chaos or revolution if he did not intervene. Finally, the Bhikku Sangh represents community, the ideal communist society.

In spite of these shifting phases, though, there is no doubt that Ambedkar's political-economic philosophy was a form of liberalism. He was an individualist and a rationalist, returning always to the basic Enlightenment values linked to Indian tradition. To take one important statement, in elaborating the morality of modern society, he argues that while in "antique society" the moral code laid down by religion is based on utility, in "modern society" it is based on justice — which he later defines as equivalent to the values of liberty, equality and fraternity: "Utility as a criterion was appropriate to the Antique World in which, society being its end, the moral good was held to be something which has social utility. Justice as a criterion becomes appropriate to the Modern World in which the individual being the end, the moral good was held to be something which does justice to the individual".

But, if Ambedkar's political-economic philosophy can be characterised as liberalism, what kind of liberalism was it? In an important essay, Ralf Dahrendorf has discussed the three main types of liberalism, classical liberalism, social liberalism and neo-liberalism. In classical liberalism, the liberalism of Adam Smith, John Locke and others, the individual is posed at the centre of society; the state is justified only because it protects the life, liberty and property (or in terms of the American Declaration of Independence, the "life, liberty and the pursuit of happiness") of individuals.

But this form of liberalism landed historically and logically into contradictions: if the claim to property is justified, as Locke did, by the fact that individuals have put their labour into it, and if the existence and power of the state is justified as protecting "life, liberty and property" — then what can be said of a society characterised by the division between those who possess inherited property and those who do not? What of the fact of actually existing propertyless and impoverished individuals who do not even have the opportunity to acquire property by honest labour? How can the state or the right to property be justified in fact in terms of human rights and human values? Volumes have been written on this by liberal philosophers; but we can simply point out here that the contradiction between inherited inequality and human rights can only be resolved if we admit an important role of state intervention to establish equality — or if we seriously weaken the effort to establish and provide equal rights for all individuals. The first is the way of social liberalism (and there are many forms of this), the second of neo-liberalism.

Ambedkar was a social liberal in this sense, as is (to take one important example), India's Nobel Prize winner Amartya Sen. He focused on state policy, including state welfare policy, arguing for its role in reducing poverty and compensating for or correcting conditions of social injustice. Whether or not this led him towards socialism (and I don't think socialist liberalism is a contradiction in terms!) is a matter of our definition of socialism. Throughout most of his life Indian communists and socialists, including those in Congress, had identified socialism with state control, and it is not unlikely that Ambedkar was becoming disillusioned with this, that he was critical of Indian leftists not only for their attitude towards caste, but for their unwillingness to accept constitutional democracy. Towards the end of his life he was apparently seeing himself more as a "social democrat" than as a "state socialist."

This can be seen in his speech presenting the Constitution which he had played the major role in drafting. There he makes several important points which deserve to be emphasised today. For example, he quotes Thomas Jefferson to emphasise the inherent right to change the Constitution. Jefferson had argued that every generation had the right to create a new Constitution for itself if it felt necessary; to refuse this right would mean that "the earth belongs to the dead and not to the living." Ambedkar cites this, adding, "what Jefferson has said is not merely true, but is absolutely true." However, he says, there will never be a need to reject India's Constitution as such, because of its flexible scope for amendment.

Then he turns to a warning about the danger to democracy in India. Here he argues first that agitation and satyagrahas should be given up in favour of parliamentary methods of trying to achieve change (in other words, he would be very sympathetic with current concerns that hartals and bandhs have gone too far!). But this is followed by an even more important appeal: that the main dangers to the existence of India as a democratic nation come from inequality, from casteism, which is a negation of India's existence as a nation, and from the tendency to worship "mahatmas" and yield to authoritarianism. It is in regard to inequality, prefacing his famous warning that "those who suffer from inequality will blow up the structure of political democracy," that he makes his eloquent statement of social democratic values: "We must make our political democracy a social democracy as well. Political democracy cannot last unless there lies at the basis of it social democracy. What does social democracy mean? It means a way of life which recognises liberty, equality and fraternity as the principles of life".

Finally, he concludes with stating that the "down-trodden classes are tired of being governed, they are impatient to govern themselves. This urge for self-realisation in the down-trodden classes must not be allowed to develop into a class struggle or a class war....That would indeed be a day of disaster." Ambedkar profoundly believed that problems of inequality and exploitation could be resolved without recourse to class warfare ... And this led him to Buddhism.

Ambedkar's Religious Views: Towards "Navayana" Buddhism

It has become familiar by now to note that in leading millions of ex-Untouchables to Buddhism, Ambedkar was singlehandedly responsible for the revival of Buddhism as a mass religion in the land of its birth — roughly a millennium after its disappearance. This would itself be a considerable feat. What is usually not recognised, however, is that Ambedkar did not simply "revive" a traditional form of Buddhism; he also took up the task of reinterpreting and rejuvenating Buddhism as a religion for the contemporary world.

Ambedkar's concern for establishing Buddhism as the religion of Untouchables comes from two convictions. First he believed that religion, in the broadest sense of a transcendental morality, is necessary for ordered social existence, and from his belief that what was known as "Hinduism" (probably the term "Brahmanism" would be more appropriate) could not serve this purpose. Both themes were present from very early. His earliest essay on religion, "The Philosophy of Hinduism" already presents his condemnation of Brahmanism; from almost the beginning we can see his sharp awareness that Dalits needed a new religion. And, though there was a period in which he seemed to waver, when for instance he argued in his challenge Gandhi that Hinduism could be acceptable if "all the shastras and puranas were given up," the condition is so rigorous as to be unacceptable. Babasaheb was a born rebel against both the traditional forms of Brahmanic varnashrama dharma and the reconstructed Hinduism pioneered by Vivekananda and Gandhi from the 19th century onwards.

In The Buddha and His Dhamma, he not only tried to present Buddhism for the masses of ex-Untouchables who followed his lead, he also put forward what I have called a "liberation theology" of Buddhism. In one of his most important last essays, "Buddha and Karl Marx," Ambedkar had posed Buddhism against Marxism, seeing Buddhism as a solution to the problems of exploitation that Marxism posed. But this is not simply an attack on Marxism, it also works the other way also: Buddhism answers, according to Ambedkar, specifically "Marxist" questions, that is, its concern is not so much the problem of religious meaning as the problem of exploitation. Thus, Ambedkar's The Buddha and his Dhamma radically challenges some of the basic tenets of Buddhism as it has traditionally existed, whether in Theravada or Mahayana or Vajrayana forms.

This his clear from his introduction itself, which presents four basic problems that Ambedkar sees in Buddhism as it has been known: Ambedkar, first, rejects the traditional version of Siddhartha's Parivraja or "going forth", arguing that the story of being moved by the sight of a dead person, a sick person, and an old person was impossible to believe since such sights must have been known to anyone.

Second, he claims that the "four Aryan truths" — sorrow (dukh), the origin of sorrow, the cessation of sorrow, and the way to the cessation of sorrow — are not part of the original teaching of the Buddha. "This formula," he states flatly, "cuts at the root of Buddhism. If life is sorrow, death is sorrow and rebirth is sorrow, then there is an end of everything...The four Aryan Truths are a great stumbling block in the way of non-Buddhists accepting the gospel of Buddhism".

Third, he asserts a "a terrible contradiction" between the doctrines of karma and rebirth, and the Buddha's denial of the existence of the soul. Finally, he claims, finally, that the Bhikku can only be the "hope of Buddhism" if he is a social servant and not a "perfect man." Ambedkar's project in The Buddha and His Dhamma is to resolve these problems.

First, in regard to the Parivraja, he argues that Siddhartha left his home to prevent a war between his Sakya clan and the Koliyas over water. The cause is social, not religious. And, after his initial wandering, on hearing that the Koliyas and Sakyas have after all made peace, Gautam determines to continue his renunciation and search, because "The problem of war is a problem of conflict. It is only part of a larger problem. This conflict is going on not only between Kings and nations but between nobles and Brahmans, between householders, between [friends and family members]...The conflict between nations is occasional. But the conflict between classes is constant and perpetual. It is this which is the root of all suffering in the world. I have to find a solution to this problem of social conflict".

Second, in regard to the doctrine of dukkha, sorrow or suffering, Ambedkar argues it is not a necessary characteristic of the existing world, and in fact the purpose of Buddhism is to end suffering in this world. [Here he links this with a denial that Buddhism is pessimistic]. As he has the Buddha say in his first sermon, "No doubt my Dhamma recognises the existence of suffering but forget not that it also lays equal stress on the removal of suffering. My Dhamma has in it both hope and purpose. Its purpose is to remove Avijja, by which I mean ignorance of the existence of suffering. There is hope in it because it shows the way to put an end to human suffering." And in even stronger words, the five Parivrajakas greet this first sermon by saying, "never in the history of the world has salvation been conceived as the blessing of happiness to be attained by man in this life and on this earth by righteousness born out of his own efforts!". Here, and throughout The Buddha and His Dhamma, Ambedkar makes very strong assertions that Buddhism is a religion (or a "dhamma") that can resolve the problems of social and natural suffering.

Third, he tries to resolve the contradiction between rebirth and the absence of a soul by interpreting karma in a socio-biological sense. The Hindu idea of karma is based on the soul and includes transmigration of soul; since Buddhism asserts that there is no soul, its idea of karma must be radically different. There is thus a similarity in words but a radical difference in meaning. Ambedkar interprets this to argue that the Buddhist conception involves rebirth, but not "transmigration", and the difference is that transmigration asserts a non-material soul which is the subject of transmigration and to which karma clings, while rebirth can be interpreted in a biological and materialistic form. Ambedkar asserts that the Buddha's whole discussion of the idea was in the context of biological-genetic inheritance and environment; that the Buddha did assert some genetic heredity but believed that environmental influence was more. Karma — or Kamma — basically refers to "causation" and more specifically to laws (niyamma) governing the social and moral order.

"The theory of the law of Kamma does not necessarily involve the conception that the effect of the Kamma recoils on the doer of it and there is nothing more to be thought about it....Individuals come and individuals go. But the moral order of the universe remains and so also the law of Kamma which sustains it'.

The fourth major innovation in Ambedkar's Buddhism was to treat the Bhikku Sangh as an organisation for social service. The fact that the Sangha was not acting so, in his experience, was to him a major block to accepting any of the already existing forms of Buddhism. (His introduction expresses his feeling that the journal of the Mahabodhi society, at that time the major organ propagating a revived Buddhism in India, was simply "dull reading". Sangharakshata's account in his study of Ambedkar and Buddhism mentions another important fact; though founded by the great Sri Lanka Buddhist Anagarika Dhammapala, the Mahabodhi society in India was dominated by Brahmans; specifically at the time of Ambedkar's conversion, Shyam Prasad Mukherjee was its chairperson! He also records the fact that at the time of conversion, Ambedkar was reluctant to take the third of the "three refuges", i.e. to accept the authority of the Sangha, and that in effect he rejected the distinction between bhikku and layman by himself administering the oath of conversion to the lakhs of Dalits in attendance).

The Social Role of Buddhism

It can be argued that Ambedkar's Buddhism, often called Navayana Buddhism, or the "Fourth Way" in contrast to the three traditional ways of Hinayana, Mahayana and Vajrayana, is based on a very important sociological understanding. Ambedkar's exploration of what religion is and what it should be began quite early; even before he came to Buddhism he was arguing that. By the time of his choice of Buddhism he was distinguishing Buddhist dhamma from religion itself, that is from Christianity, Islam, Hinduism or whatever else is classified as "religion." His argument can be upheld if we take almost all western-biased dictionary definition of religion as including a "faith in god"; clearly Buddhism which rejects notions of god and the soul, and stresses rationality and experimentation, was quite different.

If we define religion in a Durkheimian way — which has now influenced the entire sociology of religion — Buddhism would be called a religion; and it is noteworthy that Ambedkar insists that Dhamma is not only morality, but "sacred" morality. It would appear that he had read Durkheim, but thought of him as an anthropologist rather than a sociologist. Ambedkar argues that Dhamma performs the same functions for society that other "religions" do, that though there are fundamental differences, society needs Dhamma (or the moral base of religion):

> "Society has to choose one of three alternatives. Society may choose not to have any Dhamma as an instrument of Government...This means Society chooses the road to anarchy. Secondly, Society may choose the police, i.e. the dictatorship as an instrument of Government. Thirdly, Society may choose Dhamma plus the Magistrate wherever people fail to observe the Dhamma. In anarchy and dictatorship liberty is lost. Only in the third liberty survives. Those who want liberty must therefore have Dhamma".

And his summing up of the difference between religion and Dhamma is indeed an echo of Marx: "The purpose of Religion is to explain the origin of the world. The purpose of Dhamma is to reconstruct the world". This is very clearly an echo of Marx and likely consciously so; for Ambedkar had rephrased Marx's point as "The function of philosophy is to reconstruct the world and not to waste its time in explaining the origin of the world" — in his last major essay, "Buddha or Karl Marx." It was one of the four points he considered the "residue of fire" that remained of Marx.

Clearly, Ambedkar's last and culminating project was to ask Marxist questions, but give Buddhist answers.

Thus, while he has earlier and elsewhere used "religion" generally to include Buddhism, and within that distinguish Buddhism from other religions, in his final formulation he identifies Buddhist Dhamma as something that is basically other than religion. Religion is a philosophy that includes, in the language of some sociologists of religion, a "canopy of meaning" that includes theses about the origin of the universe, humans, usually their creator and so forth. It requires faith. In contrast, Buddhism works by reason, and the Dhamma is primarily morality, though a sacred morality. According to Ambedkar the result of this is that for religions (or non-Buddhist religions, depending on how the term is used), morality is only a secondary offshoot, "it is a wagon attached to it...attached and detached as the occasion requires"). Dhamma is pure morality, but since it is sacred, i.e. placed beyond the ability of individuals to change it, it can serve the function of regulating the actions of the socially "strong" individuals who would otherwise override the claims of the "best" (3xx).

Ambedkar's stress on rationalism in Buddhism is also strong. To him, the person who accepts Buddhism does so as a free individual convinced that this is the way; in fact The Buddha and His Dhamma says nothing of the "three refuges," the main "statement of faith" of the Buddhist believer. Ambedkar takes it upon himself to give his own interpretation of Buddhism in the way of almost any charismatic religious leader. (Perhaps he was similar in this sense to Gandhi, who felt free to claim that every value he approved of was in Hinduism). Ambedkar does give us a rationale for this. In arguing for Buddha's own rationalism, in stating that any contrary interpretation that seems to be in the texts was a Brahmanical insertion, he offers a simple methodology for understanding them: "There is, however one test which is available. If there is anything which could be said with confidence it is: He was nothing if not rational, if not logical. Anything therefore which is rational and logical, other things being equal, may be taken to be the word of the Buddha".

Would Ambedkar's Buddhism be acceptable to other Buddhist believers? That is a question for all of them to answer! Few religious people are willing, initially, to accept a fundamentally new "path" in their faith—which is what Navayana Buddhism is. Nevertheless it continues to guide the aspirations of millions of ex-Untouchables and other converts, and it has been hailed by many, for instance Christopher Queen, as an example of "engaged Buddhism" which has correlates in many other Buddhist countries.

The Mahar Movement's Military Component

Dr. Bhimrao Ramji Ambedkar, is famous for being "the most highly educated Untouchable in India." His education, encouraged and financed largely by the Gaikwad of Baroda, led to his role as the Untouchable's chief spokesman, the founder of a political party for Untouchables, and the moving spirit behind organisations, schools, and colleges established for their uplift. One of Ambedkar's final acts was the initiation of a Buddhist conversion movement that ultimately attracted more than 3 million Untouchable adherents.

This part of Ambedkar's story is well-known. However, his family's military service in the British Raj is not widely acknowledged for creating an environment that laid the foundation for his later success. Eleanor Zelliot, an expert on Dr. Ambedkar and the Mahar movement, maintains, "The hundred year period of Mahar recruitment into British armies may well have been the single most important factor, aside from economic reasons, in producing the Mahar movement." This article examines the importance of military service in improving the social status of Ambedkar's caste, the Mahars of Maharashtra. The focus is on their relationship with the British.

The Mahars benefited from their participation in the British Army in a number of ways. First, military service became "a significant part of caste élan and mythology." The first section provides the historical evidence they use to establish their credentials as a caste with martial traditions. The paper's second section details the advantages, especially education, that accrued from military service and discusses their access to the government that otherwise was unavailable to Untouchables. The final section discusses the British decision to recruit only "martial races," in which the Mahars were not included, for the British Indian Army and the Mahars' efforts to gain reinstatement in the Army. The article does not focus exclusively on Dr. Ambedkar, but uses him as a point of reference for many of the examples given.

Early Military Participation

Eleanor Zelliot explains that the British gave Mahars the opportunity to seek different occupations from their traditional role as a village servant. She explains that before the arrival of the British, Mahars had no special skill or craft, but performed necessary duties for the village as watchmen, wall-menders, street-sweepers, removers of cattle carcasses, caretakers of the burning ground, servants of any passing governmental official.... Mahar service was essential for the village; his status was low, his work menial, but his place was secure. With the coming of the British and the spread of new ways of administration and communication, the Mahar place in the village grew less important.

Military service provided Mahars with the opportunity to move beyond their traditional social position in the village. In fact, the Mahar tradition of being in armies precedes the British Raj.

The recorded history of the Mahars' military achievements dates back to Shivaji's Army in the 1600s. Cynthia Enloe, a noted sociologist who has written extensively on ethnic-military relationships, states, "The best of all militaries in the eyes of a state elite is one in which the most competent soldiers are also the most politically reliable, because they have the greatest stake in the continuation of the current system." The Mahars met this condition according to descriptions of their loyalty. Colonel V. Longer, author of *Forefront Forever: The History of the Mahar Regiment*, states:

> There were a number of useful functions which the Mahars performed. Their Argus eye; their daring tenacity and determination; their faithfulness, loyalty and honesty; their courage and candour, were inestimable qualities which were always held in respect and were for ever utilised to advantage by the village .... In course of time, their voice carried great weight when there were disputes over property as their evidence was considered most accurate, intimate, and trustworthy.

This sense of loyalty and trustworthiness led Shivaji to include Mahars as a vital component of his army.

Shivaji, leader of the Maratha nation, fought for a Hindu Empire, but using Untouchables did not bother him. He "found the Mahars useful, for the wily Maratha chief realised that the best way of obtaining the maximum results was to mix up various castes in his garrison forces." He used the Mahars "to watch the jungles at the foot of the hill forts, act as scouts and [they] kept the forts supplied with wood and fodder." This was the first exposure of the Mahars to an organised army that provided its soldiers with steady pay and benefits. After Shivaji's death, Mahar units continued to serve his descendants throughout the 1700s. Their experience with Shivaji and others encouraged them to seek similar employment as sepoys of the British East India Company.

Ardythe Basham, in her detailed examination of the Mahars and the military, found the perceived early martial history to be an important part of Mahar identity. She concludes, "Whether or not these incidents are historically true, they are widely accepted by the Mahars as part of their tradition, and now form part of the official history of [today's] Mahar Regiment." The Mahars have often used this martial identity, rooted in the 1600s, to legitimate their continued presence in the military.

Mahars began their service with the British in the 1750s. Stephen P. Cohen, an expert on the Indian Army, discusses the importance of Mahars in the Bombay Army in his seminal work, *The Indian Army: Contribution to the Development of a Nation*. He writes that Mahars were a sizeable portion of the armies of the Mahratta chieftain Shivaji, served as hereditary local policeman, and were thus a "natural" martial class. Heavily recruited in the premutiny years, the Mahars constituted a fifth to a quarter of the entire Bombay Army.

In addition to the size of the Mahar contingent, they were also praised for their conduct as soldiers. The Mahars rewarded the British with the same loyalty that Shivaji had enjoyed.

The Bombay Army fought in several battles, and in most, the Mahars were recognised for their skills. Longer proclaims:

> Much praise was showered on the Mahar Sepoys of the Bombay Army who endured the rigours of difficult marches when rations were low and disease was high among men and animals. Whether they were charging ahead or were besieged or taken prisoner-of-war, whether they were storming fortresses or making

> tactical withdrawals, they always stood steadfast by their officers and comrades, never letting down the honour of their Regiments.

The recorded history of their exploits, especially prior to the mutiny of 1857, supports this effusive adoration. Basham located evidence of Mahar participation in the Second and "Third Anglo-Maratha War, the Second Anglo-Sikh War and the Second Afghan War." The Mahars' exploits in these conflicts form an important part of their military lore.

The Mahar participation in the battle of Koregaon on 1 January 1818 is the most famous, and also the best documented, action involving Mahar soldiers. This battle gave the British the advantage in the Third Anglo-Maratha War. The successful defence of Koregaon by a small force of 500 men ... under the command of Capt. F. F. Staunton [who] fought without rest or respite, food or water continuously for twelve hours against a large force of 20,000 Horse and 8,000 Infantry of [Maratha Leader] Peshwa Baji Rao II who was threatening the British garrisons at Kirkee and Poona.

Mahars dominated Staunton's unit. The Peshwa's troops inexplicably withdrew that evening, despite their overwhelming numbers, giving the British an important victory. The men of the 2/1st Regiment Bombay Native Infantry, including many Mahars, who fought in this battle, were honoured for their bravery. The official report to the British Resident at Poona recalls the "heroic valour and enduring fortitude" of the soldiers, the "disciplined intrepidity" and "devoted courage and admirable consistency" of their actions. Further, the action is commemorated by a monument, with the names of twenty-two Mahars killed there, erected at the site of the battle and by a medal issued in 1851. Today, the monument still "serves as a focal point of Mahar heroism." Similar anecdotes are recorded in the written histories of the Mahar Regiment and Bombay Army. All demonstrate that most Mahars soldiers were dedicated and courageous.

In addition to Army units on land, the Mahars formed a vital component of the Bombay Army's Marine Battalion. This unit's history is well documented and provides numerous examples of Mahar actions, including several acts of bravery by Mahars in the battalion. In September 1810, during the Second Maratha War, several Mahars proved their loyalty when captured by the French

Navy. The French tried to induce their prisoners to enter their own service, a practice which enjoyed some success with Irish, Madrassi and Bengali troops. On this occasion, the Bombay sepoys [soldiers] were shown the captured Bengal and Madras Sepoys dressed in French uniforms and enjoying considerable privileges and luxuries, whereupon the Bombay Detachment started abusing them as being dead to all shame that they could forget the oath and desert their colours.

The upshot was that they were very roughly treated and some were severely wounded. To the seventeen survivors who reached Bombay a special medal was given and of this number twelve were Mahars.

This is just one of many cases where Mahars distinguished themselves as a part of the Marine Battalion and is another part of the martial history that the Mahars used to legitimise their important role in the British Indian Army. But, in the wake of the 1857 mutiny and threats from Russia, the British re-examined their recruitment policies. The Mahars were a casualty of this new thinking.

The Mahars Delistment

Despite the Mahars' long martial history, the British ceased recruiting them in 1893. The Bombay and the other Presidency Armies were re-evaluated following the 1857 mutiny. The Peel Commission first examined class composition of the armies in 1858. One report to the Commission "emphasised that 'we cannot practically ignore it (the caste system), so long as the natives socially maintain it.'" This led to the discrimination against the Mahars and other low-caste groups as well as some Brahman castes which were considered unreliable.

General Lord Roberts, while not originating the concept of martial races, was instrumental in implementing a strategy of building "class regiments." Recruiting policies were rewritten, and the Bombay Army "was notified that the Mahars, together with a number of other classes of the Bombay Army, would no longer be recruited to the Army." Lord Roberts recorded his rational in his autobiography, *Forty-One Years in India*. He writes:

> I have no doubt whatever of the fighting powers of our best Indian troops; I have a thorough belief in,

> and admiration for, Gurkhas, Sikhs, Dogras, Rajputs, Jats and, selected Muslims; I thoroughly appreciate their soldierly qualities; brigaded with British troops, I would be proud to lead them against any European enemy.

Roberts thought that the first step to making the Indian Army was "to substitute men of the more warlike and hardy races for the Hindustani sepoys of Bengal, the Tamils and Telagus of Madras, and the so-called Mahrattas of Bombay." He was convinced that

In the British Army the superiority of one regiment over another is mainly a matter of training; the same courage and military instinct are inherent in English, Scotch, and Irish alike, but no comparison can be made between the martial value of a regiment recruited amongst the Gurkhas of Nepal or the warlike races of Northern India, and of one recruited from the effeminate peoples of the south.

The Mahars believed that their martial history demonstrated their abilities as warriors, but the British had made their decision. Mahars could only enlist as bandsmen or clerks. This would not provide the same opportunities for promotion, and allow little change in their social status. As expected, the Mahars felt the British had betrayed them after over 100 years of loyal service to the British Raj.

Throughout India, there was controversy about which groups should remain in the Army. The Mahars had support from some British soldiers, including three commanders who recommended their continued service. The commander of the 2nd Grenadiers argued that:

> 'The Parwari [Mahar] is of far better fighting material than the Deccani Muslim," and suggested that the Marine Battalion might be made a class regiment of Parwaries. The commanding officer of the 9th Bombay Infantry thought that a regiment of Parwaries, especially from the Deccan, would "give a very good account of itself."

The Commanding officer of the 19th Bombay Infantry stated that:

> "They are possessed of as much soldierly quality as many castes of whom much higher opinions are entertained."

However, their assistance was not enough to overcome the sentiments of Lord Roberts and other senior officers of the British Indian Army.

Longer provides an excellent commentary on the impact of the decision on the Mahars. He writes:

> The excellent system with its cosmopolitan composition, which had worked out over the years, was dismantled and destroyed. The Mahars, who had proudly carried the Colours of various Regiments of the Bombay Army, were crestfallen and heartbroken. For years they had provided abundant evidence of their courage, resolution, perseverance, constancy, and fidelity. When they bade farewell to arms there were eight Subedar-Majors, 62 Subedars, 34 Jemadars, and a host of Non-Commissioned Officers and Sepoys of the Mahar community who had served with distinction in the Bombay Army.

The Mahars would continue to fight for the right to re-enlist in the Indian Army. They were loath to lose the benefits that the military provided. Furthermore, the education provided to the soldiers had created an educated cadre that would transfer their skills into political action. However, there were few Mahars left in the Army by the beginning of World War I.

Benefits of Military Service

Eleanor Zelliot notes that the "emergence of Mahar leaders and a new spirit of militancy in the 19th century was due in large measure to the influence of education acquired in the military." The result was that:

> During the 19th and 20th centuries, a substantial number of Mahars removed themselves from their traditional village servant role. The establishment of British rule in Bombay Presidency provided Mahars with the opportunity for service in the army, employment in cotton mills, ammunition factories, railroads, dockyards, construction work, and as servants in British homes. The 1921 Census records that only 13.5 per cent of the Mahar working force of nearly 300,000 were employed in their traditional

occupation even though most Mahars maintained strong ties with their ancestorial village.

The Mahars' ability to work among the British exposed them to Western ways, and helped them to realise that their status as Untouchables did not keep them from working in successful and satisfying occupations. They aggressively used the advantages provided by their relationship with the British.

Military service provided important benefits to its soldiers. The benefits include "pay and pensions, access to education and/ or specialised training, preferential access to employment, enhanced social status, and personal satisfaction." For the Mahars, the access to education and increased social status was the most important benefits. The best example of their results was Dr. Ambedkar. Zelliot writes that Ambedkar's experiences were "free from the traditional village role, his early life was spent among educated ex-army men, imbued with the pride of soldiers and acquainted with a more sophisticated Hinduism than that found in the village." In fact, Ambedkar extends much of the credit for the start of the movement to improve the Untouchables' place in society to contact with the British Army. He maintained:

> Until the advent of the British, the Untouchables were content to remain Untouchables .... In the army of the East India Company there prevailed the system of compulsory education for Indian soldiers and their children, both male and female. The education received by the Untouchables in the army ... gave them a new vision and a new value. They became conscious that the low esteem in which they had been held was not an inescapable destiny but was a stigma imposed on their personality by the cunning contrivances of the priest. They felt the shame of it as they ever did before and were determined to get rid of it.

It is indisputable that this access to education was helpful to Ambedkar, and therefore, to all of India's Untouchable communities.

Ambedkar's family had extensive links to the military. Additionally, his mother's "father and her six uncles were all Subedar Majors in the Army," the highest rank that Indians could hold. Ambedkar's father also was a Subhedar Major and a full-fledged teacher trained at the Normal School then established by Government for turning out teachers to impart education that was then compulsory for the children as well as both male and female relations of the military servants. For fourteen years Ramji Sakpal served as Headmaster in the military school.

Undoubtedly, the accomplishments of this family were exceptional. Nonetheless, the availability of education had a positive effect on all members of Mahars in the military, including women. Consequently, Basham concludes, "The loss of this education option with the loss of their right of enlistment was therefore a real blow, not merely the loss of a theoretical benefit which few actually received." The quality of life for soldiers and their families suffered because of the loss of educational opportunities available through participation in the military.

Mahars joined the military with the intent of improving their social status. They were successful in this regard. As Basham explains:

> Within the closed circle of the regiment, caste prejudice was, if not actually absent, at least officially discouraged. According to army regulations no distinction was made between soldiers on the basis of their caste or community .... Mahar officers were able to command men of other castes apparently without difficulty.

After growing up in this environment of equality it was a shock for the Untouchables to travel and live in situations away from the military cantonments.

Ambedkar's biographer, Dhananjay Keer, writes of young Ambedkar's shock the first time he travelled outside the military environment while he was in school. He and his brother were travelling to meet his father in a distant village. At the railway station, they hired a bullock cart to take them to the village, but hardly had the cart gone a few yards when the god-fearing touchable Hindu cartman, to his wrath, came to know that the well-dressed boys in his cart were the accursed Untouchables! In a fit of rage he threw them out on the road as one overturns the dust bins; for he felt they had polluted his wooden cart and destroyed the purity of his domestic animals!

This was Ambedkar's first experience that forced him to confront his status as an Untouchable. Life in the military cantonment had sheltered him from the prejudice and discrimination for the early part of his life.

After retirement, there was a period of adjustment for Mahars who lived outside the cantonment. Basham concludes:

As nearly as can be deduced from rather limited information, it would seem that while actually in the army, or after retired or taking other employment, while in contact with British employers and officials, the Mahar soldier was not treated in any way differently from a soldier of higher caste. Once retired and living in his native village, a Mahar soldier, although he might have a relatively high status among the Mahar community and even among caste Hindus, would nevertheless once again have to accept his untouchable status.

The important point is, even after retirement, Mahars with a military background still had access to the British government. The retired military officers were an effective lobby for Mahar rights.

Retired officers also created a group of political leaders with access to the Indian government. This was especially true near military cantonments in Poona, Satara and Ahmednagar. Basham relates an incident where Mahar children were not being offered equal educational opportunities. Local caste Hindus and low-level British education officials refused the Mahar demands for Mahar boys to be integrated into classes with caste-Hindu boys.

The dispute was resolved in favour of the Mahars. Basham argues that this demonstrates they were seeking not just education for their sons, although this was obviously important, but also an improvement in their social status. The fact that many of these parents were retired officers, and therefore could legitimately make a claim on the attention to government officials, indicates the value of military service in this respect.

Clearly, the type of access available to the soldiers, active or retired, was unavailable to most Untouchables.

All the benefits the Mahars received were the result of their ability to develop a link with the British. This helped them overcome the obstacles erected by the Hindu social system. Zelliot observes:

> It was their entry into the British army which proved significant for the subsequent history of the Mahar movement. It is important to gauge this significance. It consists not in any automatic elevation in the social hierarchy through military service, which indeed is ruled out in a hierarchical system governed by considerations of ascriptive status and ritual purity. It rather consists in the fact that military service at such an early date exposed them to British institutions much before the dissemination of western culture took place on a large scale.

Such an exposure socialised them sufficiently early to the new political order so that when new opportunities and alternatives became available, they were found prepared to use them more effectively than those groups which did not have this opportunity. Following the delistment of 1893, the Mahars would need all the access and knowledge they had gained to overcome the impact of being refused service in the Army.

The Fight For Re-enlistment

The Mahars did not give up their positions in the Army easily. The British decision of Mahar "delistment in 1893 had been a severe blow to them as a community, not only threatening their economic status, but also (in their view) giving official sanction to caste Hindu discrimination against them." Overcoming both of these threats was the focus of two different efforts to petition the Government of India to reconsider its decision between 1894 and the start of the first World War.

The Mahars used two different strategies to influence the government; with both they tried to regain enlistment privileges in the army and an improved social status. Zelliot maintains that these efforts "illustrate the importance of army service to the Mahars. This was clearly the beginning of their efforts to induce government to intervene on their behalf, and their questioning of their traditional inferior status." In both instances, the movement was led by educated, former military officers.

The first organised attempt was in April 1895. Some of the details of the petition drive presented by Zelliot and Basham are speculative. Basham, who has completed the most recent study, states it was originally presented to the Viceroy, but was later returned for resubmission through the Bombay Government. It appears that the petition was submitted by Gopal Baba Walangkar, a retired military officer, on behalf of the Anarya Doshpariharak Mandali, the non-Aryan committee for the rightings of wrongs, an Untouchable organisation. Dr. Ambedkar, following the death of his father, found a copy of the petition in his papers. Ambedkar "believed that his father had obtained the assistance of Justice M. B. Ranade in preparing the petition." The petition compares Mahar actions to those of the higher castes and requests reinstatement in the military.

The petition's pleas were simple. The Mahars believed that, in 1859, the Government had declared that the castes who fought loyally for the British were to be given due preference for military enlistment. Therefore, they demanded:

> In view of that promise, Government should employ in civil, military and police department without any discrimination these faithful and honest persons. They should also be given education and proper opportunity for suitable posts in the department.

The case they presented for reinstatement was more complicated than their demands. Much of their argument attempts to demonstrate that their identification as Untouchables was a mistake.

The 1895 petition argues that the Mahars as a group who are actually of the Kshatriya caste. This represents the Mahars attempt to change their position in the caste structure by "Sanskritisation." The petition states:

> Our ancestors were Kshatriya. In about the year 1396 there was a great famine for about 12 years which was called Durhavedi famine. That time our ancestors survived by eating whatever they could find. Therefore, they were considered low case under the Peshwa rule.

It continues by attacking the legitimacy of the higher castes. It claims, "The so-called high caste and pure people's ancestors were as degraded as our people and were used [sic] to eat flesh of cow and beef. They wrote their own religious scriptures."

Finally, the petition provides a "creation myth" about the high castes. It maintains:

> The high caste people of the South are progeny of Australian Semitic Anaryas and African Negroes whereas the high caste people from North are mixture of several castes .... Several castes of foreign origin became high caste Hindus by giving up beef-eating.

The Chitpavan Brahmins of Konkan came from the Jewish race. They fled from Africa for fear of their lives by the invaders and their ship was wrecked nearby Malabar coast. Their children and women drown and died in the sea. Those men who survived, married the native low caste women.... When they became rulers, they called themselves Brahmins.

The document's tenor shows the importance of military service to the Mahars and the use of Sanskritisation tactics to show they were at least equal to the alleged high castes.

This campaign was unsuccessful. The Mahars were unaware of the debate "over recruitment policy or the acceptance of Lord Roberts views on martial races" which was the prime component in the British decision. However, Basham shows "the government of India took the petition seriously enough to request information about the Koregaon monument from the government of Bombay (presumably to verify the petitioners' claims).

Eighteen months after the initial submission of the petition, the Indian government replied that it was "unable to rescind the orders which have been issued regarding the castes to be admitted to the Bombay Army." Shortly after the turn of the century, a second attempt was organised.

The second major petition was submitted to the government three times between 1904 and 1910. The document's "signatories included forty-two military pensioners" including Dr. Ambedkar's father. Basham's research found that "several of the signatories had also written letters to newspapers or had signed at least one other petition, suggesting a long-term commitment and a willingness to agitate for change." This petition had a broader base of support than the one in 1895.

This campaign was more sophisticated than the first. The spokesman, Shivram Janba Kamble, spoke English (Walangkar could not). More importantly, the petition's "appeal for consideration was not on the basis of the Mahars' having been demoted from Kshatriyahood, but on the grounds of former service, English justice and human worth." This pragmatic approach attracted greater support than the earlier petition, and used arguments that were later refined by Dr. Ambedkar. In fact, Ambedkar took over leadership of the Mahars from Kamble.

The 1910 petition was more polite and less argumentative than the 1895 petition. The document states, "We do not aspire to high political privileges and positions, since we are not educationally qualified for them, but humbly seek employment in the lowest grades of the Public Service, in the ranks of Police Sepoys and of soldiers in the Indian Army." It continued:

> We are making no new demands; we do not claim employment in services in which we have not been engaged before. Indeed, some few of our people do still hold positions in the Police Force, and have acquitted themselves most honourably. So also have our people been employed in the Indian Army from the very commencement of the British Raj in our country, and they have risen to the highest positions by their valour and good conduct.

Despite the reasoned arguments, this petition demands, like the first, were denied. The manpower demands of World War I had a greater effect, and beginning in 1914 Mahars, again, were recruited into the Army and given their own Regiment, the 111 Mahars. The Regiment's three battalions "were formed the towards the end of the war, but they did not see action and their martial qualities were untested." Shortly after the war, the Regiment was disbanded by the British "on the excuse of the economy."

More important, however, is that the petition drives provided an organisation for Dr. Ambedkar to use after the war to improve the social status of Untouchables. Basham correctly concludes:

> Military service had been a significant factor for the Mahars in two respects. Education and skills acquired through military service created a class of community leaders, and the wish to retain the social and economic benefits derived from military service was a powerful

> incentive to organise behind these leaders and work for a common goal. A high level of organisation and political activity in the Mahar community by the 1940s was therefore at least in part a consequence of their military past.

The long association with the military gave Mahars an issue to organise around and the movement then worked to achieve more substantial achievements than just military service.

Conclusion

The 120 years of service in the British military gave the Mahars excellent skills. Basham concludes:

> Mahar soldiers were able to establish a link with the most powerful institution in India — the British Raj — and in some instances to use that link to bypass local authorities. Military service was also a way to sever the ties of village customary law which maintained the inferior status of the Mahars. Other forms of employment could take the Mahar out of the village, but none offered long-term financial security in the form of pensions.

This case study shows how military service has assisted the Mahars to fight the stigma of untouchability. Their positive experiences fighting with Shivaji encouraged them to seek similar opportunities from the British. It is clear, that in their service they received their most tangible benefits. Before delistment, Mahars in the Bombay Army received a steady wage, housing, and education. With this, many were able to retire with a pension, which, often, eliminated the need to return to the traditional Mahar occupations following their military service. These obvious benefits were eliminated following the 1893 decision.

However, military service still influenced Mahar life following delistment. As Basham argues:

> If the army system of education had produced no effects for the Mahars other than to provide an appropriate environment for Ambedkar's early life (since his father took a very strong interest in encouraging his sons' education) this in itself would be a significant impact on the Mahar community.

Furthermore, the petition drives provided political organisations to press for overcoming the stigma of Untouchability. There were other benefits that were accrued, even if their requests for reinstatement were refused until the beginning of the war. Kamble's work in Poona that formed the base for Ambedkar's later political movements is the best example of this. Therefore, even after military service was taken away from the Mahars, the traditions and accrued benefits continued to be an advantage to this Untouchable community.

Epilogue

A Mahar Regiment was reformed in 1945 and has existed ever since. The ceremonial Colonel of the Regiment is K. V. Krishna Rao, former Chief-of-Staff of the Indian Army and current Governor of Jammu-Kashmir. The preface of the Regimental History states:

> Militarily, the Mahars faced the vicissitudes of fortune, but once the Mahar Regiment was reborn in 1945, it came into its own after India became free .... A three-battalion [one class] Regiment blossomed into a eighteen-battalion Regiment with men from all classes and communities of the country fused together to form a rich and radiant amalgam.

The Regiment has taken part in all of India's major military operations since 1947. Just as the Mahars have survived and prospered, so has the Mahars' military legacy.

Reservations and Development of the Scheduled Castes and Scheduled Tribes

The Depressed Classes, as the SC and ST Dalits were known during their long struggles were demanding not for a token foothold, but a formal Representation in the Administration, due Presence in the Bureaucracy, full Participation in the Govt. and for their Share in the Governance of the Country. They were ably led by the well learned indomitable Baba Saheb Dr. Ambedkar. It is because of Dr. Ambedkar's Struggles, even in the face of severe threats to his life and that of his followers, and in spite of the presence of strong oppositions to his demands and scheme of thinking for the good of the Country, wellbeing of the People including the Dalits, and better future of the Society including his own Dalit Sections that we find the SCs and STs present here and there, at times noticeably even if not prominently, in the visible segments of the Society, in the notable layers of the Bureaucracy, and in important places in the Govt., like the Central Secretariat of the Govt. of India at Delhi.

The presence of some SCs and STs in Services, including the Central Secretariat at Delhi is a fact, even though the SC and ST Communities have not yet really got their Dues, or a real and true Share of Power or Responsible Part in the Governance of the Country. Even this small presence, has now become possible, only because of Dr. Ambedkar's Statesmanship Vision Foresight, and his Insistence for Preserving and Continuing in Free India, if not more, at least the moth-eaten Reservations for the Depressed Classes, to which he was forced to agree by Gandhi in 1932, and entered into a formal Pact, a written and signed Solemn Agreement with the caste Hindu leaders, on behalf of the Depressed Classes. It is this Agreement, the Poona Pact which formed the basis of the Govt. of India Act 1935, and the Foundations of our Constitution. And it is these, and particularly because of Dr. Ambedkar and his Reservations — that while the Anglo-Indians, Other Christians, Muslims, Parsis, etc. of the British India, have either faded or vanished from the Central Secretariat, the then rare SCs and STs have gained some presence in Free Independent India, the caste Hindu dominated India, as many Minority and Backward Class Leaders of those days including Dr. Ambedkar also, rightly predicted and feared. Even this small presence of SCs and STs in the Central Secretariat today, is not a small achievement. And this, in short, is what the Policy of Reservation has achieved.

Many poor Backward Castes with Social Conditions, Economic and Political Standards, comparable or at times at least in some ways bad if not worse than that of the SCs, who in the early days of Independence of the Country refused and fought bitterly against any proposal or suggestion or even an idea to include the names of their Castes into the list of SCs, when the Govts. in the States were considering and enumerating various Castes to compile and declare the Lists of the Scheduled Castes for the States, have come around and made a complete about turn, clamouring for their respective individual Castes to be included in the List of Scheduled

Castes. They were primarily interested in getting the advantages of Reservations and Special Development Programmes for the SCs and STs, particularly in the spheres of good Education, especially Professional and University Education, Employment and Promotions in Services, Financial Assistances for Education and Development, such as the Grant of Scholarships Fellowships Freeships Exemptions from Payment of tuition/hostel/mess/ examination Fees and to start Business/setup Shops/Factories/ Industries, etc. Grants for Studies Abroad, Admissions to General or Special Students' Hostels, allotments of Surplus Agricultural and even Fallow or Waste Lands, Building Sites, Houses or Flats and Industrial Plots/Sheds, Political Representations, etc. through the Schemes of various Reservations and Development Programmes meant for the SCs and STs.

The demand by the Other Backward Classes and also many others, and their claim to be declared as a SC, or at times at least as a ST, even by hook or crook was going on silently almost all the times. This, even though they were all otherwise publicly opposed to the SCs and STs, and were running the SCs and STs down badly as if they were outsiders and their enemies. They were also denigrating the SCs and STs, calling them names and humiliating them openly.

The others were opposing all forms of Reservations, specifically any assistance or help by the Govt. to the SCs and STs. And they were the bitter critics of the whole Scheme of Reservations, particularly Caste based Reservations. They were arguing that the Reservations should not be on the basis of Castes, even though they were specifically asking for inclusion of their Castes in the List of SCs, only and in order to get the benefits of Reservations for themselves and their own Castes. In the public, they were always critical of Reservations, even when demanding Reservations for themselves. Such were and still are, the double standards of the Hindu society. They were claiming that the Reservations were there, and in fact were conceived only to please the SC and ST Dalits, with an eye on the hustings. They were, as the caste hinds today still are, cribbing that the Politicians upheld Reservations only due to the compulsions of electoral necessities. They were all complaining that the Political Parties and the Govts. in Power supported and sustained the Reservations, just for the sake of getting the votes of the SCs and STs, and to preserve them as their Party's solid Vote Banks. Thus, they were and others are, so foolish even to criticise and blame Democracy, and the processes of choosing the Peoples' Representatives for sending them to the Panchayats, Legislatives and the Parliament through Adult Franchise. In the end, finding the doors of entry and inclusion of their Castes into the List of the SCs closed, or at least closed tight, some of them came around to open a new front or line of similar Reservations in the name of Backward Classes.

Constitution facilitates the Govt. to provide for, Reservations to Other Backward Classes, who are not Represented in Govt. But the dominant castes who appropriate everything and take all good things in life for themselves, have been effectively and systematically blocking the Reservations for the Backward Classes all these years.

Many caste Hindus, with a criminal bent of mind and crooked attitudes, also began to impersonate themselves as SCs/STs to mislead the authorities, just to take the benefits meant for the SCs and STs. Many of them had gone up in the offices and in their lives. Many others, with the connivance of the officials themselves, even today appropriate and continue to enjoy the benefits meant for the SCs and STs, with the help of bogus SC/ST Certificates they manage to obtain falsely, and or by falsification of facts, about their birth or that of their parents, or just by paying bribes to the caste Hindu peons, clerks and the Caste Certificate Issuing Authorities in the States and UTs.

This, only because of the all round realisations that Reservations really help, and help even the lowly placed, despised, marginalised, socially suppressed, culturally physically politically, educationally and economically oppressed weaker sections and communities like the SCs and STs. This also, in spite of all the negative steps taken against the SCs and STs as well as the Reservation Policy, and the severe oppositions and silent hurdles mounted in the way of implementation of the Reservations by almost most those who are in offices and positions of power and authority. Almost all the authorities and other officials are totally opposed and are against the SCs and STs and their Development, or are jealous and intolerant of the SCs and STs getting even an iota of Progress, little Liberation, inch of Freedom, or at least a bit of Justice.

Reservations are really and truly beneficial not only to the people concerned like the SCs and STs and OBCs, but also to the whole Nation and the Society for the overall and just Development. Also, the Country's Economy gets benefited, and can achieve better and quicker results through all-round Growth and Progress. Whatever may be the shortcomings and oppositions, or behind the screen schemings that go against Reservations, the Reservations had served well, the Nation and the Indian Society. With the part acceptance in 1990, of Reservations for the Backward Classes recommended by the Mandal Commission, Reservations have come to stay, in spite of all the fury and all-round oppositions. Reservations now have become permanent.

Nobody in the Country now has the courage or the guts to scrap them, however much they may dislike Reservations and or hate the SCs and STs and OBCs. Now, there is a flurry of rush by individuals and castes to include themselves and their castes as Backward Castes. This is an ample proof, for the reality that Reservations have at last come to stay in our Country also. Reservations have been accepted by all, as the sure means to develop even the badly disadvantaged despised and marginalised sections of the society.

In fact, the Reservations for long have been recognised as a reliable mechanism to help the Weaker Sections of the Society anywhere in the World. And there is no better Model, to Uplift the Backward the Helpless the Marginalised and the Neglected Communities. It is only for this reason that, there is so much of fury and oppositions to Reservation Policy on the one hand, and the silent sabotage and subversions that we see on the other in the actual implementation. The specific details of Reservations, the mechanisms and processes of operating and enforcement of the Reservations, are silently and cunningly derailed by those who are jealous and intolerant of the Growth Development and Progress of the SCs and STs.

The Reservations for OBCs had multiple effects. They are yet to be felt or realised in full. But the immediate effects are that the dominant castes had lost their control over the OBCs, and thus an effective tool to oppress the SCs and STs, and focus their tirade against the Reservations for the SCs and STs. They had lost an effective excuse to keep the OBCs captive any more. They could no more blame the Reservations for the SCs and STs and their growth, for all the Backwardness of the OBCs, and the lack of Opportunities for the OBCs, which they had deliberately not created or allowed to be made available. They could no more turn the attention of the OBCs away from the fact that, they have always been taking away the opportunities, shares and dues of others including the OBCs, and thus have all along deprived the growth development and progress of the OBCs. They could no more divert the anger of the OBCs against the SCs and STs, to escape from the same. Hence, they could no more succeed in keeping the OBCs and the SCs and STs — the Deprived Sections of the Society - divided, and hold down the SCs and STs by using the OBCs to keep the SCs and STs suppressed.

The dominant castes till now had only contempt for the SCs and STs, and had only occasionally shown their intolerance and hatred for the Reservations They were only Jealous of the Development of some SCs and STs in spite of all the oppositions and hurdles for growth. They rarely had to deal directly with the SCs and STs, or oppose Reservations by themselves. That task, they had effectively managed to put on the OBCs. They were only operating from the back, by manipulating the Details and the Methodologies of Reservations, and the actual Processes of Implementation.

Now, for the first time, they had to handle the SCs and STs directly, and not only that have to face the OBCs fully, that too almost on the side of the former. With the Reservations for the OBCs, their hatred had increased, and the targets of hatred had enlarged from the just hopeful expectant SCs and STs, to the restless and aggressive but at the same time unorganised OBCs also. Now they had to confront both, almost at the same time and on the same issues. At the same time, they had to also carry on by themselves on their shoulders the burden of opposing the Reservations, and also keep manipulating the Reservations, so that the Reservations don't actually benefit either the SCs and STs or the OBCs.

They are thus actually playing with fire. What will happen when the OBCs fully wake up, organise themselves and get united? What will they do to face the fury of the organised OBCs? And what will happen if the SCs and STs also join them? The dominant castes apparently are not thinking beyond the immediate, and are making a great mistake. They should quickly and amicably settle themselves in a just manner, while they still hold the levers of power, without attempting to play one caste or tribe against the other, the SCs against the STs, the SCs and STs against the OBCs, or any such combination to buy time.

The significant is the fact that the caste Hindus have developed in their minds a great fear about the grouping, coming together, possible unity, and combination of the OBCs and the SCs and STs, at least as the Beneficiaries of Reservations. But instead of finding a practical and lasting solution, they still want to play their games. They don't want change or mend their ways. They want to continue with their manipulations.

That is the reason why they have Administratively and through the Courts, limited the Reservations for the OBCs, to only Appointments in Public Services by Direct Recruitments alone, and not in Promotions. Therefore, they want to avoid the OBCs and the SCs and STs joining hands, and prevent them from fully coming together. Hence, they want to preserve many areas of divergence between the OBCs and SCs and STs, and thus the disunity and conflict, particularly in Admissions to higher and professional education, at least in the Central Institutions and in Promotions in Services.

Today, the fear in the minds of the caste Hindus had grown so intense that all the dominant castes, almost without any exception, feel threatened that their days are counted, and that their dominance now is really at stake. Therefore, even some of those well placed fellows, and happy satisfied comfortable and self contented individuals, who had in the past shown some sympathy for the poor bright or the helpless and needy or capable and promising individual SCs and STs, have no more empathy left in them for the later. Their fear is now so great, intense and total. They are no more willing to help even the most needy and deserving poor SC/ST. They are now totally opposed to the SC and ST Communities, the Reservations for the SCs and STs, and the whole Scheme of Reservations. As they are in power, and in full control of the Govt., Bureaucracy, and the Administration of Public Affairs, the heat is increasingly being felt now, by most of the SCs and STs.

What have the Reservations for the SCs and STs Achieved?

Many things! And at the same time the Reservations had failed to achieve much more essential things! They have proved to be a great disappointment to the SC and ST Communities as a whole! They have failed the SCs and STs almost in all the fronts and every walks of the life!

It is not that Reservations are bad, but those who have been called to work them have proved to be really bad! The learned officials, the Public Servants of the Country, in whose hands the responsibility of implementing the Reservations rest, have deliberately let down the still poor and helpless SCs and STs! They really have no heart, neither any compassion or concern for the poor helpless and the weak, nor any interest in the Welfare Growth and Development of the People, the Society, the Country and the Nation!

We have adequate and reasonably reliable data on the Reservations for SCs and STs, and there are lots of Reports and other Writings on their actual effects. But sadly, after five decades of operations of Reservations for SCs and STs in free Indian Republic - even if we neglect the period between 1935 Govt. of India Act and 1950 when the Constitution with Special Provisions for the SCs and STs including various Reservations for the SCs and STs, in different and related spheres of Politics Education Employment and Economic Activities, like Development Growth Housing Welfare, etc. came into force — the achievements are not really worth recounting.

For, the Reservations have never been seriously or sincerely enforced, except in Politics for Electing the Representatives of the People to the Lok Sabha in Parliament at the Centre, and the Legislative Assemblies in the States. As a result, in the significant areas of Education and Employment, there is nothing we can talk of proudly, or the Govt. can take credit of.

Today, fifty years after Independence of the Country, there are only two SC Secretaries to the Govt. of India — one an IAS Officer, and the other the Law Secretary to the Govt. of India. There is no ST who is a Secretary to the Govt. of India. Not very long ago, there were about ten SC and ST Secretaries to the Govt. of India - about six or seven SCs and two or three STs, and nearly half a dozen Additional Secretaries as well as more than a dozen Joint Secretaries in the Central Secretariat. This situation instead of showing an improvement to reflect the actual presence of the SCs and STs in Public Services all over the Country, and development of an unbiased tolerant Civil Society without any prejudices and biases or contempt against the poor and the weak, had rapidly detoriated to the present sad situation of hardly two Secretaries at the Centre. And what is worse, there is no worthwhile effort to improve the situation. On the other hand, there is a strong animosity against SC and ST Officials, particularly against the intelligent hardworking honest capable and result oriented ones. Practically every one of them are suffering, have suffered and will suffer more and more problems in the days to come.

Why is this So?

The answers are not far difficult to find. One need not even search for them. They are readily available before us, and are clearly visible. They are obvious to everyone. Both the Bureaucracy and the Judiciary have been gunning for the SCs and STs, and the Reservations for them. They are aggressively intolerant, jealous and have been openly working against the Development Growth and Welfare of the SCs and STs. For reasons they can not clearly explain to themselves, or honestly speak out, or perhaps out of total ignorance, or shear stupidity and bull headedness, they are still opposing the Reservations for the SCs and STs and OBCs. And what is worse, there is no more empathy towards the SCs and STs.

Today's Political Party Leaders don't have any concern, or even show any lip-sympathy towards the SCs and STs, even for public and political reasons. They feel that they need not bother at all, or show any concern for the weak and the helpless, like the SCs and STs, Backwards and Minorities. Hence, they just don't care now for anyone. They are very sure that they can manage all of them with out really doing anything good or positive for them. They think that, with the help of a few captive leaders in their parties from these marginalised groups, or by some clever manipulations of the different leaders, weaker sections and their votes, and also by other devious methods and dubious means of managing the elections, they can win and capture power. Under these circumstances what else or what more can then we find?

Representations of SCs and STs in Public Services

SCs and STs taken together form nearly 26 per cent of the Indian Population. In absolute numbers they are more than 260 million today. It is not only significant, but is a very large Population. Most of the Nations, barring China and India are not that big. But such a large People have no place or Representation in the Country even today. In fifty years of the Indian Republic, there was only one Vice-President, and only just now we have a President from the SCs. There has never been anyone in these Offices from the STs. During the same period, there were hardly two or three Tribal Cabinet Ministers at the Centre. There has never been a SC or ST Prime Minister. Able, capable, efficient, intelligent, honest, hardworking, sincere, very senior and prospective Ministers, and probable or sure SC/ST Candidates, who would have perhaps proved to be the best/ most successful and deserving Prime Ministers the Country could have ever produced, have been pipped or pulled down and sabotaged at the final moments of reckoning many a times. Hardly ever been there any SC/ST Chief Minister in the States and UTs, and the rare ones also were not allowed to stay in office even for one or two years. The only exceptions have been in the inevitable North Eastern States. There too, the SCs and STs of Manipur and Tripura have a very bad experience to narrate.

In thirteen Planning Commissions that we have seen so far, there never was a regular SC Member, and only one ST was a Member, twice with tenures of less than one year and five years, from 1990 to 1991, and again from 1991 to 1996. The Planning Commission of India at the Centre, surprisingly does not yet have a Separate Department or even a small Cell for either the SCs and STs taken together, or for the larger group of the SCs, or for the special groups of STs, even though the conditions of the SCs and STs are pitiable all over the Country, and is going from bad to worse with each passing day, as the overall Planning and Development of the Country, Market Forces, as well as the growing numbers of greedy social elements are squeezing and forcing the SCs and STs out, even from their own traditional lands and homes. This may be surprising and strange, given their population of more than 260 million now, almost evenly spread all over the Country, save for the North Eastern States and the Tribal

Concentrated Belts and Pockets here and there on the subcontinent, and their abject poverty of homelessness, landlessness, assetlessness, powerlessness, massive illiteracy, extensive superstition, systematic suppression and planned oppression. But this is not at all shocking, given the still prevailing prejudices and biases in the Indian Society, particularly in the Hindu mind against the SCs and STs.

The Representations of the SCs and STs in the Judiciary are woefully poor, and that again shows the prevailing awful animosity against the SCs and STs in the minds of the so-called learned Judges, and other highly placed Jurists Authorities and the Govt., who choose consider select recommend and make appointments of the Judges, especially to the High Courts in the States and also to the Supreme Court of India. Some of them are not only against the SCs and STs as Judges, but are openly and blatantly against the SC and ST Communities as a whole. With such animosities biases and prejudices, what type of Justice can they do or what sort of Judgements will they deliver? No one has yet made any study of the damages they have done to the creative hardworking SCs and STs, and thus to the Country. In fifty years, there were only three SC Judges in the Supreme Court at different points of time, and not even one ST. Now no one is there, and hardly anyone is likely to be allowed to come in there in the near future. Such is the opposition against them. Hence, it is no wonder that the Courts these days are openly intolerant towards SCs and STs, or to hear their pleas. They throw out their Cases, don't have patience or want to listen anything from the SC and ST Lawyers, even for the sake of appearing to be just and show off that they have heard the Case, and are doing and would do Justice, both to the Lawyers and the Parties they represent in the Case before the Court.

SCs and STs in Academics and Education

The Representations of the SCs and STs in Academics, either as Students or Employees in Schools, Colleges, Universities, other Autonomous Institutions or Centres of Higher Learning are still very poor. Thousands of qualified Job-Seekers are deliberately refused employment in the Schools Colleges Universities, etc. Hundreds and hundreds of SC and ST Students aspiring for higher studies are turned out every year denied admissions, or even after admissions are thrown out or forced to get out under some pretext or the other from the Colleges, Universities, Autonomous Institutions and other Centres of Higher Education. The caste Hindu Lecturers and Professors are both unwilling and are actually incapable of teaching the SC and ST Students, unlike the British who produced the likes of Dr. Ambedkar during those days itself.

The Opportunities for Studies Abroad available to Indian Students are by and large still kept as a secret from the SCs and STs, even though hundreds of Indian Students are to be found in many Foreign Countries with various Scholarships and other Schemes that help them to pursue their studies abroad, without taxing their families. Even Dr. Ambedkar's Dream of educating select SC and ST Students Abroad, accepted by the then British Indian Govt., has been badly twisted beyond recognition by the Welfare Ministry over the years. A similar Scheme of Dr. Ambedkar Overseas Fellowships for Students to study abroad, through Dr. Ambedkar Foundation has been in the cold storage for quite sometime, and many students already selected for the Award of the Fellowships have not been permitted to avail of the Fellowships. A silent effort is said to be in the offing, to turn it as a facility only for SC and ST University and College Teachers already in job. Thus, the Scheme meant for the Students is being distorted, and at the same time, the UGC and other authorities would be washing off their responsibilities in providing opportunities to Train Abroad, the SC and ST Lecturers and Professors working in the Colleges and Universities. Thus, by one change, two opportunities available to SC and ST Students and the SC and ST Teachers are now being cleverly and silently closed.

The numbers of SC and ST Lecturers, Senior Lecturers, Readers, Assistant Professors, Associate Professors, Professors, etc. in the Colleges, Autonomous Colleges, Universities, Deemed Universities, Research Centres and other Institutions of Higher Learning in the Country are extremely poor. One can have a taste of this, when we find that in the whole of Delhi, the Nation's Capital, barring the Govt. Engineering and Medical Colleges to which Recruitments are made by the Union Public Service Commission and the Appointments by the Govt., today there are only five Professors — One SC and One ST, a respectable total of Two SC and ST Professors in Delhi University, Two SC Professors in JNU, and one SC Professor in the Indian Institute of Technology Delhi. This in spite of the fact that, Delhi attracts professionals scholars and teachers from all over the Country. Yet, the authorities have managed successfully so far to keep the SCs and STs at a very far distance away from Delhi. In this, the negative role being played by the University Grants Commission, etc. can not ever be discounted or forgotten.

The UGC is not even allowing or facilitating the SC and ST Students to acquire the requisite Higher Qualifications of M.Phil. and Ph.D. essential for Teaching in the Universities and Colleges. They do not provide them any Scholarships and Fellowships to pursue these long and costly studies. The Govt. and the Ministry of Social Justice and Empowerment is not helping the poor SC and ST Students wanting to go for such essential higher studies. The caste Hindu Professors and Universities are also doing their best and contributing their shares in denying the SCs and STs admissions to these courses, and also in rating them deliberately lower so that they do not become eligible for teaching, even if the SC and ST Students manage to do these essential higher Courses. Such is the situation in the Country today.

Perhaps India is the only Nation in the World where the Teachers instead of teaching the poor are denying them education, instead of equipping them with knowledge are condemning them, turning them as unfits and deliberately rating them low. In fact this has been the history of India. One could not ever afford to forget Egalivya.

SCs and STs in Government Services

The Representations of the SCs and STs in Govt. Services, even on the overall reckoning is extremely poor, in spite of operating the Reservation Systems for the last fifty years. And this, with so many brilliant and highly educated and qualified SCs and STs, duly examined and certified so, by all those caste Hindu controlled Universities and Educational Institutions, always knocking at the doors of the Govt. Offices and various Recruiting and Appointing Authorities for Jobs and Employment. The overall Representations of the SCs and STs in the Central Govt. Services all over the Country, as on 1st January 1995 are:

10.15% SCs and 2.89% STs in Group A (Class I) Services and Posts

12.67% SCs and 2.68% STs in Group B (Class II) Services and Posts

16.15% SCs and 5.69% STs in Group C (Class III) Services and Posts

21.26% SCs and 6.48% STs in Group D (Class IV) Posts

Even in the Group C (Class III) Services and Posts, the Representations of the SCs and STs in the higher grades are very very poor. Even these small Representations of the SCs and STs in Services, most of the caste Hindu authorities are unable to tolerate and digest. They therefore, go after the blood of even these small numbers of SCs and STs in Service.

All the observations and empirical data available today indicate that, on an average more than 90 per cent of Vigilance Cases are against the Employees and Officers who are weak, susceptible and are vulnerable, such as those about to retire, due for promotions, and are SCs and STs. And what is more surprising is that, more than 60 per cent of the Employees and Officers facing Vigilance Cases, or are under Suspension, caught up in Enquiries, suffering Punishments of loss of increments, reduction in pay or pay-scales, withheld increments, withheld promotions, denial of promotions, downgrading in rank or termination, are the helpless and godfatherless SCs and STs. Since these are Vigilance Cases, none is generally forthcoming or are in a position to extend any helping hand to them. The Departments and senior officials are also in a position to casually and carelessly brush aside their pleas and representations, without even taking a cursory look at them and their cases. But, the losses, being suffered by so many SC and ST Employees and Officers all around, and their Families in Physical, Psychological, Mental, Social and Financial Terms are immense and colossal. In fact it is a serious and major economic loss to the Country and a criminal wastage of well qualified highly trained productive responsible and useful manpower. And only this caste ridden Country can afford the luxury of wasting so much of scarce valuable assets and resources, that too deliberately.

Those who get poor Assessments, Reports, Gradings, and hence as a result miss their Promotions often times and repeatedly, are almost exclusively the SCs and STs. This, in spite of the fact that, many of them have been recruited through All India Competitive Examinations by the UPSC or other Commissions/ Agencies. It is often an humiliating experience for them, which get further compounded, when they find that they have lost the race for promotions and seniority, to those who are far juniors to them in service, and many times to those who are not even qualified and are from the ranks, but have managed the promotions only because they are caste Hindus and hence are well connected having direct access to their seniors who matter, either directly by themselves or through their families or with the help of other relatives, friends, or the ever important caste circles.

In the sphere of Sweeping, a category of cleaning jobs as Sweepers, an area and occupation exclusively Reserved by the Hindu society for the SCs, others are today making inroads edging out the poor SC Sweepers, even when they are unwilling to work as Sweepers. They are coming in as Sweepers, not to Sweep and work as Sweepers, but to take by hook or crook a well paid Govt. Job in Govt. Offices, where they can easily and safely avoid work, if they even otherwise choose not to work or don't want to work. These others, are coming in dubiously as Sweepers, to get into Govt. Service with a clear intention and motive of quickly migrating into other areas or cadres of Service within the Office. For them, the job of a poor Sweeper is a convenient backdoor entry into Govt. Offices, which they are otherwise unable to enter for want of requisite education, training, experience, intelligence, capabilities and such other qualifications required for direct recruitment to the jobs they desire to take. Hence, their attempts to take jobs of Sweepers is farce, and is a fraud on the Sweepers and Govt. They therefore, always refuse to work as Sweepers even for a second, and avoid touching the broom ever, even though they had applied for and joined service as Sweepers, hold the job of Sweepers, mark attendance as Sweepers, take salaries as Sweepers, ask for special facilities as Sweepers and promotions as Sweepers. Once in the Govt. Offices as Sweepers, these others with the open support help and connivance of their caste Hindu superiors hold for namesake the job of Sweepers. They are never asked to do any work as Sweepers. Even when they are allotted or have to do the work of Sweepers, they become *benami* Sweepers. They get their work done through other Sweepers in the office, or act informally as Sweeping Contractors or Suppliers of Casual Manpower for Sweeping on their behalf the offices as also for keeping clean the premises and the areas allotted to them for cleaning, for a paltry token payment which they pay from out the full Govt. Salaries they take as Sweepers.

In many offices, the system of exploiting and cheating both the Govt. and the poor lowly paid Sweepers has been formalised, and the caste Hindu Contractors are given regular Contracts to Supply Casual Sweepers regularly to the office, or get the sweeping done on a regular basis on Contract. These Contractors, employ a very small number of Sweepers, fully exploit and force the Sweepers to do the work of many, and pay them far less wages for carrying out the day to day job of sweeping and keeping the premises clean.

It is because of the ingenious dubious practices, cheating and exploitation of the helpless Sweepers, by the educated and well employed superior officials, and the realisation of the same by the regular Sweepers, the regular Sweepers are on an un-noticed continuous strike, and they are now adopting a non-cooperative go slow tactics, that they don't take their work any more seriously. Thus, the quality of their work is poor. Hence, the sweeping work suffers. It is because of these that, the maintenance of Cleanliness and Hygiene in Govt. Offices and their surroundings are very poor, and the Corridors awfully stink even many paces away from the toilets and waste bins anywhere, that sensitive and conscious individuals cannot pass by them easily.

Unless the Govt. makes peace with the Sweepers, genuinely and sincerely look into their grievances, end all forms of cheating and exploitations, and put a complete stop to the present dubious methods of employing others, the overall cleanliness and hygiene not only in the Govt. Offices but in the Country will suffer very very seriously, particularly when we take into consideration the peoples lack of consciousness and attitudes of not maintaining general cleanliness in their places of work/living and surroundings. They require a separate class of people to work as Sweepers, and maintain their homes, work places and surroundings clean, on behalf of themselves and the whole society.

With acceptance of some Reservations for the OBCs, consolidation of the OBCs which was inevitable and taking place even before the Reservations for them was accepted, and the growing consciousness of the SCs and STs, the caste Hindus are today a worried lot. Even then, they don't want to rest, or change and mend their ways. They don't want to adopt reasonable just and fair Civilised Methods of working, and managing the affairs of the society. Since the caste Hindus are still in positions of power, and always speak for the Nation, on behalf of the Nation, as if they are the Nation, they adopt such policies and practices that it appears the Nation is hitting back at the SCs and STs, the OBCs and the Reservations. Yes, they are under attack, and the attacks though systematic severe and total, are meted out silently. They are being hit below the belt and in the back at unexpected times.

It is the considered opinion of the SCs and STs and the OBCs that, the Country had adopted the path of Liberalisation, Globalisation, opted for opening up the Economy, and had slowly begun the privatisation and selling of the Public Sector Govt. Enterprises built up so laboriously over a long period, with the hard earned money and great savings of the people, only because they want to avoid Reservations at any cost, and are unwilling to part with the Jobs and Employment there, rightly due to the SCs and STs and OBCs.

The caste Hindus are palming off, as if on silver platter even the profit making PSUs. Thus, the PSUs which have formed the core of the Nation's Economy, the base of the Country's Self Reliance, the Pride of the People and the Foundations of National Development, are either being dismantled or passed off into private hands and to the Indian or Foreign Multi-National Corporations, only to reduce the Govt.'s Role and eliminate the PSUs, and hence the availability of the Jobs therein, which were till now available to the Public, and would therefore now be subjected to Reservations to the SCs and STs and OBCs. It is to avoid this, and still deny jobs with a decent salary and livelihood to the OBCs and the SCs and STs, that caste Hindus are wanting to close, sell off, hand over the PSUs to the private sector, including foreign Multi National Companies.

As a result of the above, the SCs and STs and OBCs today are foxed. There are in principle, on paper, Reservations for them in

Employment and Jobs, but in practice there is no Employment Opportunities and no Jobs! The Govt. Offices and PSUs themselves are vanishing! Employment and Job Opportunities are shrinking sharply and abruptly for the Public. Private Sector Companies do not believe in Public Employment. They make recruitments silently and privately, with out any knowledge or information to the public. Even if there is any information, the claims of the public are crudely brushed off and set aside. For, they make appointments based on personal contacts and through their own private and secret arrangements.

Steps to Integrate SCs and STs into the Main Stream?

The SCs and STs are now at the Cross Roads. Their hopes and aspirations are getting frustrated. Their sufferings and miseries are on the increase. They don't see any signs of change. And there is no such possibility in the near future. The atrocities against them, the crude criminal premeditated oppressions and offences in the Rural Areas and Urban Slums, the sophisticated silent planned white collar suppressions by the educated superiors in Educational Institutions, Govt. Offices, etc. are rapidly on the increase. Their patience is already running out. They may now go in any direction, and take any path. One side, they want to stick to the Path of Peace and Constitutional Methods, shown to them by Baba Saheb Dr. BR Ambedkar, and follow his ways. They clearly remember his exhortations:

> If we wish to maintain Democracy, not merely in form but also in fact, what must we do? The first thing in my judgement we must do, is to hold fast to Constitutional Methods of achieving our Social and Economic Objectives. It means, we must abandon the bloody methods of Revolution. It means that, we must abandon the method of Civil Disobedience, non-Cooperation and Satyagraha. When there was no way left for Constitutional Methods for achieving Economic and Social Objectives, there was a great deal of justification for Unconstitutional Methods. But, when Constitutional Methods are open, there can be no justification for these unconstitutional methods. These methods are nothing but the Grammar of Anarchy, and the sooner they are abandoned the better for us.

On the other hand, will the SCs and STs stray away in future from the Constitutional Methods of achieving the Economic and Social Objectives of the People, the Aspirations of the Society, the Goals of the Nation and the Dreams of the Founding Fathers of the Constitution pointed out by their Messiah Dr. Ambedkar, and opt out in frustration to Unconstitutional Methods of Change and bloody Revolutions warned by Dr. Ambedkar himself many a times? The signs of these are already in air, in various pockets in almost different parts of the Country. Will SCs and STs radically choose to alter the Economic, Social and Cultural Orders of People in the Society, and the Political Structure of the Country, or go for balkanising and break away from the Nation, as we see many frustrated impatient Sections of various societies are already doing in different parts of World? Will there be Social Unrest endless Law and Order Problems, as we already experience, in our Cities and Metropolises? Will there be an avoidable Civil War? We don't know! The real answers to these unanswered potentially dangerous and virtually explosive questions, ultimately depend upon the choices the Society makes and the Govt. Leaders now take, to establish a just fair and equitable Economic Order and build an Egalitarian Social Structure. And it needs to be thought as to what can We the People or the Govt., the Country, the Society and the SC and ST themselves do? We have to find an answer, and find it quickly. For, the time is really running out for all of us and the Country as a whole.

What we need more urgently now, is not Liberalisation of the Economy but Liberation of the People, the downtrodden the weak and the marginalised; not Globalisation of our Economy but Universalisation of Human Rights in favour of the poor and the helpless like the SCs and STs.

The SCs and STs are poor weak marginalised and powerless. They need Education and Employment. They want Development and Growth. They are still to get their Independence and Freedom. They are eagerly looking forward to the Day of their Deliverance. They are seeking Liberty and Equality. They have waited all these days with great hopes and patience. They are now demanding Justice and Human Rights. They want Human Rights and Life with Dignity. They are thirsting for Individual Recognitions and Equal Opportunities. They are asking for Self Respect and Fairness in Social Life. They need Good Jobs and Decent Salaries. They look for Helping Hands and Respectful Wages alright. But they may not wait for long. They cannot afford to pay bribes or bring in influences and recommendations in their favour. Hence, there is a need to implement the Reservations honestly fairly and in full. There is also a need to force the private sector companies and the Indian and Foreign Multi National Companies, to make their Recruitments and Appointments public and fair, through open advertisements and without any secrecy. They should be asked to give Representations to different Sections of the Society. After all, these are the ways of any Civilised Nation and all Civil Societies of the World. Secret Selections and Private Appointments based on personal contacts and private considerations are not the ways of a decent World.

If Reservations here in the Country are the due Rights and Shares of the SCs and STs and the OBCs in the Nation Building, Administration and Governance of the Country, even in the Mecca of the Free World and the fountainhead of all the new waves of Liberalisation and Globalisation sweeping the World now, there is Affirmative Action for the Blacks enforced by the Govt. This Affirmative Action has now been proudly accepted by the Private Sector there.

The American Educational Institutions, Universities, Seats of Higher Learning and Centres of Research, and also the big powerful and rich MNCs there, are vying with each other to show to their Society and the World their achievements in this respect. Why should the caste Hindus here then not honourably accept their own educated sisters and brothers from the SC and ST and OBC Communities? Why should they resent the SCs and STs and the OBCs even today, or feel jealous of the alters' progress or become envious of their development? And why should there be oppositions to the Reservations that only seek to provide the SCs and STs and the OBCs their proportionate share of Education, Jobs and other Opportunities in Life in the Country? Why should anyone, any reasonable or rational individual crib? One really does not know.

The caste Hindus are now forcibly taking away, what they used to silently steal all these days. Now they are openly grabbing the shares and dues of the SCs and STs and also the OBCs, in the name of Excellence, National Interest, National Security, Defence,

Science, Technology, Research, Higher Studies, Super Specialities, Development of Excellence to International Standards, rapid or accelerated Economic Development, Opening up the Economy, Privatisation, Liberalisation, Globalisation, Structural Adjustments, Financial Discipline, and the frauds of their Special Merits and Efficiencies. These are nothing but an open fraud to cheat the people, shield and cover up all their inefficiency, blatant nepotism, shameless favouritism, violation of rules and regulations as well as the norms and procedures/precedences, open corruption, lack of respect for fair open honest selections/recruitments/promotions and appointments.

The repeated jokes they are trying to play on the Country is the Superiority and Respect to, as well as the need and compulsions of having to abide by the decisions of a pack of caste Hindu individuals, who have reached their positions due to their closeness proximity and compromises with those they were and are in positions of power, with the right political authority to select appoint patronise backup and promote them all along the line.

The latest cruel joke of caste Hindus is that, they are all now waking up after fifty long years, to talk about the need to produce and support the specialists in the making, comparable to International Standards, but only from the dominant castes. What were they doing all these five decades? What happened to all those meritorious sons and daughters of theirs, whom they freely selected all these years, saying that no suitable SC/ST was available, and without giving any Reservations to the OBCs?

Why should they get this urge now, when the SCs and STs have already grown up to become Specialists, and are doing extremely well in Serving the Country with out fleeing to foreign shores, and as the OBCs are getting their Opportunities? Even now, why don't they produce such International Class Specialists from their top most meritorious scholars? Why do they need to grab or take so blatantly the Opportunities of the SCs and STs and OBCs? Why do they want to deny the poor SCs and STs and OBCs admissions to higher studies, professional courses and super specialities, and give these admissions to their third rate scholars who could not make their grade by themselves, competing with their own fellow colleagues freely and fairly, but come at the last, much behind their own caste individuals? Do they have no faith in their most meritorious fellows, who come at the top in the assessment of merits as per their own methods, standards of evaluations and the scheme of norms and scales? Do they want to play a game of choices, and gamble on those who miss out in the race, that they want to bring them in the places of the SCs and STs and OBCs? Would they then wait, hope, pray, or dream that at least one of their third-rate scholars, who had come in through the back doors, to the professional and super-speciality courses, in place of the poor SCs and STs and OBCs, to become an International Expert par-Excellence? Should we or can anyone believe them? Still, they try to fool the Country the SCs and STs and the OBCs? Have they gone crazy, or are they such big fools or so stupid to think that the SCs and STs and OBCs are such fools that they can buy their arguments and keep quiet?

Govt. should now come out with a Comprehensive Reservation Policy for the whole Country covering Govt., Public Sector Enterprises, Banks, Financial Institutions, Colleges, Universities, Centres of Higher Learning and Research, other Educational Institutions, Autonomous Bodies, Non-Governmental Organisations, Voluntary Organisations, and Private Enterprises including Indian and Foreign Multi-National Companies in the Country.

Law on Reservations for the SCs and STs and OBCs

SCs and STs of the Country strongly feel that there is no point in believing and trusting that the caste Hindus in the Govt., in Govt. Offices, and the Courts would ever be honest to implement the Reservations in an honest and fair manner. Hence, there is a need to bind them legally. The present Reservations are only Govt. Orders, Departmental Rules and Regulations, and Office Memorandums. They are easily flouted, and also can be conveniently changed. Therefore, the Govt. of India should bring in urgently, without any further delay a comprehensive Reservation Bill, and enact a Law on Reservations. This Reservation Law should, amongst other things provide for:

- Incentives and Financial Assistances to individual SCs and STs, wanting to pursue Higher Studies, particularly Post Graduate Studies in Professional Spheres like Architecture, Engineering, Medicine, Management, Law, etc. and take up Advanced Courses like M.Phil., Ph.D. and Post Doctoral Studies and Specialist Trainings .

- Incentives and Financial Assistances to the Families, for encouraging individual SCs and STs to pursue Higher Studies .
- Incentives to individual Teachers, Professors and Officials for encouraging helping developing and training SC and ST Students, Professionals, Employees and Officials.
- Incentives to Schools, Colleges, Universities and Government Departments/Ministries/Public Sector Enterprises, Banks, Financial Institutions, Autonomous Bodies and Private Sector for teaching employing and encouraging SCs and STs.
- Penalties for the Teachers, Professors, Officers and Schools, Colleges, Universities, Offices and other Establishments who/which do not follow and fail to implement the Reservations, and discourage SCs and STs.
- Reservations in all Govt. Offices, Public Sector Enterprises, Banks, Financial Institutions and Autonomous Institutions without any exceptions.
- Reservations in every Public Service, Post, Grade and Level, right from the top most Public Office to down below, without any exemption whatsoever.
- Reservations in all Educational Institutions Govt. or Private, in Admissions of Students and Scholars, and also in the Recruitments and Promotions of Teaching Faculty as well as the non-Teaching Staff.
- Reservations in the Joint Sector Organisations.
- Reservations in all Establishments where the Govt. and the Public have a share.
- Reservations in all Establishments which make use of Public Facilities created with Public Funds, or created for the use of the People.
- Reservations in all Establishments making use of Land and other Natural Resources of the Country.

- Reservations in Employment in all Private Sector Establishments.
- Reservations in all Courts, including Law Officers and the Judiciary.
- Lateral Entry of SCs and STs into various Services and Cadres at higher Levels Grades and Posts, to improve and ensure their full Representations at every level.
- Free mobility of SC and ST Professionals and Academicians, between and across Govt., Bureaucracy, Administration, Public Sector, Joint Sector, Private Sector, Voluntary Organisations and into the Universities.

This Reservation Law should be placed in the Ninth Schedule of the Constitution, and be beyond the purview of the Courts. The People are Sovereign in a Democracy. India is a Democracy, a Socialist and Secular Democratic Republic. Hence the People, their Representatives and the Parliament have the ultimate Power to make Laws.

The Courts can legitimately interfere on behalf of the People when the Govt. fails to act and Govern or Govern properly, but can not go against the People, the will of the People, and poke their nose into the Parliament. Otherwise it will be a sad day for the Country, the Society and the People. Of late, the Courts have been interfering too much and too frequently against the SCs and STs, their Development and with the Reservations for the SCs and STs, and the Govt. Policies and Procedures in this regard.

What Should the Govts. at the Centre and the States/UTs Do?

It is hightime that the Govts. take some specific steps and positive action beyond Reservations. Fifty-three years of Independence had already passed. Fifty years after the establishment of the Republic, had also rolled by. We have wasted precious long time. We can not afford to sleep any further. Otherwise, the poor people would soon lynch us all alive. It is necessary to think what we need to do, and at the sametime act fast. Honestly speaking, we have not yet really started thinking of Development of the Weaker Sections. We have only been playing soft balls with them all these days. Let us get serious now, at least a bit. The Govt. of India therefore, should bring in the learned SCs and STs and thinkers amongst them, to chalk out real Plans and Action Programmes for their Social, Economic and Cultural Development. It is only they, who can understand the needs and aspirations of the SCs and STs. As Baba Saheb Dr. Ambedkar had long ago rightly said, it is only the servile class who can lead them. Definitely not their antagonists, nor the class room city products of just the Universities, or those with foreign education, or WB and IMF trainings and mandates. The Govts. at the Centre and the State/UTs should at least now establish:

- National and State Level Administrative and Professional Training Establishments for the SCs and STs, to develop and improve their Administrative and Professional Competence and Capabilities.
- National SC and ST Housing Finance and Development Corporations.
- National and State/UT Level Centres for SC and ST Development.
- National Level Centres for Planning for, SC and ST Education and Employment.
- National and State/UT Level Task Forces, for Entrepreneurship Development amongst the SCs and STs.
- Separate Tribunals to look into and expeditiously dispose off the Cases of SC and ST Employees.
- Separate District Level Courts to expeditiously hear and decide the Cases of SC and ST Lands taken away by others.
- A Special Judicial Commission to exclusively look into the Judgements of the various Judges, who have a tendency to decide cases against SCs and STs, and make specific recommendations to the Govt. to protect the interests and Welfare of the SCs and STs.
- A Special Committee to visit and look into the working of SC and ST Student Hostels and make appropriate Recommendations to the Govt. to improve the Conditions and Working of these Hostels.

The Govt. at the Centre should also Institute:

- Awards for Selection, Recruitment and Promotion of SCs and STs, similar to those for the physically handicapped.
- Recognition of Individuals and Institutions, working for the Development and Integration of the SCs and STs.
- Special Insurance Schemes, to protect and also provide succour and help to the SCs and STs, from suspensions terminations and non-payment of salaries and wages.
- A Cadre of Rural Welfare and Labour Officers, to look into and expeditiously solve the Grievances of the Workers in the Rural Areas and in the Unorganised Sectors.
- Special Social Security Schemes, for the SCs and STs, especially the educated and unemployed
- Special Tax Concessions, to SCs and STs to educate their Children, and for sending them for Higher Studies or Studies Abroad, and or for Specialist and Advanced Courses and Trainings.
- Special Concessions, to SCs and STs for building their own homes, to eliminate the slums and the growing problems associated with them that dehumanises the people.
- Special Schemes and Concessions to SC and ST Entrepreneurs taking up self-employment, starting their own business, and setting up their own industries.
- Special Programmes, to harness and utilise the talents, knowledge and experiences of retired SC and ST Professionals, for the Development and improving the Standards of Life of the SC and ST Communities.

The Govt. should also regularly Constitute an High Power Committee, at least every two years, to review the Allocation, Utilisation, Appropriation and Diversion of the Funds meant and Budgeted for the Education Welfare and Development of the SCs and STs both in the States/UTs and at the Centre.

Similarly, in the States and UTs also, appropriate Committees should be constituted, to look into the Funds earmarked, actually made available, utilised, surrendered and or diverted by the State/ UT Govts., Zilla Parishads and down at the Village Panchayats.

Govt. Should Regularly Review, Assess and Change from time to time, both the Long Term and Short Term SC and ST Schemes and Programmes to Evolve better Schemes and Programmes. There should also be Schemes and Programmes, evolved and structured to suit Specific Communities/Castes/ Tribes, and also sub-Castes, sub-Tribes and Part of the Castes and Tribes living/settled in different areas. This is absolutely necessary, in view of Large Scale Migrations due to Education, Employment, Search of Livelihood and for Survival; and also the Uprooting/ Shifting/Relocation of whole Villages, Communities and the people of different Regions, particularly the STs and also the SCs of many small pockets, as a result of Development Programmes and Mega-Projects.

Govt. Should Classify the Schemes and Programmes meant for the SCs and STs, into specific Categories. Adequate Funds have to be separately earmarked for Poverty Elevation, Ameliorative, Assets Creation, Welfare, Infrastructure Development, Education including grant of various Freeships Scholarships Fellowships and provision of Hostels and Messes, Entrepreneur Development, Financial Assistance for Purchase of Land/House Building/ Starting Business, and for Establishing Cottage/Mini/Small-Scale/ Medium/Big/Large Industries, and such other identifiable Schemes and Programmes.

Similarly, Funds Should be Separately Budgeted, Allocated and Released to NGOs run by others for the Welfare and Development of the SC and ST Dalits, to NGOs headed or patronised by SC and ST Leaders and Individuals, and to NGOs run and personally managed by the SC and ST Dalits themselves. Their utilities and effectiveness must be carefully assessed, separately in different Areas and Regions, and for different Schemes and Programmes, for taking up timely and appropriate corrective and remedial actions, and for a better utilisation of the funds and maximisation of the results. Only this could ensure a real help to SCs and STs, today at different stages of life, and in various levels of development and growth in different Regions and Parts of the Country. The present Practices of allocating Consolidated Funds, and leaving them in the hands of Govt. Officials who are only interested in their jobs, perquisites and or the privileges of their offices and future/promotions; or in supporting, helping and patronising their friends, relatives, colleagues, neighbours, etc. are not going to deliver any results, or ever Develop and Liberate the SC and ST Dalits still living and believing in this Country and the Govts.

Poona Pact

Poona Pact, agreed to by leaders of caste — Hindus and of Dalits, at Poona on 24-9-1932. The following is the text of the agreement arrived at between leaders acting on behalf of the Depressed Classes and of the rest of the community, regarding the representation of the Depressed Classes in the legislatures and certain other matters affecting their welfare.

- There shall be seats reserved for the Depressed Classes out of general electorate seats in the provincial legislatures as follows:

  Madras 30; Bombay with Sindh 25; Punjab 8; Bihar and Orissa 18; Central Provinces 20; Assam 7; Bengal 30; United Provinces 20. Total 148. These figures are based on the Prime Minister's (British) decision.

- Election to these seats shall be by joint electorates subject, however, to the following procedure:

  All members of the Depressed Classes registered in the general electoral roll of a constituency will form an electoral college which will elect a panel of tour candidates belonging to the Deparessed Classes for each of such reserved seats by the method of the single vote and four persons getting the highest number of votes in such primary elections shall be the candidates for election by the general electorate.

- The representation of the Depressed Classes in the Central Legislature shall likewise be on the principle of joint electorates and reserved seats by the method of primary election in the manner provided for in clause above for their representation in the provincial legislatures.

Central Legislature

- In the Central Legislature 18 per cent of the seats allotted to the general electorate for British India in the said legislature shall he reserved for the Depressed Classes.

- The system of primary election to a panel of candidates for election to the Central and Provincial Legislatures as i herein-before mentioned shall come to an end after the first ten years, unless terminated sooner by mutual agreement under the provision of clause 6 below.
- The system of representation of Depressed Classes by reserved seats in the Provincial and Central Legislatures as provided for in clauses (1) and (4) shall continue until determined otherwise by mutual agreement between the communities concerned in this settlement.
- The Franchise for the Central and Provincial Legislatures of the Depressed Classes shall be as indicated, in the Lothian Committee Report.
- There shall be no disabilities attached to any one on the ground of his being a member of the Depressed Classes in regard to any election to local bodies or appointment to the public services. Every endeavour shall be made to secure a fair representation of the Depressed Classes in these respects, subject to such educational qualifications as may be laid down for appointment to the Public Services.

  (Adult franchise but reservation has been provided for Dalits on population basis, till 1960).
- In every province out of the educational grant an adequate sum shall be ear-marked for providing educational facilities to the members of Depressed Classes,

Vows of Dr. Ambedkar

Dr. B. R. Ambedkar prescribed 22 vows to his followers during the historic religious conversion to Buddhism on 15 October 1956 at Deeksha Bhoomi, Nagpur in India. The conversion to Buddhism by 800,000 people was historic because it was the largest religious conversion, the world has ever witnessed. He prescribed these oaths so that there may be complete severance of bond with Hinduism. These 22 vows struck a blow at the roots of Hindu beliefs and practices. These vows could serve as a bulwark to protect Buddhism from confusion and contradictions. These vows could liberate converts from superstitions, wasteful and meaningless rituals, which have led to pauperisation of masses and enrichment of upper castes of Hindus.

The famous 22 vows are:

1. I shall have no faith in Brahma, Vishnu and Mahesh nor shall I worship them.
2. I shall have no faith in Rama and Krishna who are believed to be incarnation of God nor shall I worship them.
3. I shall have no faith in 'Gauri', Ganapati and other gods and goddesses of Hindus nor shall I worship them.
4. I do not believe in the incarnation of God.
5. I do not and shall not believe that Lord Buddha was the incarnation of Vishnu. I believe this to be sheer madness and false propaganda.
6. I shall not perform 'Shraddha' nor shall I give 'pind-dan'.
7. I shall not act in a manner violating the principles and teachings of the Buddha.
8. I shall not allow any ceremonies to be performed by Brahmins.
9. I shall believe in the equality of man.
10. I shall endeavour to establish equality.
11. I shall follow the 'noble eightfold path' of the Buddha.
12. I shall follow the 'paramitas' prescribed by the Buddha.
13. I shall have compassion and loving kindness for all living beings and protect them.
14. I shall not steal.
15. I shall not tell lies.
16. I shall not commit carnal sins.
17. I shall not take intoxicants like liquor, drugs, etc.
18. I shall endeavour to follow the noble eightfold path and practise compassion and loving kindness in every day life.
19. I renounce Hinduism which is harmful for humanity and impedes the advancement and development of humanity because it is based on inequality, and adopt Buddhism as my religion.

20. I firmly believe the Dhamma of the Buddha is the only true religion.
21. I believe that I am having a rebirth.
22. I solemnly declare and affirm that I shall hereafter lead my life according to the principles and teachings of the Buddha and his Dhamma.

Constitutional Safeguards for Dalits

Safeguards in the Indian Constitution for Scheduled Castes and Scheduled Tribes

The important Constitutional safeguards for SCs and STs are mentioned below:

(a) Directive Principles of State Policy

Article 46 is a comprehensive article comprising both the developmental and regulatory aspects. It reads as follows:

> "The State shall promote with special care the educational and economic interests of the weaker sections, of the people, and in particular, of the Scheduled Castes and the Scheduled Tribes, and shall protect them from social injustice and all forms of exploitation".

(b) Social Safeguards

Article 17: "Untouchability" is abolished and its practice in any form is forbidden. The enforcement of any disability arising out of "Untouchability" shall be an offence punishable in accordance with law.

To give effect to this Article, Parliament made an enactment, viz. Untouchability (Offences) Act, 1955. To make the provisions of this Act more stringent, the Act was amended in 1976 and was also renamed as the Protection of Civil Rights Act, 1955. As provided under the Act, Government of India also notified the Rules, viz. the PCR Rules, 1977, to carry out the provisions of this Act. As cases of atrocities on SCs/STs were not covered under the provisions of PCR Act, 1955, Parliament passed another important Act in 1989 for taking measures to prevent the atrocities. This act known as the Scheduled Castes and the Scheduled Tribes (Prevention of Atrocities) Act, 1989, became effective from 30.1.1990. For carrying out the provisions of this Act the Govt. of India have notified the SCs and the STs (Prevention of Atrocities) Rules, 1995 on 31.3.1995.

Article 23: Prohibits traffic in human beings and beggar and other similar forms of forced labour and provides that any contravention of this provision shall be an offence punishable in accordance with law. It does not specifically mention SCs and STs but since the majority of bonded labour belong to SCs/STs this Article has a special significance for SCs and STs. In pursuance of this article, Parliament has enacted the Bonded Labour System (Abolition) Act, 1976. For effective implementation of this Act, the Ministry of Labour is running a Centrally Sponsored Scheme for identification, liberation and rehabilitation of bonded labour.

Article 24 provides that no child below the age of 14 years shall be employed to work in any factory or mine or engaged in any other hazardous employment. There are Central and State laws to prevent child labour. This article too is significant for SCs and STs as a substantial portion, if not the majority, of child labour engaged in hazardous employment belong to SCs and STs.

Article 25(2)(b) provides that Hindu religious institutions of a public character shall be thrown open to all classes and sections of Hindus. This provision is relevant as some sects of Hindus used to claim that only members of the concerned sects had a right to enter their temples. This was only a subterfuge to prevent entry of SC persons in such temples. For the purpose of this provision the term Hindu includes Sikh, Jaina and Budhist.

Educational and Cultural Safeguards

Article 15(4) empowers the State to make any special provision for the advancement of any socially and educationally backward classes of citizens or for SC and ST. This provision has enabled the State to reserve seats for SCs and STs in educational institutions including technical, engineering and medical colleges and in Scientific and Specialised Courses. In this as well as in *Article 16(4)* the term 'backward classes' is used as a generic term and comprises various categories of backward classes, viz. Scheduled Castes,

Scheduled Tribes, Other Backward Classes, Denotified Communities (Vimukta Jatiyan) and Nomadic/Semi-nomadic communities.

Article 330 provides for reservation of seats for SCs/STs in the Lok Sabha.

Article 332 provides for reservation of seats for SCs/STs in the State Vidhan Sabhas (Legislative Assemblies).

Article 334 originally laid down that the provision relating to the reservation of seats for SCs/STs in the Lok Sabha and the State Vidhan Sabhas (and the representation of the Anglo-Indian community in the Lok Sabha and the State Vidhan Sabhas by nomination) would cease to have effect on the expiration of a period of ten years from the commencement of the Constitution. This article has since been amended four times, extending the said period by ten years on each occasion. This provision was to expire in January 2000.

Service Safeguards

Article 16(4) empowers the State to make "any provision for the reservation in appointments or posts in favour of any backward class of citizens which, in the opinion of the State, is not adequately represented in the services under the State".

Article 16(4A): Nothing in this Article shall prevent the State from making any provision for reservation in matters of promotion to any class or classes of posts in the services under the State in favour of the Scheduled Castes and the Scheduled Tribes which, in the opinion of the State, are not adequately represented in the services under the State".

Article 335: "The claims of the members of the Scheduled Castes and the Scheduled Tribes shall be taken into consideration, consistently with the maintenance of efficiency of administration, in the making of appointments to services and posts in connection with the affairs of the Union or of a State".

Article 320(4) provides that nothing in clause (3) shall require a Public Service Commission to be consulted as respects the manner in which any provision under *Article 16(4) & 16(4)A* may be made or the manner in which effect may be given to the provisions of *Article 335.*

Statutes and Legislations

There are a number of laws, both Central and State, which provide for safeguards to SCs/STs. Some of these emanate from the various Constitutional provisions. An illustrative list of such laws is given below:

- The Protection of Civil Rights Act, 1955.
- The Scheduled Castes and the Scheduled Tribes (Prevention of Atrocities) Act, 1989.
- The Bonded Labour System (Abolition) Act, 1976.
- The Child Labour (Prohibition and Regulation) Act, 1986.
- Acts and regulations in force in different States to prevent alienation of land belonging to SCs/STs. In some States such provision exists in the Land Revenue Code.
- Acts in different States for restoration of alienated land to SCs/STs.

What is "Dalit" and "Dalitism"?

We have received many letters asking us the meaning of the word Dalit. The same question is also being put to us at meetings. What gives us great pleasure and pride is this word has become popular all over India and abroad in such a short timegiving expression to the anger of the Untouchables. And gathering so much of charisma.

We are also happy to note that not only the militant Dalits but even some Hindu press have stopped using the hated word, Harijan, a Gandhian humbug, and switched on to Dalit. This awareness of their identity is itself a big step forward in the Dalit liberation struggle. The word Dalit symbolises the mood of this explosive commodity and connotes and denotes their protest. Hence, the switch-over to this new word is itself a great improvement indicating a big leap in the search for their roots.

Only three years back people barring those in the Hindi belt did not even know this word. It was not in their vocabulary. But as soon as they came to know this word and discovered its intrinsic value, its magic, its melody, they readily adopted it. Literally embraced it. "National" newspapers like the Times of India are using this word even in headlines. Even the Malayala Manorama, the largest circulated language daily of Kerala, has started using this word heeding our appeal. We call upon all our Dalit and other persecuted minority comrades to use only this word and persuade others to popularise it. If the English and language dailies start using the word, Dalit, in headlines it will soon catch up. Therefore, Dalits and their co-sufferers must go to newspaper offices and meet journalists and prevail upon them to use Dalit instead of Harijan or SC/STs. We will suggest the Oxford, Webster, Cambridge and other dictionaries to include it.

Now its meaning: The root word of this word Dalit is Dal. The adjective of dal is Dalit. We find this word dal on page 471 of the prestigious Oxford Sanskrit English Dictionary, new edition, 1964, edited by the world-famous Sanskrit scholar, Sir Monier Williams.

"Dalit" is found in many Indian languages and even a Dravidian language. The meaning given to 'Dalit' in the dictionary is: burst, split, scattered, dispersed, broken, torn as under, destroyed, crushed. All these English words sum up the exact position of the Indian Untouchables and also tribes. We are crushed and cramped and made mincemeat by the Hindu religion. That is why we are Dalits. Be proud to be a Dalit, the original inhabitants of this ancient land. Let us walk with our head high. Let us be proud of our Dalit culture. Black is beautiful.

The famous word, 'Daridra', which is popular in many Indian languages, is derived from 'Dalit'.

Since 'Dalit' sums up our mood, we call upon all SC/ST government employees, public sector SC/ST unions to change their names into Dalit Employees Association. The first to popularise this word were our militant Dalit Panthers of Bombay. Their manifesto has defined this word. Though this word has now come to mean Untouchables, the Panthers have included Tribes, Muslims, Women and all those persecuted minorities.

Along with 'Dalit', another word is also getting popular: Dalitism which is both the ideology and nationalism of India's persecuted, suppressed masses. It is rooted in Ambedkarism. Dalitism or Dalit philosophy is developed to pave the way for a liberal tradition against casteism and untouchability. The new revolutionary philosophy of Dalitism also stipulates that Dalits alone can liberate Dalits from the Ruling Class. Even in such a short time Dalitism has attracted millions. It is the living spiritual principle of India's Untouchables. The object of Dalitism is to attract the youth all over India and make them understand the culture and history of India's submerged masses.

The ruling class historians and writers have given little or no attention to the history of our life and culture. Historical evidences are either destroyed or simply neglected for lack of interest. Dalits were simply marked under slavery and serfdom in India. The only meritorious scheme now on the anvil is the all-round flowering of Ambedkarism. Truth cannot be suppressed for long. The human mind is the most potent instrument in history. Words are more powerful than weapons. Dalit thinkers and writers take stock of all this time-bombs to bombard the citadel of the Ruling Class that mismanaged the Indian history and culture founded by us.

Tradition is not the prerogative of a particular caste/class. The tradition the Ruling Class claims for itself is of a recent origin compared to the Dalits. It is this tradition that make up its power-structure, politics, economics, religion, education, art and culture. The tradition that vouchsafe for the culture and history of Dalits originated with the beginning of life in India. From this strong whirlwind developed the Dalit life, history and culture that got down to 1980s with an uninterrupted impact upon evolution. That is its novelty. It is the strongest living spiritual force in the entire life-history of man and universe. What happened to this truth? Dalit writers should ponder over the subject.

The Indus Valley Civilization was the finest specimen of the ancient Dalit wisdom. Dr. Ambedkar gave its modern version, democratic spirit and a scientific culture. With their new awakening, the Dalits are marching forward fully aware of this line and demarcation.

It is an indisputable fact that India lives in two worlds, has two cultures — Dalits and that of the Aryan oppressors. The national will of the Dalits, reawakened with the spirit of Ambedkarism, is really soul-searching. Now, on one has got the courage to dislodge the truth and validity of Dalit life. The Dalit culture was drawn from the myriad forces of history but got sidetracked and dissipated over a wide spectrum of life and activity under the aegis of Hinduism, Islam and Christianity.

Religion has got the better of life in India. All religions flourish under the name of tradition, idealism and the enthusiasm of the Ruling Class. But the human in Dalit life and activity lost all the meaning. Caste and untouchability became the ruling norm of India's traditional society. Modernism and Marxism is only a mask. Only the dalit intellectual can give vent to the crusading spirit of Dalit national identity and culture. The word, Dalit, is the other extreme of the word Brahmin. So, the task before all Dalit writers is a challenging one. With all the oppressive machinery at their command, the Ruling Class is making inroads into Dalit unity, culture, struggle and progress. This assault will take a vigorous turn shortly. We must hit back. It is against this cataclysm of Indian life that Dalits should revolt. Dalitism is the only alternative to national degeneration. Even Marxism has missed the bus in India. Any one who wants regeneration and rebirth of Idna, he must seek the spirit of life and culture of Dalits. Dalits alone can lead the Indian Revolution. Truth can come out only from the innermost depths of their mind, whereas sycophancy rules the Ruling Class. India has ceased to be a nation because of this.

Hinduism has become the repository of another cult called anti-Dalit. The Ruling Class is up against the reservations. If possible it will destroy Dalitism, root and branch. Dalits should make all-round effort to ward off this machinations of the Ruling Class. It failed in its political as well as religious maturity. The Dalits are the worst victims of this tragedy. They were dethroned and lobbed to the lowest depths of life. Dalitism is, therefore, a revolutionary philosophy and a guide to action. The Brahmin cult should be destroyed and buried 100 fathoms deep. Reason will not dawn on the Ruling Class with its present bigoted spirit. Anti-Dalitism has become a way of life with the oppressor. Therefore, the Dalits should meet this challenge. They must revolt. They must explode. Now is the time. The dawn of 21st century is the triumph of Ambedkarism. With the close of the 20th century Gandhism will end and Ambedkar Era will begin.

Dalits have suffered a lot in India, their forefathers were exploited and destroyed. Their growth was stunted. Dalitism is the answer for all this. It will not only save the Dalits but India as well. Possibly, it may avert a Third World War. India can attain its real self and liberation only with Dalitism.

Bibliography

Abarill Chandra: *Social and Political Ideas of B.R. Ambedkar*, Alekh Publishers, Jaipur, 1977.

Agarawal, S.: *Dr. B.R. Ambedkar: The Man and his Message*, Prentice-Hall of India, New Delhi, 1991.

Ahir, D. C: *The Legacy of Dr. Ambedkar (Bharat Ratna)*, B.R. Pub, Delhi, 1990.

————: *Buddhism and Ambedkar*, Ajay, New Delhi, 1968.

————: *Dr B.R. Ambedkar: Buddhist Revolution and Counter-Revolution in Ancient India*, B.R. Publishing, Delhi, 1996.

————: *Gandhi and Ambedkar*, Study Circle, Jullunder, 1979.

————: *Gandhi and Ambedkar. A Comparative Study*, Blumoon, New Delhi,1995.

————: *Life of Dr. Ambedkar*, BR Publishing, Delhi, 1990.

Aluwalia, B.K. and Shashi: *B.R. Ambedkar and Human Rights*, KK Publishers, New Delhi, 1981.

Appadorai, A.: *The Substance of Politics*, Oxford University Press, Delhi,1965.

Ardythe, B.: *Untouchable Soldiers, Ambedkar* Sahitya Prakashan, Bangalore, 1980.

Baisantry, D.K.: *Dr. Ambedkar, a Pioneer of Labour Welfare*, Buddhist Publishing House, Jalandhar, 1982.

Bakshi, S. R.: *B.R. Ambedkar: His Political and Social Ideology*, Deep & deep publications, New Delhi, 2000.

Balley, L.R.: *Thought On Ambedkar*, Bheem Patrika, Jullundhar, 1972.

Bamfield, J.A.M.: *Thoughts on Dr. Ambedkar*, Bheem Patrika Publications, Jaladhar, 1972.

Barill, C.: *Social and Political Ideas of B.R. Ambedkar*, Aalekh Publishers, Jaipur, 1977.

Basavalingappa, B.: *In the Foot Prints of Dr. B.R. Ambedkar*, Karnataka Buddha Dhamma Samithi, Bangalore, 1990.

Bhagwandas: *Thus Spoke Ambedkar*, Bheem Patrika,Jullundur, 1969.

Bharathi, K.S.: *Foundations of Ambedkar Thought*, Dattson's Publishers, Nagpur, 1990.

Bharill, C: *Social and Political Ideas of B. R. Ambedkar*, Aalekh, Jaipur, 1977.

Chavan, Sheshrao: *Bharat Ratna Dr. Babasaheb Ambedkar*, Vimal Publications, Aurangabad, 1990.

Das, Bhagwan: *Revival of Buddhism in India and Role of Dr. Baba Saheb B.R. Ambedkar*, Dalit Today Prakashan, Lucknow, 1998.

Fitzgerald, T.: *Ambedkar, Buddhism and the Concept of Religion*, Vision and Values, New Delhi, 1999.

Gehlot, N.S.: *Dr Ambedkar, Mahatma Gandhi and Dalit Movement*, Indian Journal of Political Science 54, 1993.

Gore, M. S.: *The Social Context of an Ideology: Ambedkar's Political and Social Thought*, Sage, New Delhi, 1993.

Iyer, V. R. Krishna, J.: *Dr. Ambedkar and the Dalit Future*, B.R. Publishing Corp., Delhi, 1990.

Jadhav, N.: *Dr. Ambedkar's Economic Thought and Philosophy*, Popular Prakashan, Bombay, 1993.

Jaffrelot, Christophe: *Dr. Ambedkar and Untouchability: Fighting the Indian Caste System*, Columbia University Press, New York, 2005.

Jatav, D.R.: *Dr. Ambedkar's Role in National Movement*, Boudha Sahitya Samelan, New Delhi, 1979.

————: *Dr.Ambedkar's Role in National Movement*, Boudha Sahitya Sammelan, New Delhi, 1979.

Jatav, D.R.: *The Political Philosophy of B.R. Ambedkar*, Phoenix Pub. House, Agra, 1965.

————: *Political Philosophy of Dr. Ambedkar; Social Philosophy of B.R. Ambedkar*, Phoenix Publishing Agency, Agra, 1967.

Jondhale, Surendra and Johannes Beltz: *Reconstructing the World: B.R. Ambedkar and Buddhism in India*, Oxford University Press, New Delhi, 2004.

Kadam, K. N.: *Dr. B.R. Ambedkar: The Emancipator of the Oppressed*, BR Publishing, Delhi, 1994.

————: *Dr. Babasaheb Ambedkar and the Significance of His Movement: A Chronology*, Popular Prakashan, Bombay, 1991.

Keer, Dhananjay, *Dr. Ambedkar: Life and Mission*, Popular Prakashan, Bombay, 1962.

Khabde Dinkar: *Dr. Ambedkar and Western Thinkers*, Sugava Prakashan, Pune, 1989.

Khadbe, D.: *Dr. Ambedkar and Western Thinkers*, Sugava Prakashan, Pune, 1989.

Khairmode, C. B.: *Dr. Bhimrao Ramji Ambedkar*, various publishers, Bombay,1988.

Kuber, W. N.: *Ambedkar: A Critical Study*, People's Pub. House, New Delhi, 1991.

Lobo, C. H. J. J.: *Dr B.R. Ambedkar: The Champion of Social Democracy in India*, Hilerina Publishers, Bangalore, 1984.

Lokhade, G. S.: *Bhimrao Ramji Ambedkar, A Study in Social Democracy*, Intellectual Pub. House, New Delhi, 1982.

Narain, A. K. and Ahir, D. C.: *Dr. Ambedkar, Buddhism and Social Change*, BR Publishing Delhi, 1993.

Narwade, S. S.: *Dr. Babasaheb Ambedkar Ani Hyderabad Sanathan*, Sugava Prakashan, Pune, 1988.

Omvedt, G.: *Dalits and the Democratic Revolution: Dr Ambedkar and the Dalit Movement in Colonial India*, Sage, New Delhi, 1994.

————: *Ambedkar: Towards an Enlightened India*, Penguin, New Delhi, 2004.

Patwardhan, S.: *Change among India's Harijans, Maharashtra: a Case Study*, Orient Longmans, New Delhi, 1973. lrlr

Rajagopalachari, C.: *Ambedkar* Refuted , Hind Kitabs, Bombay, 1946.

Rajasekharaiah, A.M.: *B.R. Ambedkar: the Politics of Emancipation*, Sindhu Publications, Bombay, 1971.

Rajshekar, V. T.: *Ambedkar and His Conversion*, Dalit Sahitya Academy, Bangalore,1980.

Rajshekaria, A. M.: *B.R. Ambedkar, The Politics of Emancipation*, Sindhu Publications, Bombay, 1971.

Raju Ganni, G.: *The Life of Dr. B.R., Ambedkar*, Dr. Ambedkar Memorial Society, Hyderabad, 1979.

Ramaiah, P. and K. Sateesh Reddy: *Dr B.R. Ambedkar's Economic Philosophy*, Delta Publishing, New Delhi, 1994.

Robbins, Jeanette: *Dr. Ambedkar and His Movement*, Dr. Ambedkar Publication Society, Hyderabad, 1965.

Sampla, B. R.: *Yug Purush Ambedkar*, Bheen Patrika, Jullundur, 1978.

Sangharakshita: *Ambedkar and Buddhism*, Windhorse Publications, Glasgow, 1986.

Santhanam, K.: *Ambedkar's Attack*, The Hindustan Press, New Delhi, 1946.

Sharma, Kusum: *Ambedkar and Indian Constitution*, Ashish Pub. House, New Delhi, 1992.

Shetty, V. T. R.: *Ambedkar and his Conversion: a Critique*, Dalit Action Committee, Bangalore, 1980.

Suman, R. D.: *Dr. Ambedkar: Pioneer of Human Rights*, Bodhisattva Publications, New Delhi, 1977.

Teltumbde, Anand: *'Ambedkar' in and for the Post-Ambedkar Dalit Movement*, Sugava Prakashan, Pune, 1997.

——————: *Dr. Ambedkar, Pratik, Vastav va Nava Anvayarth*, Krantisinha Nana Patil Academi, Pune, 1998.

Thorat, S.: *Ambedkar's Contribution to Water Resource Development*, Central Water Commission, New Delhi, 1993.

————: *Ambedkar's Role in Economic Planning and Water Policy*, Shipra, Delhi, 1998.

————: *Ambedkar and Nation Building: Reflection on Selected Themes*, Radiant, New Delhi, 1999.

————: *Ambedkar and the Economic of Hindu Social Order: Understanding Its Orthodoxy and Legacy*, Indian Social Institute, New Delhi, 1997.

Tope, T. K.: *Dr. B.R. Ambedkar, A Symbol of Social Revolt*, Maharashtra Information Centre, New Delhi, 1964.

Vakil, A. K.: *Gandhi-Ambedkar Dispute*, Ashish Pub. House, New Delhi, 1991.

Varale, B. H.: *Dr. Babasaheb Ambedkarrancha Sangaki*, Shrividya Prakashan, Pune, 1lrlr988.

————: *Dr.Ambedkarancha Sangati*, Shrividya Prakashan, Pune,1988.

Wilkinson, T. and Thomas, M.: *Ambedkar and the Neo-Buddhist Movement*, Christian Literature Society, Madras, 1972.

Zelliot, E.: *Dr Ambedkar and the Mahar Movement*, University of Pennsylvania, Unpubl, 1969.

Zelliot, E.: *From Untouchable to Dalit: Essays on Ambedkar Movement*, Manohar, New Delhi, 1992.

————: *From Untouchable to Dalit: Essays on Ambedkar Movement*, Manohar, New Delhi, 1992.

————: *The American Experience of Dr. B.R. Ambedkar*, Bodhisattva Publications, New Delhi, 1977.

————: *The Leadership of Babasaheb Ambedkar*, Vikas, New Delhi, 1977.

————: *The Political Thought of Dr. B.R. Ambedkar*, Sage Publications, Delhi, 1986.

Index

❑❑❑